Tom Petty
and Philosophy

Popular Culture and Philosophy®   Series Editor: George A. Reisch

IN PREPARATION:

For full details of all Popular Culture and Philosophy® books, visit www.opencourtbooks.com.

Popular Culture and Philosophy®

Tom Petty and Philosophy

We Need to Know

Edited by
RANDALL E. AUXIER AND
MEGAN VOLPERT

OPEN COURT
Chicago

Volume 124 in the series, Popular Culture and Philosophy ®, edited by George A. Reisch

To find out more about Open Court books, visit our website at www.opencourtbooks.com.

Open Court Publishing Company is a division of Carus Publishing Company, dba Cricket Media.

Tom Petty and Philosophy: We Need to Know

ISBN: 978-0-8126-9465-9

Library of Congress Control Number: 2018962707

This book is also available as an e-book (ISBN 978-0-8126-9467-3).

Contents

Foreword

LUKE DICK

Petty is the best American rock and roll has had to offer. Period. I've applied a load of hairbrained metrics to come to that assessment. But metrics aren't important to songs. What's important is this: Petty has somehow made a lifetime's worth of songs that have somehow gotten to the heart of the American everyperson in the simplest and purest form.

What of Dylan? Springsteen? I'd bet a hundred bucks at this very second that of the umpteen million cars rolling in America, there's more Petty billowing out of them than the other two combined. What he did with songs is the most beautiful magic of getting to you by getting into you. He gave us the luxury of not thinking and just absorbing the song. They're songs to get high and low to. Songs to windows-down escape to. Songs to smart-assed yell to. They're three-minute teardrops: Small. Saturated. And they hold inexpressible worlds in them.

What's the everyperson? Fuck if I know. But everyone from Maine to Muskogee has had dreams of not driving forklifts or working in shitty diners. Somewhere someone in Indianola is longing to leave that crummy town and find love and fortune somewhere better. And those who made their way to Hollywood for a better life are there right now heartbroken, thinking about what a sham everything is and wishing they were back in a somewhere-else town with less bullshit and cheaper gasoline to drive them to the next new ray of hope. Tom Petty is for all those people, because he is, was, and forever will be one of those people. He doesn't conceptualize it—he just distills it. So easily.

There's something about American experience that wants you to both be something glamorous and also to find all the notion of glamour and fame ridiculous at the same time: Visualize the dream. Chase down the dream. Get the dream. And then realize there's a new dream that you have to chase.

Most rock stars keep chasing new dreams until pop culture wads them up and sells their records back, but Petty seemed to realize it was all just a perpetual mirage to begin with. One of his greatest tricks was taking the feeling of futility and somehow making it fun when it should be sad. His whole catalog seems to be sung with a smart-assed grin. Go ahead—look at the lyrics to "American Girl." Look at "Mary Jane's Last Dance." It's that kind of drawled defiance that Americans fell in love with, and he became part of the rock and roll canon because of it. Even the losers get lucky sometimes.

What of Dylan and Springsteen? Of course they're brilliant. But they're dense and austere. They require wading. Petty gave us riffs and melodies and songs that rolled off our tongues time after time. We didn't have to think about them if we didn't want to. He gave us something so easy that felt like a perpetual summer night. But it isn't bubblegum, either. It's that beautiful in between. He gave us music to help us forget everything and it will remain to me a communion, like music was to begin with.

So why are you here? Is there any way that a bunch of philosophers are going to make you feel as good as Tom Petty can? Of course not. But you're here for the same reason they are. Because you love him. And sometimes we just need a way to appreciate and eulogize and try to understand it from another lens rather than from another set of speakers. If nothing else, reading this book can be a communion of Petty fans having erudite conversations about un-erudite songs. The words you're about to read are fun and interesting and insightful. But make no mistake, the chapters ahead will be hard pressed to beat Petty's simplicity and the worlds they hold.

I've never cried when a celebrity died. But something about Petty got to me. I turned on "American Girl" and was ugly crying by the chorus. So hard it was almost embarrassing. I actually had to buy Visine from the corner store to cope. I've been asking myself why ever since his death. I think it's because I saw *myself* in there somewhere in the melody. I felt *myself* trying to get out of my shitty little town and make something of myself. I felt *myself* getting up the next hill only to see a new mirage.

And in the middle of all that I loved him for being the greatest musical companion and making me feel like I had a friend who understood that. I mean *really* understood that. What did I do with my tears? I walked into a music store barefooted and bought a twelve-string electric guitar on the spot.

The good news is, this book is cheaper than the guitar I bought, so you can take the kind of triumphant tears Petty gave you and unpack them with these philosophers. If you get bored somewhere along the way—and Petty knows that life and books do get boring—pause your reading and sing "Refugee" at the top of your lungs.

Keep a Little Soul

October 2nd 2017: the world got still, didn't it? Tom Petty died on a Monday, one week after closing the encore of his final fortieth anniversary tour date with "American Girl." It was the same way he closed hundreds of other shows for dozens of years. We loved him for his constancy and his consistency.

Coming down from that is a damnably difficult thing, so here we are, trying to keep a little soul. But we are heartbroken, after all. That was the hard promise they made, back when it felt like heaven. We were always gonna get it. We should have known it, because nobody could ever say quite what Tom Petty was doing. Was it New Wave, Southern rock, folk revival, pop? Was it southern California or northern Florida? Was he a writer, a musician, an actor, a performer? If Andy Warhol was good at being famous, Tom Petty was good at being bad at being famous. That is sort of post-pre-post-modern, crammed into a forty-year fifteen minutes.

The Heartbreakers and the family—and, heaven help us, the (*%#$@*!) record company execs—got together and began sorting through the archives in search of what ultimately became the box set, *Tom Petty: An American Treasure*. A treasure indeed, Petty had a special knack for big compilations like this. *Playback* remains a gold standard for how to catalog rarities. Both *Anthology* and *The Live Anthology* charted, and *Greatest Hits* went all the way to number two. New tunes on these albums stood toe to toe with beloved classics. When "Mary Jane's Last Dance" debuted on *Greatest Hits*, it turned out to be the last thing recorded with Stan Lynch on drums, just as when "Surrender" debuted on *Anthology* and turned out to be the last thing recorded with Howie Epstein on bass.

It's tempting to say Petty always had impeccable timing—so much so that he often seemed prescient. But we have a much bigger compliment to offer, the truth of which became undeniable when "Keep a Little Soul" launched as his first posthumous single: Petty worked hard to be timeless. An outtake from the *Long After Dark* sessions that got shelved in the haze of album cycle fatigue, the song's context should mean it's a piece of trash from an album that isn't too fondly remembered anyway. And yet, his seeming throwaway from 1982 sounds snug at home in 2018. But the thirty-six years there isn't the reach. Roger McGuinn sometimes heard Heartbreakers tracks on the radio and genuinely mistook them for his own stuff with The Byrds from a decade prior. Maybe "Keep a Little Soul" is just timeless.

We're not afraid to depend on the way timeless stuff flattens out the future, the present, and the past. Petty always lived what he believed: that everybody has dreams we ought to keep running down, despite the accompanying heartache it may earn us, because they never would come to us. If we just try to stay up on our feet, nothing else matters. Perhaps this wonderful track got cut from the album because the morning of Ronnie Reagan's presidency did not seem like a particularly kind moment to sing about how nothing really matters anymore. So while the kids hit the political snooze button, Petty turned up the volume instead.

Well, Nietzsche would've appreciated the gesture—which brings us to what we're doing here. Petty was never too fond of explaining to people what his songs were about. And yet, many of his turns of phrase have entered our common lexicon as shorthand for some ideas that are rich in philosophical value. As soon as *An American Treasure* was announced, half the comments on social media joked that waiting for it is the hardest part. How many times have we swatted the dog away from the toilet bowl, reminding him not to live like a refugee? Even the great puns in cover band names speak to this witty intellectualism, too: Heavy Petty, Petty Larceny . . .

So it's high time we start discussing Petty as the philosopher he clearly was. So what if he never made it through college? He didn't need it. But we did, and we've put together this rocking little box set of big ideas in order to begin filling out some leaves on this branch of his legacy, the one that we're most equipped to examine. This branch has sprouted five nice, green buds—one each on epistemology, aesthetics, and ontology, plus two on ethics, one a little more political, one a little less political. Learning to fly is never easy, but we attempted to answer these questions: What does Petty want to know, and how does he resolve uncertainty? How does Petty make the music, and what does his process say about creativity? How did Petty conduct himself in the world, and why does he value equal partnerships? How did Petty battle the music industry, and what is his sense of artistic freedom? How did Petty undermine other systems, and what is individualism worth to him?

He lived his life the way he wrote and the way he played. It was grit, drive, and just enough finesse, to make things nice, at least where they need to be nice. On stage, he put the *schau* in *Anschauung*. He stood up to corporate assholes in a number of precedent-setting legal maneuvers and album concepts, risking his career and fortune, but never backing down. He was the center of a musical community that endured over four decades. We see it in the Heartbreakers, but also bookended by Mudcrutch and his collaborations with his elders, such as Bob Dylan, George Harrison, Roy Orbison, and Johnny Cash. His ability to cultivate new generations of listeners while connecting himself backward to the heroes of his own youth has made him universally respected by the widest range of music fans.

Maybe the secret was that Tom Petty knew when to stop talking and start playing. His message is smart common sense. If you have to explain a song, it probably isn't a good song. If you have to explain yourself, you probably aren't living free. Everyone is selfish, but we really have to work on that. And every family is dysfunctional and everybody has to fight and there is no free lunch. So Lucky marries Luanne and tries to mend his ways. There really is better and worse. And more to the point, nobody *has to be* an asshole. They choose it. You don't owe them any mercy. Why gab on about that if you can put it into a few choice words and sing it? No, Tom Petty was a doer, not a talker. He owned his mistakes and pushed ahead, until he couldn't.

Tom Petty may be gone, but our fascination with his body of work runs on anyway. We explore a whole gamut in here that exists on a continuum between Folk and Rock, between New Wave and Americana, between Southern simplicity and West Coast chic. The songs hook and they captivate, but they are often profound in their understatement, their stark minimalism. Petty's insight into the human condition adumbrates a powerful philosophical anthropology with a metaphysics of tragedy, gravity, and levity. His theory of knowledge is psychological and interpersonal, both deeply meditative and delightfully skeptical.

His ethics focuses on dilemmas of the outcast, downtrodden and heartbroken with a view to the fallen and the sinful as our redeemable antiheroes of the everyday. Some want out, some want back in, some won't move. His political thinking is that of the artist, enlivened by Southern hostilities and Californian futilities, culminating in a deontology that puts duty to the fans first. The dialectic of love and hate, abuse and recovery, poverty and power, triumph and loss provides the genuine objects of knowledge. Above all, Petty's songs are the confessions of a poetic mind interpreting a wounded soul.

This volume helps to keep that soul, regardless of how wounded it may be, by exploring Petty's thoughts and the thoughts we have while we listen. That ain't nothing. It matters.

PART I

Making Art

1
Free Falling into Postmodernism

JOHN SEWELL

Alas, my misspent youth. The teenage years are a metamorphic era of grappling for identity—and, baby, I really went through some ch-ch-ch-changes in my teens. 1979 was my junior year in high school. And that year I was deep into my New Wave phase, full of skinny ties and wraparound shades. (Yes, I'm *that* old.)

I remember one time in '79 when I was visiting my cousin in a small college town about an hour from Big, Bad Atlanta. This was well over a decade before the Internet, when radio was king. So we were listening to 96 Rock, a powerful Atlanta FM radio station, in hopes of hearing something new and exciting from the far-off radio station in the big city.

After about an hour of the station's ceaseless iteration of "album rock" staples like Foreigner, Toto, Fleetwood Mac, and of course Led Zeppelin—and doubly of course Lynyrd Skynyrd (after all, this *was* The South)—we decided we'd had enough. So we seized our destinies and actually called the station's request line.

Asked by a couple of smartass, teenage mooks to play some New Wave music, the DJ was a bit, ahem, terse. "We've got Petty coming up," was all he said. And then he hung up. Boom. Just like that. We wanted New Wave. So we nervously called the big city rock station, just trying to be cool. And all we got was an abrupt hang-up. And Tom Petty. Oh yeah, and the Heartbreakers, too. I mean, we *really liked* Tom Petty. But still . . .

We were hoping for something herky-jerky like Devo or the B-52s. Or even the Cars or the Police, two nakedly careerist bands riding the New Wave train en route to platinum—but still considered "edgy" at the time.

This slice of my young life is a paradigmatic example of the daily struggles faced by thousands of courageous New Wave teens in the American suburbs of 1979. *And* it also illustrates Petty's position along the classic rock continuum of the time. Yes, there *is* a connection.

(And, by the way, my skinny tie New Wave period lasted for only about a year—to be followed by umpteen other stupid haircuts and fleeting subcultural affiliations. Now I'm a boring old man, droning on and on about "back in the day" or whatever. My stupid haircut years are over. And in the process of becoming a boring old man, I've gained a real appreciation for all things Petty. *C'est la vie* and all that.)

The late 1970s was a musical era where anything could happen—and did. Granted, the (then) extreme sounds and styles of the Ramones, the Sex Pistols, and the Clash that would later become canonical cultural touchstones were ignored by Mainstream America. But somewhat-more-palatable-but-still-edgy artists like Elvis Costello, Patti Smith, Graham Parker and (especially) Bruce Springsteen had somehow crashed the FM rock party and were achieving real momentum—and sales.

With an eponymous debut in 1976, Tom Petty and the Heartbreakers emerged into a pop music milieu that was changing its ethos: The musical innovations of the Sixties peace and love generation had long since been commoditized—repackaged as bloated, over-processed progressive rock (Emerson Lake and Palmer, Yes), high-gloss, hippy-dippy California singer-songwriter schmaltz (Jackson Browne, the Eagles, America) and dumbed-down, hypermasculine stadium rock (Grand Funk Railroad, Bachman Turner Overdrive, KISS). So, by 1976, what was "old" became new (or at least refurbished and repackaged) again: Punk and its euphemistic cousin, New Wave, were rearing their spiky heads to deliver concise, three-minute teen anthems that were funny and fun—and angry and sexy.

This was the fortuitous era when Petty made his debut. Petty's success was underpinned by his deft construction of a liminal persona—both traditionalist and iconoclast, a rock classicist who was reverential of his antecedents (Elvis, Roy Orbison, the Byrds) *and* in sync with the new wave of (then) contemporary rockers who were retooling and subverting youth (sub)culture from within.

Tom Petty Begat Tom Petty

Let's face it: Rock'n'roll is as much about tight pants, cool hair, and a sneer as it is about music and lyrics. Basically, what you get from *any* rock act is some variation of the youth-as-rebel persona, a performance of authenticity that is just about as "authentic" as the hall of mirrors of youth-as-rebel personas that preceded it.

And it goes a little something like this: Marlon Brando and James Dean begat Elvis; Elvis begat the Beatles' Frankfurt and black-leather-jacket phase; the "bad boy" Beatles begat actual bad boys the Rolling Stones; the Stones begat wild children like the Stooges and the New York Dolls; the Stooges and the Dolls begat punks like the Ramones and the Runaways—and so on, ad infinitum. Oh, and by the way, didya notice that black leather jacket that Tom himself was sporting on the cover of the debut album? And what about that sneer? Rude!

I concede that maybe this genealogy of rebel-posing, rock'n'roll icons might be just a wee bit oversimplified, but you get my drift, right? Now, don't get me wrong here. The prefab, performed "authenticity" of rock identities is *not* a bad thing. There's a rich history of rock'n'rollers who acknowledge, and *celebrate*, even, the vacuity of the pop persona—and of themselves. But my hunch is that when all the aforementioned bad boys and bad girls and bad boy-girls (Tom Petty among them) donned their tight pants, tousled their hair just so and strapped on their guitars, they really meant it, man.

Real rock'n'rollers don't just play songs. Sure, the songs are great. But each song kind of serves an episodic function in the grand tapestry that is the rocker's life, performed in public. In a way, it's almost as if writing and performing songs is a precondition for the rocker to do what he or she *really* wants to do—which is to preen around on a stage, sweating and spitting, crotch-thrusting, and affecting some kind of surliness that is so simultaneously mesmerizing and repulsive that, well, it makes people wanna fuck. *Or* it makes people wanna strap on guitars and do it themselves.

Tom Petty wanted to do it himself—and did. Tom Petty was a careerist. Tom Petty was a deft image manipulator who also just so happened to write and perform great songs. And Tom Petty was well aware that the process of constructing a persona was part of the deal—the deal-sealer, in fact. And all of this is really, *really* cool.

Petty's Postmodern Pop Product

Petty was twenty-six years old when his debut album was released. A journeyman musician who'd already racked up twelve years in the business, most of it as a semi-successful, regional quasi-star, thank you, Petty wasn't *old* per se—but he certainly wasn't young by rock'n'roll standards.

There was an upstart quality to Petty's schtick. Petty's short, sharp songs had snarl and swagger that defied the sonic conventions of FM rock, but at the same time hearkened back to the pithy Sixties sounds of Creedence Clearwater Revival, the Byrds, or anything Phil Spector had a hand in producing. So, on the one hand Petty was defying the pretentious, proggy bombast of 1970s album rock while on the other he was delivering the sound of the 1960s—a repurposed sound, perhaps, but still steeped in the antiquity of the previous decade. (Remember, rock culture was evolving really, *really fast* in the two decades that stretched from Elvis to Hendrix to the Sex Pistols.) Both in terms of his music and his image, Petty bestrode the Rock of Ages, as it were.

An astute student of all things rock'n'roll, Petty personified careless cool from pretty much square one. Just take a look online for photos of Petty with his second band, the Epics, in 1966. He was only sixteen then, but he already looked like he was bored shitless. My hunch, though, is that he was *absolutely thrilled* to be posing for a pic with his band. That surly little blonde punk in the photos, well, that's the careless cool affectation. He'd already nailed it.

By late 1976, Petty was an old pro with a new twist. As the faintest, nascent ripples of the new wave were escalating into a stronger current that would eventually affect a sea change in mainstream rock, Petty was on the proverbial beach, at riptide, board (or guitar) in hand, ready to hang ten and ride that gnarly wave to stardom. (Okay, with that I'll dispense with the "wave" thing for a while.)

When *Tom Petty and the Heartbreakers* first came out, Petty had perfected an asynchronous image. He was "punk" enough to appeal to the sullen, leather-jacketed, rebel-posing rabble-rousers of rock's (then) wannabe avant-garde. But he also had this "everyman" thing that somehow appealed to the "Regular Joes" of the mainstream and to the post-hippie bunch who still wore flare-legged jeans, still worshipped Dylan and the Beatles, and still read *Rolling Stone*. This Petty, he was a man for all seasons. Petty was both of the times, and *of no time*. And it worked. This image was believable—and it sold.

This music, an amalgam of 1960s folk-rock jangle, 1970s heartland rock and just the slightest hint of punk's gritty, attitudinal and sonic insouciance, was as asynchronous as the image of the man who performed it. Petty's contrastingly edgy and accessible music had a ring of truth to it that was believable—and it sold.

In these ways, Petty was something of a postmodernist, even though he may well not have known or given a damn about postmodernism. And Petty's pop product, a product that was every bit as much himself (or some prefab, performed and proffered version of himself, anyway) as his music, was (and still *is*) postmodern.

So What Is Postmodernism, Anyway?

Well, postmodernism is a philosophical movement that, predictably, emerged after modernism. (So, this begs the question: what is modernism? That's a whole 'nother enchilada, a Pandora's Box we won't open here.) Postmodernism is a cultural dominant, a *condition* that occurs whenever grand narratives come into question or whenever new mutations emerge in aesthetics.

Postmodernism is *not* a particular era. It is *not* a point on a timeline that comes after ("post") a certain epoch or before ("pre") a subsequent epoch. Whenever styles and genres are broken down into core components and then recombined to produce *new, different* styles and genres, well, that can be said to be a postmodern occurrence. Whenever worldviews collapse, well, that can also be said to be postmodern.

In his 1984 article, "Postmodernism, or the Structural Logic of Late Capitalism," political theorist and literary critic Frederic Jameson asserted that postmodernism erases distinctions between "high" and "low" art, celebrating kitsch and the culture industry itself. For Jameson, "postmodernity" is marked by pastiche ("new" artistic works produced to mimic other, earlier works) and a crisis in historicity—the sense that "history" in the present has been supplanted by a commodified version of history delivered via cultural products, such as songs, albums, and even the artists themselves, for example.

So now this *all* makes total sense, right? Well, I think it *will* make sense, really, when we use postmodernism as a theoretical lens through which to examine Petty's life and work, and to explain *how* and *why* he became such an important, influential figure in American pop culture and iconography. You got lucky, babe, when I found you.

Mixing and Remixing

Jameson says a state of postmodernity occurs when aesthetic production and commodity production are merged. In postmodernity, "art" becomes "product," eroding distinctions between "high" and "low" art in the process. "Serious," highbrow art is found in museums, opera houses and in Literature (with a capital "L") that spout forth from *artistes* who hover above the omnipresent gravities of consumerism and the almighty dollar. "Unserious" or low art is the louche, vernacular drivel produced by hayseed hacks whose only motivations are the flesh, "fun" (How *gauche!*) and, of course, filthy lucre. In contrast, critics of Jameson, and of postmodern theory in general, have argued that the very notions of high and low art are elitist—and that to regard a creative work (such as a song or album) as a "cultural product" is an utterly cynical, dismissive, and condescending view. Well enough.

But this melding of the high with the low, this merger of aesthetic production and commodity production, and this delivery of artistic works that were indeed products designed to sell (and *sell BIG*), well, that was exactly Tom Petty's gig. And to our collective benefit, the end result of Petty's aesthetic-plus-commodity production was a canon of timeless "classic rock" songs that are indeed classic.

Key to Petty's popularity and success were the ways that both his music and his persona were *of* the time and *out* of time. His music was a kind of cut-and-paste amalgamation of stylistic elements from the various eras of rock music that preceded it—*and* from other strands of musical Americana like folk, blues, and country. Again, it's likely that Petty wasn't aware or didn't give a damn about postmodernity as he was cobbling together his songs. But this cobbling-together is a paradigmatically postmodern approach, and it is the very thing that imbued his music with a quality of timelessness that is, well, classic.

Jameson lamented that in the postmodern milieu, that affect (that's affect with an "a," mind you), induced through exposure to high modernist art, had waned—or disappeared, even. Jameson argued that the feelings expressed in postmodern cultural products are in and of themselves free-floating—or freely fallin', if you will. In effect, postmodern cultural products elide or erase the individual from the artistic equation. The consumption of postmodern cultural products (such as Petty's music) doesn't produce a *particular* affective response, but more of a vague, amorphous, catch-all sentimentality which certainly *seems* important—but is perhaps lacking in depth. Postmodern theorists aver that cultural products are all surface and no substance.

Throughout his songs, Petty uses a quality of lyrical imprecision that Jameson might term "depthlessness." Contrastingly, one (such as myself) might see that same lyrical imprecision as universalizing. We can project our own stories onto Petty's depthless, catch-all hymns of love and longing to produce our own, form-fitted interpretations. And for each individual, what could be more profound than to "hear" their own story as sung by Petty and backed by a great band like the Heartbreakers?

So, in a nutshell, Petty's songs are postmodern because they recombine different genres in timeless ways, because they are indeed cultural products designed to appeal (*and sell*) to all kinds of people, and because, through their universality, their interpretation is arbitrary for each individual. Petty's music is both one-size-fits-all, and bespoke for the individual at the same time. And that's cool with me.

The Image: Mastering and Remastering

So, I hope we've established that Petty made a bunch of great songs, delivered as cultural products, assembled from fragmentary shards of various styles, genres and eras. And of course Petty's songs were the building blocks of his albums, which were the proverbial units being moved—the bulk of the things that were bought and sold in his career.

But this is rock'n'roll. And to sell songs in rock'n'roll, you've got to sell an image. Petty wasn't just selling songs—he was selling *himself*, or at least a version of himself that was pre-constructed. It was a postmodern cobbling-together of various strands of cool archetypes, cool attitudes, and cool comportments designed, just so, to maximize customer appeal and salability.

Sure, by the time of his 1976 debut, Petty's careless cool was effortless—or at least appeared to be. And furthermore, at twenty-six, Petty was a music biz veteran who had already been cool for so long, well, it probably came "naturally." Or something.

Judith Butler, a philosopher and theorist associated with postmodernism who is known as much for the baffling complexity and what-the-hell?-ness of her writing as for her brilliant ideas, coined the term "performativity" to explain how we come to understand socially constructed gender identities as innate.

Butler explains that gender is a sex-associated way of being that we are socialized in from birth. Gender is in its way a form of drag. We "do" gender. We perform gender, not only for the rest of the world, but also for ourselves. We "do" gender so ardently and so convincingly that, with incessant repetition, we come to believe that the learned, gendered comportments we *perform* are "natural," instinctual and of essence.

In the thirty-odd years since performativity's coinage, Butler's concept has been expanded to explain not only gendered identities, but identity in general. Whatever socially-constructed identity we assume, we perform it so incessantly for others—and for ourselves—that we convince ourselves that we've been that way all along. Constructs like race, class and (of course) gender are in this way performative. Now, let's take this concept a step further, even. Let's expand performativity to explain the construct of coolness as personified by a certain Tom Petty.

Coolness is a comportment that Tom Petty *learned*. He didn't do so great in school, but Petty was an adroit scholar of rock-'n'roll—and, thus, a scholar of cool. He learned how to be a rocker, so he learned how to be cool. And with incessant repetition, he became a dexterous performer of cool—so much so, that he came to understand his own coolness as being natural and innate. And while he was busy convincing *himself* how to be cool, he convinced everybody else, too. In this way, he was too cool for school. (Sorry, I can't help myself sometimes.)

Anyway, let's rein this in and return to the bit about Petty's persona-as-product. Sure, we love rock'n'rollers because we love rock'n'roll music. But after a while, the coin flips and we start loving certain rock'n'roll music, really, because we love the rock'n'roller who made it. Case in point: Did you buy that Mudcrutch album because you just had to have a hard copy of their number-one hit that you just couldn't pry out of your brain? Of course not. You bought that Mudcrutch album because you love Tom Petty.

You might've ended up loving the album as a byproduct of its purchase, but you bought the album because you love Petty himself—or his stylized persona, anyway. We bought the album because we "bought" the persona. (And I'm betting that you listened to the Mudcrutch LP a couple of times, liked it well enough, and then stuck it in the shadowed recesses of the stack—over there in between the Traveling Wilburys and Benmont Tench's solo album.)

What I'm getting at is that Tom Petty's persona itself is a postmodern cultural product. Through practice, Petty mastered the performance of cool. Then, through his career, Petty continually retooled his persona to *stay* contemporary-yet-timeless, to stay timelessly cool, and to keep selling more cultural products. Tom Petty's freely fallin' persona was (and *is*) a commodification, a free-floating signifier of Petty-ness that continues evolving (and selling) today. We love the Petty persona because, in its ever-changing facets, we see reflections of ourselves—or who we want to be. And that's cool.

Into the Great Wide Hyperreal

Tom Petty was no stranger to psychedelia. And I'm doubting he would've objected that much to our analytical use of the psychedelic prism of post-structuralism in the final segment of this essay. Then again, maybe I'm just projecting here—or maybe I'm seeing some reflection of myself (or the prefab "me" that I want to see) in some facet of my own interpretation of the Petty persona. Here we go into yet another hall of mirrors where way-out, groovy theories intersect, reflect and refract upon one another. Like, wow, man. Far freakin' out.

Jean Baudrillard (1929–2007), a French philosopher and theorist associated with postmodernism and, later, post-structuralism, introduced the concepts of simulation and the hyperreal to explain how the radical, postmodernist notion that meaning and meaning-making is only decipherable within the context of the symbols and symbol systems that surround it impacts the world. Sure, that's confusing. But here's where the hall of mirrors thing really comes to the fore.

Baudrillard defined the hyperreal as the condition of reflection and refraction where the reference eclipses the referent—as if there *ever were* a referent, that is. Hyperreality is a faux reality that is all surface and no substance. For Baudrillard, "reality" is only an ever-fluctuating contingency. In other words, everything is a copy of a copy of a copy: There is no foundational, *a priori*, core thing (the referent) that "has it."

A simulacrum is the copy of the copy that supersedes, defies and denies the original artifact, as if there ever were one. Even the self is a flexible construct, a facsimile with no fundamental, original, of-essence presence as its base. Following this tack, one might conclude that there is or was no "real" Tom Petty, only a *version* of Tom Petty that was an approximation of the prior version of Tom Petty, that was an approximation of the prior version of Tom Petty, and so on, and so on, ad infinitum. Icons like Tom Petty have no basis in "reality," just as we, ourselves, have no basis in reality.

Critics of Baudrillard (and of postmodernism and of post-structuralism) have asserted that all the aforementioned conceptualizations are nihilistic hogwash that denies the existence of truth, being, the self and, well, anything-and-everything. But bear in mind, these theories are only theories—sincere attempts to explain how things work most of the time, and to the best of our abilities at the time.

Runnin' Down Our Dreams

I repeat yet again that Tom Petty may well not have known or given a damn about postmodernism—*or* post-structuralism, or the hyperreal or simulacra. Nevertheless, these postmodern constructs function as valuable tools with which we can hopefully better understand Petty's timeless cultural resonance. And as to whether or not Petty's artistry and persona were "really true," well, who can say? And does it really matter, anyway?

What *does* matter is that Petty imbued his work with the auras of sincerity, truth, and authenticity that we experience and perceive as real—about as real as it gets. And if we perceive something as real, if we perceive something to be empowering, then it may as well *be* real and empowering, right?

Petty's music, persona, and artistry functions as a site for knowledge production—not only for knowledge of who Tom Petty was or purported to be, but also for knowledge of identity in general and of "who we are" (especially as Americans) in particular. After all, what we perceive in the present *is* reality in the present, or as close of a facsimile of reality as we're gonna get.

If it feels real, it *is* real—or at least real enough, anyway. And that's cool.

So sleep tight, baby, we're alright for now.

2
Echoes of Past and Present

MATTHEW CRIPPEN AND MATTHEW DIXON

Most of us have been through a bad break-up, maybe even one that took far too long in coming around. What album, fired up extra loud and on constant repeat, helped you to get through it? Now that you've hopefully moved on, how often do you reach for that album? Likely never.

Tom Petty finally ended his first marriage around the time he was composing *Echo*. In interviews with biographer Warren Zanes, he described this time as a dark, despondent phase. Wounded, he fell into heroin use, his health degrading to the point that he took to using a cane; his therapist even remarked that people with his level of depression usually don't survive.

Like most people would want to do, Petty went to lengths to repress this period, avoiding videos for the album and its songs on the follow-up tour and reporting little memory of its making. The crisis Petty experienced during the writing and recording of *Echo* was arguably the worst in his life, and the thoughtfulness and self-reflection that traumatic circumstances spur pervade the album. So too does the tendency to look backwards in times of crisis, whether in hopes of finding solidity in the past or just out of an exhausted inability to cope with the present. When you have no way of knowing what lies ahead, why not settle into the dream of a long time ago?

In history, this sort of thing occurs regularly. We see cultures reverting to old gods and traditional ways during moments of great upheaval. Existentialists and psychoanalysts have noted that the same happens on an individual level, and the retrospective feel of *Echo* is one of looking to the past for

the sake of surviving the present. This is to suggest two dominant themes, albeit without reducing the album to just these:
crisis and reversion.

Throughout the album Petty sings of suffering and recovery,
being knocked down and rising, getting high and coming down,
all different ways of expressing similar traumas, signaling the
crisis. The reversion shows up in the form of recurring lyrical
and musical references to bygone eras—echoes of the past, as
it were, with some songs specifically gesturing at critical periods in Petty's life. This nostalgic style in fact typifies Petty's
catalog. Throughout his career he made music steeped in past
rock traditions, and Southern rock, which loves nothing quite
as much as declaring how much better things used to be, claims
him as a seminal figure.

Petty clearly associated *Echo* with personal grief, refusing
to listen to it for years. As with many other examples of art,
however, the album was also a way of surviving and growing
beyond a clear and present trauma. It compelled him to
acknowledge and confront important parts of his past, including his wife of twenty-plus years and perhaps even an abusive
childhood. For Petty, clinging to fragments of the past—musical
and otherwise—appears to have been a way of coping with a
difficult present and the relentless march of time.

Same Sad Echoes

The experience of crisis reverberates internally throughout
Echo, with phrases and sentiments bouncing around and reap-
pearing in multiple songs. The album simultaneously looks
outward and backward, cataloging events from Petty's life and,
to some extent, the shared experiences of those living through
the same periods as him.

Perhaps the most dominant theme echoing through the
album is that of being up or down, high or low, and needing
eagle wings to get over things, as Petty tells us in "Rhino Skin."
The same song emphasizes the struggle of life—needing thick
skin and elephant-sized balls if you don't want to crawl and get
broken and lost. Earlier in the album in "Counting on You," he
laments that somebody is going to let him down.

"Free Girl Now" has an upbeat melody and instrumentation, but is schizophrenically contrasted against a story of a

woman pushed down, held under the thumb of her boss, sexually harassed and forced to keep her mouth shut. This is something Petty understood to some extent, insofar as any musician battling record execs like he did can be said to have suffered some kind of emotional abuse. At the same time, the song looks to an unrealized future when she will no longer be a slave, made to suffer and forced to crawl, this last sentiment exactly repeating what is said in "Rhino Skin."

"Accused of Love" has legal intimations in the title and mentions a grinning attorney, possibly in reference to Petty's divorce. Most songs contain passages about day and night, moonlight and the Sun. Although some of this is trivial, especially given their repetition, images of sinking and setting suns form a persistent trope that underscores the sorrow of the album.

The constant talk of being knocked down, let down, getting up, sinking into and rising above troubles—in addition to connoting elevated and deflated moods—points to the highs and lows of drug use. "Rhino Skin" emphasizes that you need a tough exterior or else you'll give in to needles and pins. "A Room at the Top" is a somber tune about love and refusing to come down, and its first verse speaks about drinking and forgetting what went wrong. Its pleading sentiments, which have Petty begging for someone to love him because he's not so bad, are echoed in "Lonesome Sundown," which concludes with the line: "Please believe in me."

In the title track of the album, Petty sings about the same sad echo and likewise speaks of pills and poison liquid. But he needs more validation, more safety among his fellow humans, than he could find in his drug-addled stupor in the chicken shack.

The highs and lows of trauma and drugs are difficulties people battle through, and the question of whether or not to keep fighting resounds in "I Don't Wanna Fight," "Swingin'," and "Billy the Kid." The last two of these songs exhibit nostalgia for past American icons, with protagonists going down hard like the Old West gunfighter who died at twenty-one; or going down swinging like prizefighter Sonny Liston; or again like Benny Goodman, Glenn Miller, and Sammy Davis in punny references to the Swing era. Petty chose his examples from among the old-timers as opposed to a more contemporary figure like Mike

Tyson or Michael Jackson, seeming to find a balm by mostly dwelling in the past and long familiar.

Is He about to Give Out?

The song "About to Give Out," in addition to connotations of being on the brink of losing a fight, likewise tips its hat to past icons. It does so in a way, moreover, that appears to chronicle critical periods in Petty's life. Davy Crockett in a coonskin town gets repeated mention, with Roy Rogers referenced near the end of the song. Rogers was a singer and actor, particularly known for westerns, a genre obviously emphasized in songs such as "Billy the Kid" and "Swingin'," with the latter's line about silver spurs.

Rogers was extremely popular during Petty's childhood in the 1950s, just around the time Disney produced its wildly successful series about Davy Crockett and marketed coonskin caps to children around the Western world. Petty claimed to Zanes that television educated him and saved him during his early years, and TV gets an additional mention in "A Room at the Top." Zanes adds that Petty and his brother Bruce obsessively watched westerns.

These songs—and especially "About to Give Out," with its focus on TV—accordingly return to Petty's early years, and he perhaps took solace in childhood references, as many do when dealing with trauma. Something similar may hold for the biblically named Abraham and Moses, who also show up in the song, but with the latter drinking and everyone finding themselves beaten up and naked in the bushes. As it happens, Petty's father was a drinker too, and physically and emotionally abusive to his children, so this may be another reminiscence about childhood, an echo of the past brought to the fore by trauma Petty experienced while making the album.

"About to Give Out" looks to other periods in Petty's life, in this case, happier times. Petty opens the track by singing about Ricky and Dickey, names of two of his 1960s bandmates from his teen years in Florida. The state itself is brought up in the first verse, specifically with a mention of Daytona. A little later, the song moves to the next decade, referencing the 1970s hit "Delta Dawn." This tune is nostalgic—a mix between country, gospel, and folk in the vein of the traditional song "Can the

Circle Be Unbroken?" This song, moreover, was one that was on heavy rotation during Petty's formative years, with hits recorded in 1972 and 1973 by Tanya Tucker and Helen Reddy, along with numerous others in the same period, including Waylon Jennings and Loretta Lynn.

The early 1970s was an exciting period for Petty, who arrived in Los Angeles in 1975, and he surely remembered that time nostalgically. This was just when his career was taking hold. It marked the birth of his first child, Adria. Shortly before this, his first marriage occurred, too—the relationship that finally gave out right before *Echo*.

Arriving at endings often throws the mind back to beginnings, and this is a plausible explanation for Petty's reflections on the early 1970s in "About to Give Out." At the same time, he may have simultaneously sought comfort in the good times, not just in the 1970s, but the previous two decades as well. Given that earlier decades also contained the trauma of having an abuser for a dad, the current crisis likely reminded him of that earlier one, pushing his mind back there for this reason as well. This fits with the internal echoes in the album, which clearly meditate on distressing circumstances.

Looking to a Higher Place

Being down often leads us to dwell on better times, and we see this at various points in the album. One of the high points in Petty's career came nearly fifteen years after the release of his first album, when he experienced a renaissance working with Jeff Lynne in the late Eighties and early Nineties. During this period, he produced *Full Moon Fever*, *Into the Great Wide Open*, and two albums with the super-group the Traveling Wilburys, comprised of himself, Bob Dylan, George Harrison, Jeff Lynne, and Roy Orbison. The streak continued into the post-Lynne period, with *Wildflowers* released in 1994, considered by many to be the artistic highpoint of Petty's career.

In *Echo*, the referencing to Petty's period working with Lynne is no more evident than in "Accused of Love." Shades of *Full Moon Fever* can clearly be heard in both the instrumentation and mixing of this song. Along with the blend and style of guitars, bouncing acoustic rhythms and embellishments, unpretentious drumming and non-syncopated guitar solos without string bending, its clean, layered and airy production specifically bring to mind "Yer So Bad," co-written with Lynne. Both songs also combine uplifting yet jaded lyrics, although admittedly less jaded in "Accused of Love."

The musical homage paid to this period is further reinforced by lyrics pointing to the Heartbreakers' time as Dylan's backing band on the 1987 Temples in Flames Tour, just at the beginning of Petty's collaboration with Lynne. In "Accused of Love," Petty sings about London and Mayfair, an area near Hyde Park and in which the Beatles shared a home in the early 1960s. The final leg of the Temples in Flames tour was in London, and the Beatles reference is fitting since George Harrison and Ringo Starr showed up for it. Lynne was also there, and hence—with Dylan, Lynne, and Petty—all of the Wilburys, except for Roy Orbison.

The song also mentions driving through rain, and a borderline hurricane hit the city immediately after the last show, leaving a lasting impression on Petty, according to the Zanes biography. Taken with the musical style, the song points to the late 1980s and specifically to last stops on the Bob Dylan tour that marked the beginning of a new musical period for Petty. The production values and general tone of this song also point just beyond this period and particularly to "A Higher Place" from *Wildflowers*.

At the same time, "Accused of Love"—like so many others on the album—contains sad echoes. It does, to begin with, because Petty does not speak of being in love, but being accused of it. Moreover, it's in this period that Orbison died, shortly before he could enjoy the success of his hit "You Got It," co-written with Lynne and Petty, and on which they both performed. This early death may have been on Petty's mind because others were imminent.

It was during the recording of *Echo* that his longtime friend and Wilburys bandmate Harrison was diagnosed with the throat cancer that would take his life in 2001. The production of *Echo* also coincided with the time that the Heartbreakers' bassist and backing vocalist Howie Epstein was beginning a final descent into heroin addiction that eventually led to his death in 2003. Petty indicated that he saw this on the horizon too, and the pain of this may have been amplified by his own struggles with addiction and life in general.

Musical Refugees

The internal and external echoes to the past are not just lyrical. While melancholically creative and hence not derivative, the album mines fragments from the musical past and to some extent the present (and even from itself), dwelling in this way on good times and bad.

The soft guitar strum, pacing, keyboards and general mood make the introduction of "Echo" nearly interchangeable with the beginning of "A Room at the Top," for example. The use of reverb, minor harmonies, the earthy keyboards and overall production qualities in "Rhino Skin" go a little further back in time and recollect "Asshole," a bleak Beck cover from Petty's previous album. "I Don't Wanna Fight"—a Heartbreakers performance composed and sung by Mike Campbell—returns to the hard-driving rock of *Damn the Torpedoes*. The straight-laced drums and layered drones of electric guitars in "Free Girl Now" go back further to "American Girl," itself influenced by psychedelic music.

The musical references continue in the sprightly mix of acoustic and electric guitars, the backing vocal harmonies and the stories of loss in songs such as "Won't Last Long," "This One's for Me," and of course "Accused of Love," which all harken to Petty's style in the late Eighties and early Nineties. Specifically, these songs bring to mind Petty's collaborations with Lynne when he made some of his best recordings, including the Wilburys albums. *Wildflowers* was another artistic high point that he often said was his best album, and this period also gets echoed in the appropriately titled song "Echo." Specifically, the soft electric guitars, sparse piano and harmonic progressions dominated by minor chords recall the composition and arrangement of *Wildflowers*' "Good to Be King."

"About to Give Out" likewise offers a musical chronicling of the past. This time buttressing what goes on in the lyrics, it points to two or three eras, and goes back much further than the Lynne period. The piano tracks simultaneously typify 1950s icons such as Jerry Lee Lewis and 1970s staples such as BTO, Billy Joel, and indeed the Heartbreakers. The guitar work could be from the late 1960s or the 1970s. All of this is lyrically reinforced by stanzas about 1950s TV shows and icons, along with references to bandmates from the Sixties and the early Seventies repeat-hit "Delta Dawn."

Petty was again probably seeking consolation in these bygone musical eras, some of them artistically formative, if not remembered fondly. At the same time, thinking back must have caused pain. His childhood was not especially happy. Returning to the 1970s when his marriage began was presumably a way of pondering its end. Even the late 1980s, while artistically defining and a time of renewed commercial success, simultaneously marked endings, with Orbison dying at the end of this period.

A little closer to home, a rupture also occurred with longtime Heartbreakers bandmate Stan Lynch. This happened during the 1987 Dylan tour when a bitter fight occurred between Lynch and Campbell, the latter being the glue that kept the former connected to Petty during their strained relationship, as Zanes documents. This ultimately pushed or pulled Lynch out of the band, who was especially resentful of Petty's projects with Lynne. Though not directly connected to Petty's divorce, it does relate to endings and the fact that new beginnings often bring them about.

Trauma Trauma Trauma Repeats

Although some scholars and especially those discussing fine arts put too much stock in psychoanalytic perspectives, it may nonetheless be as psychoanalysts say: that people suffering trauma relive the past in unacknowledged hopes of bringing about different outcomes.

Psychoanalysts such as Sigmund Freud and Jacques Lacan have proposed that we are fated to repeat traumatic experiences. Repetition can manifest as dreams or flashbacks in which the person afflicted feels that they are reliving their trauma, and that can be sublimated into art. It can also appear in the more disturbing form of re-enactment where someone who suffered trauma, particularly during developmental phases, keeps falling into similar problematic patterns, which, however much despised, seem impossible to abandon. This occurs when we find ourselves in troubled relationships resembling those from the past, but it too can be sublimated into art.

Such perspectives seem to capture at least some of what is going on in *Echo*. But this is not because Petty was re-entering troubled relationships. It is instead because he was creating music almost obsessively fixated on difficult events from the past, whether in the form of his marriage or childhood. At the same time, many of the songs focus on high points and pleasurable moments, whether by turning to childhood memories of westerns or the Jeff Lynne years and other formative periods in his career.

That said, reasons for Petty's fixation on the past might be more straightforward. To begin with, making art draws on our past, good and ill, albeit not necessarily to the extent Petty explicitly relied on it in *Echo*. Some of the repetitiveness may have resulted from his suppressed capacity to generate new material because he was simply exhausted. Without criticizing the aesthetic of the album—which is somehow uplifting and somber, refined and gritty, resigned and pleading, all at the same time—there is a sparseness to the lyrics. "Counting on You" has only three two-line verses, plus a chorus. Six out of eight lines in the verses begin with the phrase "I want you to be," followed by various completions. "Won't Last Long" recapitulates phrases, many relating to being down and out, but with hopes of getting up again.

Some stanzas in fact draw attention to repetition in a self-reflexive way, as when Petty repeatedly says "over and over" and "over this ground again." Other recurring phrases in the song are: "I can't explain," "Don't let me down," "I'm down but it won't last long" and "Half my brain has gone." This last sentiment reappears in the soulful and deeply sorrowful song "One More Day, One More Night," which contains the line, "What goes on in my brain is not clear." Though composed by Petty's bandmate Mike Campbell, the song "I Don't Wanna Fight" fits this pattern too, repeating a relatively small number of stanzas and musical motifs. The sparse aesthetic continues in "No More," albeit not because lyrics repeat, but because of their sheer brevity. The instrumentation here is also simple, and on a musical level, there is a descending call and response—or echoing—throughout.

Will-to-Power Chords

The exhaustion that the album's sparseness points to indicates that Petty must have been experiencing a need to conserve depleted energy. This is along lines described by Friedrich

Nietzsche, often compared to his slightly younger contemporary Freud.

Nietzsche conceived life as will to expansion, or what he called power. Organisms grow in ways to increase their field of domain, as when moss covers more space, a cat explores new territory, or we gain greater mastery over skills like playing guitar. Though it is conceived as growth, Nietzsche also understood that endless expansion is self-destructive, as when continually taking on additional things until falling apart and suffering a breakdown.

Thus, in this scheme, conserving or preserving phases are part of healthy cycles if they allow for the next push forward, outward, or upward. On the other hand, endless self-preservation—here defined as merely maintaining yourself—is symptomatic of illness. For Nietzsche, the past is what is already settled and thus conserved, so relying exclusively on it is indicative of illness. Endless, repetitive bouncing in the present indicates the same thing. Petty of course did not *merely* rely on the past, nor *endlessly* echo the present. However, the album displays a situation of distress in Nietzsche's sense, more so if the sparseness is grasped as a conserving of energy in the face of exhaustion.

One More Album, One More Fight

Nietzsche's notion of illness is carried through the album and exemplified in its closing song, "One More Day, One More Night," a moving expression of deep anguish and hope. The song opens with laid-back folk and blues tones in the electric guitars and some mournful stanzas. Petty's voice sounds tired as he pleads to God about how he's had to fight night and day to keep his sight on what's real, and also about his fears of losing his way and touch with what he feels. Petty then repeatedly laments breaking down and being alone.

After this, the lyrics grow more hopeful, with Petty singing about a night when his eyes will reflect light and come upon something bright in the distance. At a climactic moment in the song, the meandering downward melody and instrumentation shift abruptly to numerous and forceful punctuations. At this point the language also switches to repeated imperatives to hold out for one more day and one more night. Again, merely holding on is symptomatic of illness. However, the closing verse of the song, and in fact the album itself, becomes even more hopeful than earlier, with Petty singing that "there'll be one more night and things will be made right" and adding that he'll "soon be far away from here." The closing guitar work is more aggressive, growling and weeping.

Even while Nietzsche claimed preservation is symptomatic of illness, he also maintained that it can arise from an instinct to protect life in decline. This seeming denial of life can, as Nietzsche explained, be among the most conserving and affirming forces, and indeed a way of recovering for growth, as when we rest in anticipation of a personally expanding trial. Although Petty was likely at the lowest and darkest phase of his life, with *Echo* reflecting this, the last song and indeed entire album in many ways manifest Nietzsche's definition of health. For Nietzsche, health was not freedom from psychological and physiological malady, but the strength to go forward and expand in the face of obstacles, including those conventionally understood as illnesses.

Nietzsche also said that we possess art lest we perish of truth, the latter understood as stasis and hence antithetical to life, growth, and health. *Echo* exhibits life-affirming aspects of art specifically because Petty's crippling depression and health problems were not a barrier. Instead, these difficulties spurred him to one of his most creative and aesthetically subtle albums—an album, moreover, not myopically focused on pain, and sometimes even unapologetically upbeat, if not happy. Petty was not giving up on his fight to recover, as he expressly sums up in "Billy the Kid." And he did recover after *Echo*, kicking his heroin habit and finding love with Dana York, whom he credited for saving him and who later became his second wife.

Though focused on personal grief and survival, *Echo* simultaneously emphasizes high points in Petty's life, looking to the past for the sake of self-preservation in the present. The album manifests life-affirming impulses to expand beyond present and past traumas. Mining fragments of the past, musical and otherwise, and building creatively with them—like a painter producing a masterwork with a limited palette—may have offered ways of dealing with a challenging present and a difficult and fading past.

3
Don't Come Around Here, Mary Jane

RANDALL E. AUXIER

This is a tale of three years: 1979, 1985, and 1993. It was the not yet, the middle, and the end. This is the story of the MTV era.

It's impossible to talk about Tom Petty's videos without writing a whole book, so we will bring the three crucial moments to life, and then we will kill them, in order to save them for eternity, to rescue them from being just *things*. (What is he talking about? You'll see. Depending on when you were born and whether you had cable, maybe you've already seen.)

The Great In-Between

It's 1979. It's the not yet. I have to get you there (or then) in your imagination. It's tougher than you may think. Most important, MTV isn't a thing yet, but (surprise surprise), music videos are everywhere. People get this order of events confused. If you were thinking MTV *caused* music videos, it was really vice versa.

In my personal case (apologies for this self-indulgence), I'm fresh out of high school. I'm not very cool, but the coolest music club in Memphis is called Antenna Club. I go. They don't card me. The club features live punk and New Wave music *and* music videos in between live sets (and these videos also play without sound during the show, which is unusual—TVs in bars were not then as they are now, unimaginable as that may be).

Now, in 1979 you couldn't see music videos on television, except once in a while, as part of a network variety show, or on

27

the edgy new late night shows like *SNL* and the doomed ABC *Fridays*. That is also where you'll get a glimpse of Blondie and the Clash and Elvis Costello, and pretty much anything else that the kids think is cool. Cable TV was new, but they hadn't figured out what to do with it, and most places didn't have it. For God's sake, they only just now had channel-numbers above 13. Weird Al's *UHF* movie was still a full decade away. So we're talking primitive times. Times of yore. Oh, and VCRs are still a great novelty, and Beta/Max, VHS and the short lived video disc are having their *battle royale* to the death. (Tom makes excellent use of that time-slice in the video for "Yer So Bad.")

I don't want to belabor the point about being there. I guess I will anyway. You may think you have this time in your head, but do you really? Even if you're old enough? Are you sure you aren't confusing it with the Eighties? There is no U2, no Go-Go's, *but* disco is dead. *Saturday Night Fever* both capped it and killed it in '77. Disco died of over-exposure and of a case of the Heebie-Bee-Gee's (in skin-tight spandex and satin). Disco's rebel running mate, Southern Rock, was also dead. Without disco to hate and with Ronnie Van Zant moldering in his grave, Southern Rock's *reason-to-be* became only a *reason-to-have-been*. Seeing the writing on the wall, certain other musicians departed fertile north Florida for fairer prospects. I have five musicians in mind, in particular. We will get to them. See my essay "The Boys of Summer."

What we have, then, is a moment, and we are melting in modern English, while New York is also eating to that beat. The Brits and the Big Apple are rocking along parallel lines. There are rats on the Westside, bed bugs uptown, what a shattered mess! And video hasn't killed the radio star. It's the great in-between. No one *knows* that because no one knows what's next (i.e., "the Eighties"). I wish I had understood it was "the Eighties" when the Eighties were actually happening and I was in my twenties, the perfect age to enjoy "the Eighties." But the Eighties didn't become "the Eighties" until the late Nineties. So we all sort of missed it. Until it was long over. Then we missed it in a different sense. I don't think "the Sixties" were like that. People *knew* it was the Sixties—they just can't remember it *now*. So they say. Kind of a blur of cotton candy and *Gilligan's Island* for me, to be honest.

Working Class Heroes

In the heartland (that *other* great in-between), it's mainly silence. Silence and a surviving niche for the working-class heroes, Springsteen and Seger. (I have to mention Cheap Trick in here somewhere, since they are lighting up the fly-over at this precise point, but they're a little too much like a cartoon cereal box cover right now to appeal to the working class—they're like the Archies on cocaine. The working class will figure out that Cheap Trick is the real deal quite a bit later.) Out west, Van Halen is still a *rock* band (they haven't jumped off that track yet). And during one of those nights at the Hotel California, the Eagles have morphed from a progressive country act into a sort of rock band (thank you Joe Walsh—you'll come up again later). What a moment. You might say it's musically the great wide open. But some stuff is afoot. The next big thing is nexting, or is next to nexting.

At just this moment, Springsteen shelved his "wall-of-sound double album," *The Promise,* and sold off his planned singles: "Because the Night" to Patti Smith and "Fire" to the Pointer Sisters. It must be nice to have "extra" songs like that. (Springsteen finally released that double album in 2010, when, as he said, it couldn't do any damage.) Springsteen and a few others from E Street made the journey from AM to FM album-oriented rock with that decision. So the world zigged and Springsteen zagged. Seger kept zigging. He would not grow a new audience in the Eighties, although he kept the one he built in the Seventies, and kept them mightily entertained.

You know damn well why I'm telling you all this, because you know that 1979 was Tom Petty's year. It was *Damn the Torpedoes* time. Yes, there were videos, but the album that made him a star was a radio phenomenon. We liked the way it sounded, and not the way it looked.

So here we are in the great in-between. What will soon happen hasn't happened yet. Soon commercial music will be forever altered by MTV. But Tom Petty and the Heartbreakers are making a bit of noise, and no one knows quite what they are. They get famous in England, so they have that kind of cachet, and they are being confused with New Wave. They're all from

north Florida, so some people see this as Southern Rock. They
live and record on the West Coast, so some people associate
them with that scene and sound—especially since everyone can
hear that they sound like the Byrds (after the acid wore off but
before Barstow).

Here Comes My Girl?

So, you've heard it, read it, that when MTV arrived, Tom Petty
and his band were sitting there waiting for it. It is true, but if
you weren't alive yet, or old enough to grasp 1979, you've still
not quite got the picture. Music videos are really cool and popular in 1979 and had been shipped to us from England for several years. Some people say Bob Dylan invented the genre with
his iconic "Subterranean Homesick Blues," but you know how
kids are. In 1979 we don't remember 1965 because we were,
like, four. We'll discover Dylan later. Right now he's sort of a
second-rate gospel singer. Or ghaspel more accurately. Tom
Petty has been to England, is a rock star there, and he noticed
what to do. So yes, he's ready, but it's not that remarkable. Still,
his videos are different.

And this band (and its leader) are serious about using
videos in a serious way. It's true that they want to sell music,
but I believe these guys knew that having a video that people
wanted to watch over and over was the key to pushing the
music itself. It started with images to accompany the music, a
sort of afterthought, and by the time MTV hit, videos were
already becoming the cart that pulled the horse.

And I'm like every other eighteen-year-old kid, but something is changing. All of a sudden, if I like the images, I
remember the songs. Not the other way around. And it used
to be that I remembered the song from the radio if I liked it.
And, same as every other kid, if I remember the songs, I buy
the songs. But now my memory is as much (and maybe
more) visual than aural. There's been a *cha-eyay—eyange*.
No? And (most importantly), when I hear the songs, I now see
the images before my mind. That means that how the band
looks in the videos becomes a crucial part of whether I like
the music. That judgment used to be made without visual
images, but now the "economy" of judging has actually
reversed.

General Economy

There once was a very creepy philosopher named Georges Bataille (1897–1962). He's so very much creepier than Tom Petty ever could be that it makes Tom entirely non-creepy by contrast, even with consideration for "Don't Come Around Here" and "Mary Jane's Last Dance." We both know Tom could be very creepy. "Creepy" is a good example of something you get *phenomenologically* (again see "The Boys of Summer" for that story in full). Very often you can't say *why* something creeps you out. But it usually has to do with that line between dark and light and what is sacred and profane, and, well, it's about eating the other. And sex. But let's wait on that one for a bit (or a bite).

Bataille says that death and life have this ultra-disturbing relationship. To be alive is *not* to be a *thing*. *Things* belong to the land of the dead. You can be physically alive and still be a *thing*. To be a thing is to be used as a thing and to fall into the world of things, of mere use, of meaningless instrumentality. But such meaningless existence can be redeemed and even things that are not physically alive can come to life. Take a guitar, a twelve-string Rickenbacker, for example. It's a thing, until someone who knows how to make it come alive reclaims it from the pawn shop or the storage unit. In the right hands, it is reclaimed, redeemed, rescued. It sings, it becomes personalized, and then the player dies and now the guitar is sacred because of the way it rang when Tom was playing it.

But what if the thing isn't a tool but a person? What happens to people who become things for the use of others? You realize Tom Petty hated that more than any other human habit, the degradation of others into mere things? He would rather have been poor and nobody than to be treated as a thing by his record companies and managers. And he wouldn't let his fans be treated that way either. He stood up for anybody and everybody who was being commodified and wouldn't back down, as we all know. So, my point: things have been sent to hell already, because it's hell to be a thing. There is nothing worse.

But here is where it gets weird. Bataille says that for all of human existence, pre-dating history, we understood that living beings who had been reduced to things were "dead" even though they were still alive. They were, in a way, un-dead, zombies, beings in the dark and in hell, with no way to reclaim themselves for light and for life. Such beings must, Bataille believed, die in order to be returned to the cosmic order of life and the sacred. That's why it's *merciful* to shoot zombies. And you know that, deep in your oh-so-delicious guts. To fall into hell is to fall away from the gods and the sacred order. It is banishment from the presence of the divine, and whole communities can fall under that shadow.

This is why we sacrificed human beings for most of our time on earth, Bataille says. Only in the last few thousand years has that practice been effectively questioned. And only in the last hundred or so has it been widely rejected—we were, after all, still hanging witches and then lynching others until quite recently, and ethnic cleansing hasn't exactly disappeared. Why do you think we (until recently) executed criminals for many, many offenses—and in a handful of countries (such as Afghanistan, Syria, Saudi Arabia, and the United States), we still do? Only a few years before the advent of MTV did we even bother to declare some execution methods cruel and unusual. At least in the Middle East and Central Asia they are honest with themselves about what they are doing and why. We'll definitely kill your ass, but it won't be cruel and it certainly isn't unusual, *for us.* Either way, the feeling is that criminals have made themselves into things for us, and we reclaim them for the sacred order by depriving them of the life that can be regained in no other way. And we "protect" (re-sacralize) our community from the deeds they brought to us by sending them to their makers, be they the gods or the demons.

Now, this is not an endorsement of the death penalty, it's an explanation that charts the practice. Last I checked, Jesus got the death penalty for something less than murder and kidnapping, and we celebrate by eating his flesh and drinking his blood, more or less constantly. The king must die, and if he doesn't have the decency to do it on his own, we have to help him. Bataille has quite a disturbing little explanation of "The king is dead. Long live the king." It goes deep in our general economy of life and death. As I recall, Jesus had a conversation with a couple of thieves, once. They weren't exactly murderers either, but one is with Jesus in paradise, so I've read. Creepy? Well, it's human. Say what you want, but the only thing new in the Jesus story is that he was supposed to be the last and sufficient sacrifice of that kind. Didn't really work out that way, for most people, I guess, in light of what followed the killing of Archduke Franz Ferdinand, for example.   Being in France, Bataille had noticed the First World War. He later noticed the Second.

For most of the time humans have been on Earth, they have killed each other ritually in order to set right the cosmic order. Jesus had to die just as surely as Nathan Hale and Ted Bundy did. It isn't about criminality, although all three were duly convicted by the authorities. It's about *things* and life and how death restores an order, a kind of "general economy" of heaven and earth. When you're convicted and sentenced, your thinghood is pronounced, and death is your reclamation. You can't get religion going without this. Achieving Nirvana isn't so different. Ask Kurt Cobain.

Bataille says that when a non-thing becomes a thing, that thing must die *as thing* in order to become a non-thing again. So a criminal is a kind of thing. Things want to live again. Death frees them to do that—I mean to live, sort of, cosmically, eternally. Or so we obviously still believe, somewhat opaquely. Without this economy of life and death, we are *all* just things. That's why religion is better than science. Science renounces the eternal and therefore sentences everything to thingdom, and makes every non-thing a thing. Science is hell. For science, you already are a sort of zombie. Religion agrees. Science is mm-bad. For religion, Christianity for instance, you are dead because of sin and can be resurrected by the death-life ritual (baptism, extreme unction, last rites, illumination, conversion, whatever). For Buddhism, you are unenlightened and suffering. But you can escape. And so on.

Science doesn't offer you a path away from thingdom; it just tells you to "get over it. If you want to be more than a thing, you want too much. Now eat your vegetables." But I admit I want to be more than a thing. In fact, I insist on it. So actual death might be welcome if eternal thingdom is my other choice. That is the bet religion always makes. It's "join us or be just a thing." Hell of an economy. Gimme that communion wafer, and make it rare, bloody in fact—whose body did you say it was? Do you have any A1? And maybe you thought capitalism was a bad economy. Actually, it still is. It's sort of like every dehumanizing and thingifying aspect of human experience rolled into one pointless waste machine.

But here we come to the point. And it gets weirder. Bataille says that the only way we can really free a thing is to *waste it*. That's right. We indulge, we behave in completely gratuitous fashion. Then and only then is the thing not a thing at all, because it has been released from all utility, from any and every practical use. We save you by wasting you, if you have become a thing. Call in Rambo. It's time for 1985.

Eat Me

No one is comfortable with this "economy" of sacrifice, even when it masquerades as some sick kind of justice. Bataille calls this energy that must be wasted "the accursed share." It arises from the excess of our bodily energy and our social energy that exceeds usefulness. We just have more energy than we can use constructively. We must waste. That is why we create culture, but even then we can't use it all. It builds up and it must be wasted because it cannot be used to achieve anything with it, so we kill each other, waste each other.

The only difference between us and our primal ancestors is the bullshit stories we tell ourselves about *why* we kill each other in massive numbers. In our more honest remote past, we embraced the sacrifice and ate the god in each of us. Of course, my Protestant brothers and sisters do this symbolically about once a month, eating Jesus. My Roman Catholic friends do it at every mass, and, according to them, non-symbolically. We have made an economy of that too, eating the god and being in communion with the divine. It isn't wrong if you do it right, right? Having wasted thee, I must get for myself as much of thine energy as I can stomach.

Now, as if you didn't know, this brings us to Alice. It isn't 1979 anymore. Our crew of Florida refugees has passed through a development, a growth. They rediscover that they are rebels, after all, except for Howie Epstein, who is Canadian and doesn't fit. They try hard to pretend he fits, but, well, he isn't long for this world and everybody knows it. Ron Blair will be back after Howie has sacrificed himself to the rock gods. Still, in 1985 he has a while to remain and has injected a new energy into the band—more than they can really handle. They will spend the Eighties with something running all around their brains, and it's gonna get weirder before it reaches a limit and begins to waste its substance.

Speaking of weird, at just this moment when the boys are reclaiming their rebel roots, the strangest dude in the English-speaking world appears in Tom's life: Dave Stewart. He isn't normal. I mean, he's devoted to Annie Lennox. That's not sane. But Tom likes him and Tom needs a single, so he goes down the rabbit hole. Dave has heard Stevie Nicks screaming at Joe Walsh not to "come around here anymore!" He is producing her album and needs a fresh ear. Tom is wandering around the studio. He and Stevie are tight, so he wanders in. Stevie leaves to get dinner. Four hours later Dave and Tom have a the demo for a new song—for Tom, not Stevie—and it's a can't miss hit. Tom takes it. Dave follows him to the studio at Tom's place.

Southern Accents now has a single, and that is far more important than having a coherent concept album. Why? Because it's 1985, silly rabbit, not 1979. Concept albums were for the brief sojourns on Earth of prog-rock and AOR-FM (may they rest in glorious peace, having now been wasted for no reason, except that it was necessary), and now an outrageous economy of images has replaced the Wagnerian prog-economy of sound. In short, your concept album isn't shit without an MTV-able single. And it's like always: we must out-do whatever went before. Time to eat Alice.

In the infamous cake-eating finale of the video for "Don't Come Around Here No More," MTV made Tom *remove* a leer he gave at the camera while Alice is being eaten. Biographer Nick Thomas reports that Petty said that MTV "actually made me edit out a scene of my face when we were cutting her up. They said it was just too lascivious. It was just a shot of me grinning, and they were like, 'Well, you can do it, but you can't enjoy it that much'." But we know very well what Tom looks like when he grins that way and, well, it creeps us out. He was very, very good at that. Too good. We are moving into decadent waste. Yum. It's gonna get worse before it gets better.

So this guy Bataille, well, when his own mother died he masturbated over her corpse while his pregnant wife slept in the next room. This goes beyond grinning lasciviously. We can agree on that. But how far beyond the video for "Mary Jane's Last Dance" is it? You see, the general economy of life, death, and wasted energy is sort of what rock music was always about. The leader of the pack, well, we'll never forget to tell Laura he loved her, teen angel that she was, and give her J. Frank's last kiss while you're at it, you black-painted bat out of hell, so don't worry baby, if you ever come back from dead man's curve. I'm guessing you get the point. "Hello, Death; this is Rock Music, and Rock Music, this is Death . . ." a pause. "It's okay dude. We've met."

They ate Alice. So it goes. Wish Foley thought it was funny, and her opinion counts, since she was dessert. Just boys messing around, she said. She would surely know. After all, she did spend the next five years with Stan Lynch, to prove her sincerity about being okay with being eaten. That is surely all anyone could be expected to endure. Stan is an asshole, even by his own admission. In the general economy of eating Alice, Stan sort of got the corner piece with the extra icing. You can't have your cheesecake and eat her too, I guess, but it isn't forbidden to try. It's not all that creepy until you think about it too much, as we have now clearly done.

I Release You, Mary Jane

This brings us, always and inevitably, to the creepiest video ever made. It isn't 1979. It isn't 1985. It's the swan song of the video era, and everything has been done. TP and his HB's have dominated the video market, making one smash after another, vids that still hold up and bear multiple watchings. And that turned out to be the key to the kingdom. Hypothetical: Can I watch this four minutes five hundred times and still think it's cool? Yes, and by the way, yes. Give me the dead Kim Basinger. The dedder the bedder. She said it was actually a tough role. Director yelling at her "you're dead, dammit, be deader." I totally believe her. Tom said when they were talking about casting that it needed to be someone desirable enough to keep around even dead. When someone suggested Basinger, Tom reportedly said "Yeah, I'd keep her around for a day or two." The general economy of necrophilia. Bataille would love it.

By the way, if you ever wanted to know what happened to Bart, the roadie, after Eddie Rebel's fall, here's what happened: he bought a Victorian mansion on psycho hill and got a job working nights at the LA County Morgue, and not because he needed the money. Hell, Eddie took care of his own. No, Bart's tastes had grown exotic during the great wide-open years. And then Bart read Bataille somewhere in there, and saw the animated movie *Heavy Metal* and that was all she wrote. Next thing you know, it's a date with Mary Jane.

You'll say "Tom was acting, playing Bart, but Bataille was not." But aren't we all acting, pretty much always? Tom had a ritual for releasing the soul of the beauty—or resurrecting her. (Remember her eyes at the end? Same as his eyes at the beginning?) Bataille had a ritual, too: Mother is primal. We owe her the full measure of the life force. Her death releases her from baby-maker into the cosmic all. We all have rituals and they always point to primal and unspeakable aspects of our desires and fears. We spend our lives trying *not to know* this stuff, but we feel these fears, these desires.

Therefore: Alice *wants* to be eaten (So, "no" doesn't always mean no in the general economy of sacred and profane; Bataille would be both personally and professionally destroyed in the #MeToo era—but he'd be totally into being destroyed, which is extra icky). Mary Jane *wants* to be dressed in white, wedded, "danced with" (uh-huh, you know what I mean), and released. I guess Bart takes Mary Jane home because that is what she really wants. She's just the quiet type. These desires cannot be wholly suppressed, and when they begin to take on visible form, we *feel* the order they suggest. It is general economy.

What an odd way to navigate the line between what is absolutely required and what is absolutely forbidden. Phenomenology helps us see what we don't really want to see. That is a good word for MTV in the 1980s. It shows us what we know but didn't really think about until it was on the TV. Mary Jane doesn't like TV. She's old-fashioned. MTV is an extended group experiment in what it is like to appropriate rock music through the mediation of visual images. And no one is better at it than Tom Petty.

A Thing about You

Bataille began his infamous career by explaining this "general economy" thing. I fear it is a thing. We may have to kill it to save it. Let me sharpen my knife. The weird dude doesn't have in mind the growth of the GDP or the price of eggs when he chooses the word "economy." I want to see if you believe this as deeply as Bart does. Consider: everything the humans do revolves around collecting, storing, and expending energy. We kill in order to transfer energy and live off of it. As the philosopher Whitehead said, the order of life is based on robbery. Our very physiology (as with all vertebrates) is a matter of taking in forms of energy—food, light, water—and expending that energy when the need arises.

But we always take in more than we can use and our bodies and minds and communities must blow off the extra steam. Our rituals help with that, channeling dangerous extra energy into highly controlled and repetitive activities. (It is very good for everyone concerned that Stan Lynch became a *drummer*. His energies were not well controlled and were maximally overcharged. Wish Foley wanted such a beast, for a bit anyway.) So we have the dance and the story and the frenzied carnival and the other mating rigmarole, and yes, finally, the war. We do all we can to direct the extra energy into accepted forms, and then we just have to waste the rest. I hate throwing food out when I consider something had to die for me to have it. So I give it to the cats. And what they don't eat I offer to a neighborhood dog. And what the mutt doesn't eat disappears. Some being eats it at night when I'm asleep. Maybe Bataille eats it.

All that effort? *That* is where culture comes from, from that extra energy and what we do with it. MTV is culture. Sort of. We don't *need* art or religion, or even language to *survive*. But we have extra energy in our bodies, so we use some of it to create what no one actually needs, like MTV, and then we pass around the results, like songs and music videos and essays on Tom Petty. But even when we have done our best to be constructive with our energies, there is still a shitload left over. MTV can't save us, heartbreaking as that may be, in spite of its awesome, gnarly waste of excess energy. So we fight and kill and rape and pillage and eat Alice while grinning and dance with Mary Jane even when she doesn't really dance back. We must.

The Rips

It's 1993. The MTV era has run its course. VH1 actually has more viewers. It's hard to be hip forever. The tweenagers have become thirty-something and don't let their kids watch Tom

Petty videos. Their energy is directed into childcare and having affairs with their co-workers. There is still extra energy, apparently. Only about half of them will still be married to the same person in ten years. You are succeeding. You are surrounded by things. You are becoming a thing.

Have you ever seen a cat get the evening crazies? (We call it "the rips" at our house.) Well, that's you too, my friends and neighbors. You get the rips, and sometimes you *want* to be so bad. You smoke a cigarette and that makes it worse, so then you down a slug of Jim Beam and you're about even. About. Not quite. So you might wonder where the action is and wake up in a stranger's bed. Or a co-worker's. You might even hit a wall with your fist for no reason you can explain and break your hand for a year, and you *might* do shit like that even if you play guitar for a living. If you want a reason, you want too much. Eat your flank steak, and to bed without dessert.

What you really want, Bataille says, is to be a thing *so that* you can be released (in death) from being a thing. And *that* is what you *will* do. You will make your body the instrument of your work until you can't do it anymore, and in your spare time, you will find ways to kill yourself or someone else. That's what we do in the suburbs. We drink, collect guns, and vote for Republicans who will send us to kill foreigners. And if the Republicans refuse to kill people, we'll militarize the police so they can kill more people here, and we ask Democrats to please bomb somebody. And they do. Then, well, then there's the drugs, whether you're twenty-seven or almost sixty-seven. Almost. From 1993 to now, it's pretty much one deadly party. Thanks, Mary Jane. (Mary Jane gave us that stupid *Purge* movie franchise.)

Under Pressure

"General economy" follows laws. We don't have time for all the laws (you can look them up), but there is a relation the weird dude notices that I have to bring up. He calls it "pressure" and "expansion." Pretty much it's what Freddie and Bowie are describing in the relevant song, but Billy Joel has a phenomenology of it in his song about pressure, too. When we push some part of what is living into what is just thinging, we put it under pressure. Time brings expansion, and expansion brings excess.

This is the proportion of energy that *must be wasted*. It is the general economy of sex and death, and it is why the Twenty-Sevens Club is supposed to live hard, die young, and leave a beautiful body.

Now, when you arrive at the accursed share in anything, you will get creeped out. That is why MTV made Tom edit out the grin over Alice. It cuts too close to the bone. Way too close, boys and girls. You don't have to be Freud to see what's happening to the little girl here, and throughout this video, do you? Even Tipper Gore could see it.[1] Imagine the Alice vid without the three moaning women in unitards. It's pornography without them, isn't it? Then, in the economy of eating Alice, there is a bit of misdirection to keep you from seeing the structure of, well, they used to call it "carnival." One supposes the Heartbreakers are carnivorous carnal celebrants. Glad those three women are moaning along in that video. Otherwise I might notice what's really going on.

This is what you see when you've been reading your Bataille. By the way, Bataille would creep out even Freud (who did not live long enough to read Bataille's work, but Bataille most definitely studied Freud—and thought him far too tame). It's also why, in the extreme time, Jimi and Janis and Jim Morrison and Kurt Cobain and Amy Winehouse are creepy. Geez, Prince and Michael Jackson too. They got pretty addled at the end. They are on the edge of wasting themselves, and is that not, somehow, *necessary*? *They* felt it was.

So we have before us that moment when we're creeped out. Tom had an uncanny command of it. His sense of it grew from 1979 to 1993. He always turned it to the comic, but in a way that just makes it worse. The setting makes a huge difference and for Tom, as for Bataille, the general economy of the creepy is always *the circle*. This is part of the reason a circus is presented in rings, run by a ringmaster. And you know as well as I do *that's* what Tom is, in his ubiquitous top hat. You know it, but you probably never really thought about it. Video after video, circles and cycles.

---

[1] But, no hard feelings, Tipper later played percussion for Tom, and she looked a bit like Wish Foley with a mid-life spread, so, still good enough to eat I guess. On the other hand, her husband had just conceded the presidency and the country was swirling in the toilet, so *someone* should be sacrificed before the big suck, when the Towers are toppled.

When Tom puts on the top hat, it draws our attention to what will happen in one ring or another of the Petty and HB's Circus, and it's definitely going to have some of that circus atmosphere. There's the Midway, you know, and then there's the sideshow, and then the freaks, and somewhere behind the tents is a guy who pulls all the strings, and his name is Petty. He's serenading us as large men in diapers dance around a giant wedding ring, waving full-sized video disks, in a half-built house, while a frustrated yuppie drives his convertible into the sunset with a blow-up sex doll by his side. Tom, yer so bad. Best we ever had.

From Fifteen Minutes to Eternity

It's hard to know how much artistic input Tom had on the videos, but given the way he worked on most things, I'm guessing it was a lot. I've been talking as if Tom alone made the videos, even though we all know that's not true. The fact is that they're Tomvids, whether or not he was the *auteur*. So, when I said "Tom," I meant "Tom and everybody else who helped Tom make the Tomvids." They wouldn't be much without him. But we can all agree, I think, that as a body they stand well above any other body of work from the time period. This was excellent, interesting art. And the songs were great, too.

Without knowing how much of it was Tom, we know that Tom liked to dream up characters. Bart and Eddie, the Ringmaster and Lucky. He liked to watch his characters take on cinematic form, with Faye Dunaway and Johnny Depp and Kim Basinger and Wish Foley stepping into the personae. He welcomed his band to the tea party. He thought in terms of characters and very often said so in interviews. To him, making up a song was a matter of making up characters, sticking them into a situation, and then waiting to see what the characters would do. That's the hardest part, as we all know, because sometimes it goes nowhere. But sometimes it learns to fly. A lot of stuff is just the middling mediocrities—the character doesn't grab us or grabs us and then doesn't do anything interesting. Tomvids are like this, too. They are not all great works of art, although they always stood out during the MTV generation, a cut above the Loverboys and Benatars. I may not be the right person, because I like Eighties videos a little too much, but someone should write a book on the first video generation and the end of the rock era.

Now, it's a swirl of images. Tom Petty videos really make you dizzy. Most of the music videos that were made for the MTV generation haven't stood up well to the vicissitudes of time and insults of age. During that bygone age they were seen by the corporate assholes as elaborate commercials for the music, made by the industry for the teenyboppers and tweenagers who haunted the malls and public parks. But Tomvids hold up pretty well through the changes in aesthetic consciousness that we've all, well, we've *mostly* welcomed them. The MTV era had a look, fun and campy, overblown and ridiculous, but it was a thing. And here I am killing it. That's only because I love it and it wants to be sacrificed to the written word.

4
Tom Petty and the Meaning of Life

CHRISTOPHER M. INNES

Suppose we look at Tom Petty much as we might look at the uniquely free-spirited Lucky he played in the Fox TV network cartoon *King of the Hill*. His honest outlook gave normal people, such as Hank and Peggy Hill, a lot to feel uneasy about, I tell you what!

Both Petty and Lucky told their bosses to "take a hike" and rose above those social and moral things that most people naively feel make them feel safe in life. They went on to pursue new moral and artistic freedom. The moral and artistic expression offered by wider society just seems so jaded, shallow, lacking in dynamism, and should be avoided.

Friedrich Nietzsche's *The Birth of Tragedy from the Spirit of Music* looks at music in much the same way. Nietzsche wanted to get an understanding of what an existential tragedy in music is. Life is pointless if it doesn't have any meaning. To have meaning we need to be creative. A fully creative individual is one who is ready to doubt or to seriously question traditions in human conduct.

Music should be a creation that gives life meaning, Nietzsche says. He thinks the "spirit" of music enables us to see our lives as meaningfully tragic. It's an abyss, for sure, but the fall into the abyss is free and creative and it is ours; it's not the bosses' free fall. I think tragedy needs to be reintroduced into the creation of music.

Twilight of the Idols

Nietzsche viewed his buddy and later nemesis Richard Wagner's creations of music as being chained to rhythm. Its form is decadent in a way that relies on a traditional understanding of life, which kowtows to an audience's need to easily understand music, lyrics, and themes. The form is unsophisticated and empty, with Wagner being an idol in the eyes of a bunch of teenyboppers. In a word, Dicky Wagner just did the twist for the crowd, and the crowd praised his surprisingly successful ditties. Such a performance made Nietzsche want to throw up in the flower bed.

For Nietzsche, music needs more creativity and getting down with the crowd. To achieve it, he summoned the Greek gods. The Greeks had lots of gods giving them moral, political and in this case, aesthetic guidance. In rocking out, some creative gods are needed. Enter Apollo and Dionysus. Apollo is the strict, rational thinker who wants his music in a formal tone and rhythm. Dionysus encourages lots of baby-making and its regular companions, of wine, revelry, and frenzy leading to . . . ummm, other things, and music that is free and adventurous. This is the forbidden fruit that Apollo tells us not to eat.

Neither the Apollonian nor Dionysian view, alone, is going to produce music that really rocks us. They need each other. Imagine the Heartbreakers with no rhythm section. It's folk music, after all. Now, take away Tom and Benmont and Mike. Where's the forbidden fruit now? Nietzsche considered music as a heartbreaking means of individual aesthetic expression. Such expression in our day is restricted by the pandering to the dilettantish Friends of Apollo (the FAPs), and I dare say we need more of the Dionysian influence. The FAPs have their idols, for sure, but they make hopelessly dire music.

Does this suggest that today's musician is excessively restricted by expectations of how songs should be written? Do we think the singer's performances are chained to the expectations of Apollo, the written word, music tone, and the music industry? Petty is a singer who, much like Dionysus, sees music as a frenzied creation. Even though there are many reasons for saying that Petty is the ultimate individualistic, free-spirited songwriter and singer—one who's in line with Dionysus—we still must understand that he remains restrained by Apollonian considerations.

We might be tempted to ask as well if the likes of Jeff Lynne of Electric Light Orchestra, similar to Tricky Dicky, are more in line with Apollo and the music industry; they give us the similar free-spirited music but with much less of the resistance? We might like a love song, but the soppy ones are a fate worse than death. So be prepared! Jeff Lynne might be along later to give us a contrast to Petty, as Wagner might have been a contrast to Nietzsche's need for real colorful music.

Nietzsche admits that his *Birth of Tragedy* is inspirational rather than founded on rock-solid reason. His understanding of Apollo and Dionysus as tragedy is Nietzsche's way of grinding his ax to cut off Tricky Dicky's head. He's more like a philosophical motivational talker. We can imagine what sort of a *Ted Talk* Nietzsche would have given.

What Is Tragedy in Music?

The modern meaning of a tragedy leans toward a moment when something terrible happens. The older, Greek meaning of tragedy is when an individual strives for freedom from something, but that thing from which they wish to be free is actually a necessary precondition to being free. The freedom is in sight, but it can never be achieved. In Greek tragedies, this flaw in the hero's character inevitably moves them toward their own doom.

In a similar way, Petty's song "Trailer" is about high-school sweethearts who get married too quickly, move into a trailer, and miss out on all those things they could have done. They could have gone into the Army or Navy, but they live in a trailer instead. They had their freedom in sight but their impulsivity was their tragic flaw that stopped them from being free. For them, they were so young but the game was up. Perhaps impulse is needed to achieve those good things in life; however, the impulse needs to be directed in the right way.

For Nietzsche, there is the god Apollo and the god Dionysus. Apollo is rational and sees the world as an understanding of reality. He is the image maker and creator of beautiful things like sick synth beats and Disney cartoons. Apollo is aware that the world of knowing is probably beyond human capability. We can see Apollo and Dionysus much like a comedy duo. We need the straight guy to set off the funny one. They act together and never succeed alone. The funny guy is never funny without the Doubting Thomas straight guy as a contrast. This is where Socrates, who is seen by Nietzsche as the earthly manifestation of Apollo, enters the historical stage.

Socrates carried on the Apollonian tradition and saw his life as the rational pursuit of wisdom, dialogue, and beauty. Nietzsche understood that Socratic rationalism's drive for unified creation of non-opposing forces dulls the human aesthetic. It's like having the straight guy without the funny guy. It's not funny! Socrates ventures on the philosophical mission to find reality. He understands that what we see is possibly just a perception. Beyond this perception is the real thing. To him, music is to show this real thing, a unified thing that is rational and almost a linear flow of sound—but for Dionysus, it lacks that real rock feeling.

As far as Nietzsche's concerned, humans are aesthetic by nature and any hampering of creativity is an evil. The world is all about constant change and excitement. In *The Will to Power*, one of Nietzsche's later publications, it is said that there is little need for what some might see as this thing called *political correctness* in musical arrangements and ideas. In the Dionysian world we create tunes to send a deep meaning that lyrics alone could not convey. The mealy-mouthed music critics are not our friends.

At the same time, we need to curb our enthusiasm. We can be creative—but not too creative. The tragedy is the balance of Dionysian subjective creation, the transgression of limits, wild and uncontrolled behavior in chorus and singing on the one hand with the Apollonian view respecting boundaries, distinction, moderation, and an individual's self-control on the other hand. A tragic hero is the brave one who takes on the challenge and leads us on this journey, causing us to see the Dionysian process in all its glory.

More than Just Makin' Some Noise

Dionysus is flamboyant and creative—but not in the showy and glitzy way. Here we imagine every limb in movement in a full expression of joy. This is an extravagant scene rather like what we might see at The Isle of Man Music Festival, where Tom Petty and the Heartbreakers played in 2012.

The music festival is real where we create art in the expression of the joy of the music. Music spurs revelry and wonder, and it is given full consent by the audience. They are involved no matter their social class, education or political beliefs. Hippies, punks, lawyers and everyone else is welcomed.

Here I can imagine being in the audience of the Tom Petty and the Heartbreakers gig in Oakland Coliseum in 1991 while they played "Makin' Some Noise." This is a basic rock song, but it is played as if it is their first and last time. Most of all, as we see him at the Docks in Hamburg in Germany, the crowd is dancing, singing along, and doing this right up near the stage. The audience is included.

The audience thinks this concert is for them. Even the Germans get the point of the frenzy and think it's for them. This is real, but at the same time, Nietzsche makes it clear that the art of music is our creation. The reality is each of ours, belonging to Tom and his bandmates and each ticket holder in attendance. There might be no universal reality as seen by Apollo and Socrates, but this won't stop us joining in with someone else's musical act of creation.

I am going to be daring and say that Petty's music creation is in the genre of folk-rock. True to the Nietzschean spirit, Petty did not like to have his music categorized. In England, his music was classified as Power-Pop, New Wave, and even Punk. We might be wrong to categorize Tom Petty as folk rock by the genre standards of rock'n'roll, but by Nietzschean standards, folk music is the union of Apollo and Dionysus. Folk music has become more intense in every one of its rebirths caused by Dionysian currents, as music that holds a mirror up to the world in a meaningful way.

It is the best art that speaks to others with such depth. This we can imagine to be the tragedy that honored Dionysus. We need to escape, but we are reliant on that which we wish to escape just like Petty needed to escape the troubling authority of the exploitative music industry. Music is a free entity restrained by the bosses. We see this in *The Last DJ* where mediocre music is demanded by Petty's fictional higher-ups. He needs the execs to have his music distributed to many people; nonetheless these execs are in the way of his free expression. This is tragedy.

The Traveling Wilburys are likewise all about delivering the music, with no massive egos attached. This is part of

Nietzsche's idea that the individual becomes a full human when they join the community. The shallow person is a rational one who holds on to the words or dialogue without joining the frenzy of creation. Sigmund Freud later adapted this idea as the selfish id, the creative ego and the community-based super-ego. The great Scott Thurston of the Heartbreakers also set his ego aside for the music. Petty often commended bandmate Thurston as being the glue that could fill in anywhere because of his having no ego and being happy to do whatever best served the band's creation.

What Is Decadence in Music?

Nietzsche didn't see Wagner as a hero. He understood him as holding on to the Apollonian ideal of music. Just like Socrates, he is not that adventurous. In fact, Nietzsche identified him as decadent. To be decadent, in Nietzsche's view of music, is to have lost much of the Dionysian quality of music and to have declined into religious references or pandering to the audience. Much like being at a cringe-worthy junior high school music recital, Nietzsche is viewing his buddy's music as pretty difficult to get excited about or dance to.

As far as Nietzsche is concerned, there are three reasons for seeing Wagner's operas as degenerate. The first is that opera is a recitative performing art where there is text and music, and the music follows logically from its dependence on the text. The second reason is that within opera there is an idyllic world of primitives that placates us with its charming nature, but it can't satisfy our intellectual needs. The third reason is that the opera sees everyone as an artist and it must kowtow to the lowest common denominator of everyone's tastes. It does allow the individual audience member room for personal interpretation, but only in way that the music wants.

This is like the school recital. You have to accept the music as it's played. This adds up to a shocking epiphany where Nietzsche could no longer revere his buddy as producing worthwhile music. Much like Petty's "Sins of My Youth," where there is someone not grasping the singer as they really are, we see Wagner not taking Nietzsche or anyone else for whom they really are. Wagner's work reveals him as a dilettante, uncaring about audience response or participation.

Just as we fashion our own lives, Nietzsche saw music as a creation of you by yourself. There is a world in which you live, but that world is a fake one in which our language, politics, thought, and music are created for us—and we accept them without complaint. This is the world of no self-creation and no truly great music. It is a world where a song is churned out with little artistic merit for the sake of entertaining the masses.

Petty rises above the hit factory mentality and creates a new way of looking at the world. His funny song, "Yer So Bad," is also somewhat cynical about traditional romantic relationships going well. This is a creative critique of what is normal in marriage as an institution, where life is a bit dull and a bit sleazy. The wild tale of a swinger who gets married to a singer gets an audience's attention and shows Petty's oddball way of seeing the world.

By contrast, Phil Spector produced modern rock'n'roll music with a Wagnerian approach. He would think of the music production with artistry and creativity, but with Nietzsche in mind, we have a feeling that only a ditty has been created. These ditties are to entertain the kids in three-minute bursts, similar to Wagner churning out what Nietzsche saw as degenerate operas to entertain the audience.

These operas were frequently ditties with religious references and tales of heroism. Certainly, they were very long ditties, with *Götterdämmerung* going on for over four hours, but the story is of a gross modern world with its bloated view of romanticism. Nietzsche viewed these operas as an Apollonian appearance of reality, and with no progressive involvement of the audience in a Dionysian way. There is beauty, splendor, emotion, and feeling, which merely appeals to the audience's shallow view of the hero and of virtue. This is at best naive and at worst decadent.

Thus Spake Tom Petty

Fans of Tom Petty are probably aware of his desire to create authentic music and to be free from the industry that wanted more popular music. For Nietzsche, words never express the stylishness that music shows. Apollo and Dionysus together make a music that sounds simultaneously both brand new and very familiar. The popular makes more money by stirring the trivial and momentary attention of the listener. An example of a fairly Wagnerian Petty tune might be "Anything That's Rock'n'Roll," as it was just a rocking song for the kids. We can take Petty as saying this song was naïve as a sign of the Apollonian and Dionysian influence present in his music. Petty wanted to produce music that was more than just an outward appearance of artfulness clinching the Billboard Top Ten.

In the 1980s, a decade of illusion in music genres like New Romance and the last strands of New Wave, Petty also noticed the advent of the Yamaha DX7 synthesizer as a naive attempt to allow the audience to see things for real. He said he wouldn't use the DX7, so here we might see the synthesizer and the soppy love songs of the Eighties as decadent. It's the McMusic scene that needs to be rejected. Much like a cheap burger, we are soon disappointed with a cheap performance. Petty makes it clear that his music is meant to be more timeless, and influenced by the Dionysian age of the Fifties and Sixties. He certainly avoided trends of the Eighties.

We also see his blustery relations to the music industry in Apollonian and Dionysian terms. Shelter Records was bought by MCA. Petty had a contract with Shelter and was frustrated when they bought and sold his music like a piece of meat. He sued the record company for contractual freedom and won. MCA then wanted to sell the *Hard Promises* album for $9.98, instead of the normal price of $8.98. Petty fought this also, realizing that his music belonged to the people, not just himself or the record company. The music, as a collision of craft with inspiration, is bigger than he is.

The tragic songwriter wants to express the notion of wonder, but can't if held back by the music industry. Adrenaline needs to flow freely to forge new ideas. We see how they work out. Chords are played in a way to find the best song. I might become spellbound and all-inspired by "Mary Jane's Last Dance," because the need to wonder is apparent. Petty said that he was in the zone when writing the song. He had an eight-track and knew the composition before going to the studio. Here Petty reconnected with old ideas and did the whole song at once. A tape recorder was used as a memory aid so he would not forget some of the old ideas. Petty felt that it's best to avoid becoming a critic and overly good, technically proficient musician and instead stick to being more of an inventive songwriter. Here we see technology and artistry in the right balance. Like a seesaw, if one side is too heavy then no one has any fun.

ELO and Apollo

Is Jeff Lynne the contemporary Richard Wagner, the twenty-first-century Degenerate Dilettante? As warned, he has returned as a foil for Petty in our analysis of tragic music. His popular songs are great for a look back at a failed, soppy love affair. Our Nietzschean interpretation is that the modern music industry might show Jeff Lynne's ballads as conforming to Socratic rationalism. This is much like Nietzsche seeing Richard Wagner's operas as decadent while at that same time seeing the worth of his contribution to the progression of music, even if it's still in the grip of Socratic domination.

Do we see Jeff Lynne as worthy of being congratulated for making a contribution? Lynne conforms to the Socratic Form without resistance. He might be seen as crushing intuition, so can we admire him as we do Petty? Petty's acceptance of the traditional ballad and his legal compromise with the music industry was part of tragedy because he dissolved boundaries with a directness and individuality, even though it was restrained. For Nietzsche, we should have faith in the human soul and accept the culture of Dionysian music. What has ELO done, compared to the Heartbreakers?

I listen to Petty's "Between Two Worlds" and I think of my relationships. I am compelled to think as he thinks. The stability of Apollo and the adventures of Dionysus are forcing me between two worlds. It's like the Saturday morning flicks of yesteryear. I see it relates to me as well as those around me. The chorus is of the view that he loves her but she is only flesh and bone that he can't leave. This is the Dionysian material view of the world. In opposition, Apollo talks of the need for stable relationships—but we see that there is only appearance, leading to the singer being unconvinced that he should commit to this relationship. We have Dionysus here, who I can feel involves me. It is as Nietzsche says: we are allowed to get at the truth of the primordial reality offered in the Dionysian world. We should revel in relationships. We should enjoy the tragedy of being attached to other people, but not being sure why, because we are all just flesh and bone.

I listen to Jeff Lynne's "Don't Bring Me Down." It's a hit song with a lot of whining about having crazy friends, being untrustworthy, and the feeling of a need to run away. This might relate to some people. Possibly some relate to "Evil Woman," but this is his break-up song with his lady. Just as Carly Simon sang "You're So Vain" about Warren Beatty many years before, it's been done over and over again. The scene is a copy about other people and their view of relationships. I don't relate to it and I'm sure there are others who don't either. It's a nice ditty. This said, is this ditty just an Apollonian appearance, with little of Dionysus to create captivating tragedy?

Can we say that the abstraction of Socratic dialogue alienates us from the Lynne experience? In the tragic culture we may see it as more like a narrative where a story is told, questions are asked and knowledge is gained. As with Socrates, for something to be beautiful it must be recognizable. For Socrates, there's no truth in tragedy. This means that tragedy was not seen as of interest to the philosopher. I might try and be drawn into "Turn to Stone" with thoughts of her not coming home, feeling down and having only memories, but it does not speak to me. If it did, I might not want to listen.

Just as he sings "Telephone Line," which speaks of some guy talking to his woman on the phone, I'm glad it's not me. It just sounds far too depressing, like most Seventies and Eighties love songs. There is little tragedy in the Lynne experience. It might have been a journey, but that's all. It is simply pastiche, passing as a cheerful song about sad times had. Socrates saw tragedy as not telling the truth, and thought that the philosopher should only deal with the truth. The sad dialogues will use strict argument forms. Alternatively, as we noticed with Petty, there is a lot of reliance on instinct and insight into the tragic scene. The Dionysian influence pushes Tom Petty to create an authentic music.

Like Socrates, Lynne lacks authenticity and thus cannot really access tragedy. Knowledge and narrative is not enough. We need to step out and escape sometimes, even if we eventually have to step back into the Socratic dialogue. We might say Lynne's music is degenerate in the same way Nietzsche regarded Wagner's music as degenerate. We might certainly see it as mediocre.

Like Wagner's opera, there is no unified consciousness. There is only the hero. You may say that you like ELO and Lynne—as long as you also feel like proclaiming you're into the pop group Abba. This does not remove the fact that the superficiality of his songs do not deliver us very far into the Dionysian world. It is a shallow, self-absorbed world that is enjoyed by hitmakers like ELO. I can listen to his songs and forget them. There seems to be more surrendering to Apollo here than serenading Dionysus. We need both to have good music in tragedy.

Tragedy Handled with Care

It might be just an opinion that Tom Petty created ultimate Dionysian music. It might be just an opinion that Jeff Lynne didn't. And what of their eventual collaborations, both on production for a couple of Heartbreakers records and in the Traveling Wilburys? We have to admit, as Nietzsche did, that our analysis is somewhat personal. It might be that music should be short and sweet and uncomplicated, but it is nonetheless the Dionysian experience we have described as crucial. Tom Petty might have created the occasional ditty here or there, but we see the majority of his music as based on the balancing act between Apollo and Dionysus.

We may like to think Petty's music takes part in another rebirth of tragedy. The problem is that music is supposed to be a creation shared by us all. It should be tragedy understood as life explored. Life is the engagement of Apollo and Dionysus in the creation of music. Music is an expression of us humans being in a creative and joyous union. It is the height of humanity.

This is tragedy that gives us a good life, and we might say that Tom Petty did this very well. He brought together Dionysus and Apollo in his music, and he brought together the audience in our revelry with his band.

5
The Boys of Summer

RANDALL E. AUXIER

Tom Petty stumbled across his band, so the legend goes, at a studio in LA. He heard them rehearsing and thought to himself "Hey, that should be my band." He knew two of them, since they came to LA with him. Two he didn't really know, but knew of, since they were from Gainseville as well.

They were the opposite of a Mötley Crüe. Tom's intuition in the moment he heard them was the same super-power he exercised throughout his career, that insight that defies full expression. You just see something and you know it works, even if you can't say why. Everybody has these moments, but very few people live by them. The sort of person who claims a stake in the world by feeling, and whose sense of things is right over and over, will become a challenge to understand and even harder to live with.

I will now attempt a post-death interview. When I talk to Tom in my mind, this is what it sounds like.

> **RANDY:** Tom, what was it all like, now that you see how it all worked out? Especially about the band, with them on one side and you on the other.
>
> **TOM:** You know I hate shit like this, but I'll try. It was very hard for me to *want* what I had, with the band or anything else. I would work like a slave to have something I wanted, but once I had it, I put it on a shelf and expected it to stay there. It became part of the furniture of my life. The band was like that for me. I didn't want to lose it, but I rarely thought about whether the things on my shelf *want* to be on my shelf. Of course they do, you know? I have some of

the best shelves and anyone with any sense wants to be part of my collection.

RANDY: Yeah, it seems like people could be satisfied with that, right?

TOM: The handful of friends I lost in my life probably wanted more from me than to be part of my collection. But I didn't know how to do what they needed. At the relevant level, professionally, it's always about me and it has to be. They just have to trust me, even though I screw up sometimes. Anyone who wants a piece of my life has to accept my terms, and that means my shelf. I won't sit on anyone else's shelf, but I have lots of room on mine. So, this oversimplifies things quite a bit, and it is admittedly selfish. But my justification, that I give to myself, is that I am different, maybe even special, in a few ways that required this arrangement.

RANDY: Is it the cost of genius?

TOM: No, man, that's not the word. There are other people like me. That's what the Wilburys was about. Creative people can do amazing things with the support they need—emotional, financial, professional. And the band and my family are the main pillars. My self-confidence can be broken and I depend on it for all the things I do that most people don't do. Benmont and Mike and Howie and Stanley, man, those guys are incredibly talented, but they aren't made to front the band and find the next thing. They were there to make it real and help me find it.

RANDY: And they just need to be okay with that?

TOM: In order to do the good things, I have to find a balance between taking more than I give when it comes to those who love me most, and giving all the things I give to, well, everybody. I know it isn't fair and that bothers me. A lot.

RANDY: Does the end justify these means?

TOM: My needs are often (it seems to me) excessive, more than a person ought to need. But that's me.

RANDY: I can't understand you here, but I do understand not being able to want what you have. But what about the people who care about you?

TOM: So, I have to admit that people in my life get taken for granted, in practice, even though I don't feel that way about them. Meanwhile, no one gets to take me for granted and if they do, I bite. And so I have had my heart broken, irreparably, twice, because I met someone I had to have in my life, and then did have, and then they wouldn't conform, forever, to the pattern I needed. And so, with my first marriage, I tried for a while to be the one to conform and became pathetic and then I hated myself and did a lot of drugs. And there was no fixing it and I was sucked into a vortex that swirled for years. I got numb. Eventually I crawled out. The band suffered. The second was Howie. He went to that same place. We couldn't get him to come back. We mostly came out of it at about the same time, but not him. So we put it back together with Ron and went on. But it was never the same.

RANDY: The public has never seen you in any condition like that.

TOM: Yeah, well we didn't exactly advertise it at the time.

RANDY: You are pretty tough. Your upbringing probably helps.

TOM: The less said about that the better. I got lucky, especially when it came to the band. I now see that when Ron left we had been leaning too hard on him. I now see that I let that happen because I wanted a new sound. I just wasn't conscious of it. I saw Howie playing with Del and I wanted his sound. When Stan left, I was being passive-aggressive and he was being aggressive-passive. I guess it really was mutual, but I now see that his sound and feel was the foundation of what worked. Steve is like the greatest drummer ever, but the sound and feel, well, it's great, but it's not the same. I wouldn't do anything different. I made mistakes and I got some things right. No regrets.

Boys Will Be, Well, You Know . . .

Now that we've had Tom's take, let's look at the boys in the band, one by one. A quick index. I'm doing this by feeling, of a certain sort. But we know Tom didn't think the thing Campbell had written was quite right for his band, you know, the tune that became "Boys of Summer"?

We want to say Tom wasn't right that time. But now imagine Tom, at any point between childhood and, say, 1994 ("Mary Jane Era"). Tom himself isn't quite "right." The dude looks like an emaciated cross between Greg Allman and Edgar Winter, and frankly he's kind of creepy (I said more on this in my Mary

Jane chapter above). Mike Campbell looks like a member of Blondie, like one of their revolving bass players. Benmont Tench belongs in Loverboy. (And everyone wants a name as cool as "Benmont Tench"—even if you do get your ass kicked in elementary school, it's worth it later). Ron Blair must have gotten lost with Lovin' Spoonful in the late Sixties and emerged ten years later with his leather vest intact. (They never said what it was a spoonful of. Brown acid maybe. Might make you lose a decade, if you're not careful.) Stan Lynch just looks like (and just is) a redneck. On the other hand, Wish Foley went home with him for about five years. That seems a testament to something. I'm not sure what. But make this variation: dress Stan just a little differently and he's one of The Ramones. He would fit.

These guys are a band? Seriously? It's a dissociative mixture. And yet, undeniably, something is working. You know it, somehow. In the days before MTV, it was surely *the sound* that worked. But *after* MTV, they were like the Monkees, Eighties version, walkin' down the street, getting the funniest looks from everyone they meet. They were a roving gang of post-apocalyptic strangers. They belong together but only as visual fiction. We don't see the interior, where that sound comes from, we see an exterior that reminds us of the music, somehow, but doesn't quite *create* that music. Somewhere down in there, there must be actual musicians, but the view is from all around without ever being from within. So, they're cool and a bit mysterious. They aren't exactly boys in a treehouse, but, as Tom said when Stevie Nicks wanted to join, the band took a vote: "No Girls Allowed."

I Feel It in the Air

How do you know these quick descriptions are right? (Be honest. They are. Even if I'm an ass.) You do it *phenomenologically.* That's a fancy word for paying attention to what it is like to *have* an experience of something and then reflecting on the experience. It's sort of "had" and then "re-had" in short term memory. Like this: Your lover says you're a liar. You now have two choices. One is to defend yourself, the other is to say "Hey, what's it like to be called a liar, like that, just now?"

It's that second one I'm talking about. Sounds like an evasion, but it's a legitimate moment in our experience. It's relevant to the accusation, but no answer. You might say it even if you *aren't* a liar, but if you are one, it's recommended. Of course, everybody lies, so you might try that path too, but providing your lover a little context, reminding us all what it's like to be accused, is one path to dialogue. That space of imagination, shared in describing ourselves to each other, that's phenomenological space.

Now, back to the band. I want to bring an image to your mind—Benmont playing the keyboard part in "Working for the Weekend," with Loverboy, and you think "yeah, I can see that," and we're golden. You did that phenomenologically. So did I. Part of it is anticipation, part memory, part comparison and analogy, part sensation. All of it comes together with some dominant quality that maybe you can *name*. Let's call this one "LoverBen."

Let me give another example. Say you bite into something. You thought it was a chocolate bourbon breadball, but it was a sausage ball instead. (Yes, this happened to me.) You expected it to be sweet but instead it was savory. You expected a bread-like texture, but you got a ground meat-like texture. You expected alcohol but you got grease. That's a great violation of expectation, so you spit it out. (Or at least I did.) Why? Especially since you really like sausage balls—in fact, you like them far better than chocolate bourbon balls. But the *surprise* was too much all at once. Your expectations and anticipations, as well as your memories and habits are very, very powerful in determining, in advance, and in hindsight, what an experience should be and what it was. So you sit back and reflect on the experience and say hmmmph. What was that all about? I shall name it "yuck." But that's not quite right because sausage balls are good, so I adjust my description. I shall call it "wtf?" That may be closer. But I can keep adjusting and getting closer to a good name for the experience.

I Can See You

With the Heartbreakers, individually, it's a process for me that ended with the short descriptions above. EdgarAllmanTom, LoverBen, BlondieMike, SpoonfulRon, and RedneckRamone. That's who they are, when I ask what they're like and I reflect and analogize and describe and then name. That's how I have the experience of them in reflection—not so much in sensation.

And now here's something weirder. Now that I have named them like this, when I return to the music, to how they sound, I can pick out little Blondie pieces in Mike's guitar style and a little Tommy Ramone in Stan's drumming, and so on. That spreading effect from naming the reflection is one of the coolest things about phenomenology. It really helps you judge more clearly what is similar and what is different in things. It's a talent and some people are better at it than others, but even without a lot of phenomenological talent, you can learn to get good at it. Wine tasters do this when they make up their elaborate vocabularies to talk about tastes and smells.

Never Look Back

The entire song "The Boys of Summer" is driven by phenomenological reflection. It isn't nostalgia, it's memory bringing the past into the present and naming the experience over and over. The descriptions are so powerful that we see them and we need no help at all from the video. As good as the video is, the feel of the song and the lyrics carry the experience. "TheOneThatGotAway." The resolution to get her back and show her what you're made of shows that this is not just rumination. The purpose of the naming exercise when he "sees" her top down, radio on, Wafarers, brown skin, smile, the purpose is to get her back.

To describe the way you actually *have* an experience, you have to be able to put the anticipation on hold, for just a moment, and try to neutralize the habits and the memories and *just see* what you're seeing, *just smell* what you're smelling, *just taste* what you're tasting, *just feel* what you're feeling, and, most important, *just hear* what you're hearing. And then describe that *and only that*. That is what Tom failed to do when Mike played him the demo tape of the music for "The Boys of Summer." God I wish I knew what lyrics Tom and Mike would have written to that music. But Don Henley is the one who just let himself hear what he was hearing, and suddenly, there *she* was. And the lyrics wrote themselves.

So this phenomenology thing is sort of hard to do, but sometimes the key to what you're experiencing perches its skinny ass right there in that moment and determines how you feel about something. It isn't coming from the past and it isn't luring you toward some future. Not yet. It's sitting right there in front of you, but usually you don't see it because you aren't working hard enough to neutralize the past and the future. Still, together we can do this. It leads somewhere. Sort of. If going in circles is somewhere.

I Wonder if It Was a Dream

Tom's videos give you a sense of The Heartbreakers that you couldn't get from just listening. Before we could see the band, we couldn't really tell what they were *doing*. We could only hear it. That was a magical passage from ear to "imaginary seeing." And we have to admit that looking at them individually or grouped together, without hearing them, doesn't help us categorize them. But somehow the center holds when we *just hear* them play.

That's what sold them, not the look, initially at least. With our ears alone we buy them *as a band*. But why? All those players in Blondie look like they belong in the same band. Same for The Clash and Talking Heads. But what is it about these guys? Actually seeing them, once we did see them, does not bring *recognition*, not from the sound alone. If someone played the whole of *Damn the Torpedoes* for you and then showed you ten random pictures of bands in a line-up, could you pick out the real makers of that music?

The spreading effect, if you *name* the experience of that music, is what you're trying to use to do that task. But I think Tom and the boys were vaguely aware that their look and their music were different. I think that is why their music videos often had nothing to do with the songs. Yes, Tom did act out the story of Eddie Rebel, and there are a couple of others that seem like the visual images enact the lyrical themes, but most often they just went some crazy direction that wasn't suggested by the music or the lyrics. Notable examples are the two most famous vids, for Alice and Mary Jane—which have nothing to do with the two songs. But look at "You Got Lucky" or "Make It Better," or even early ones like "Refugee" or "Here Comes My Girl." Tom and the boys saw that it was an advantage to not look like their sound, to let the sound carry what the sound needed to carry (the radio, the albums), and to let MTV and the videos carry something else. Tom knew he could get away with this. The boys were willing accomplices. They turned an incongruity into a space for creative marketing—and for art. How?

A Little Voice Inside My Head

Time for some phenomenology. I think I get something about this you probably never noticed. It's about circles. It was always about circles. I think Tom always saw his band as a circle and he was the middle. So in their earliest videos, like "Refugee" and "Here Comes My Girl," he arranged the boys in a circle. In the second of these he "presents" the band members one by one, making a circle, and flirting with each of them as he goes. He begins with Stan, then goes over to Mike, then Benmont, then Ron (he even hugs Ron) and then shares a "virtual kiss" with Ron, before returning to Stan to complete the round.

Let's pause on that kiss for a minute. A little voice inside my head is telling me to do that. Ron is the one who got away, and Tom got him back. The virtual kiss is interesting because the image is a deliberate "quotation." So there's something extra, something to consider, going on in these artsy-fartsy videos, which is called "quotationalism." It's this tendency in popular culture to reconfigure its own earlier images in new settings and new ways. Tom's videos did this all the time, usually light-hearted and as parody.

People act like quotationalism is a fairly recent thing, but it goes way back. In the video for "Here Comes My Girl," Tom and Ron stand at right angles a few feet apart in a quotation of the Abba video for "Knowing Me, Knowing You," which was directed by the rising film director Lasse Hallström. Go watch it. You will know, as I do, that Tom's crew was paying attention to what images worked in that video and why. I don't have to remind you that these guys were going to make some of the most enduring and controversial videos of the Eighties and Nineties. That sort of thing doesn't *just happen*. They were paying attention to what worked. The video for "The Waiting" is a quotation of any number of Sixties American Bandstand lip-synchs, which they make obvious at the end when Stan and Benmont switch instruments while the soundtrack plays, making light of the lip-sync habits of that era.

But the circles repeat from video to video. The most obvious one is "Yer So Bad" where absolutely every scene is dominated by circles, ending with Elvis imitators in diapers dancing in a circle around a giant wedding ring on a circular cake while waving large round video disks. In "Insider," Tom surrounds himself and Stevie Nicks with the band—a cage without a key. The video for "You Don't Know How It Feels" is just a merry-go-round of developing scenes while Tom stands in the middle. It's in every video, just about. Watch for it.

So these videos are full of circles, and they are just packed with imagistic quotations. Watching for them helps us understand the band's creative process and it's easier to analyze than music. The music is full of quotations too—they're everywhere—but you almost have to be a musician to hear what's going on. I have met some non-musicians who can pull music into its pieces using their ears and description alone, but it's much easier with videos, when we can see how each band member is presented. But let's try a little ear phenomenology and see if we can get inside of that process.

The Summer's Out of Reach

Some of you got my chapter title right away, because you know the story. It's 1983. Mike Campbell buys a drum machine, and is messing around with his four-track recorder. Finds a groove on the machine, pulls out the guitar, invents an arpeggio that would work as a sig lick, adds a chord progression that avoids the tonic (substituting the six chord, minor, for "home"). It's not unusual. Just a groove, a lick and a chord pattern The effect of all three is a *chord circle* that feels, well, I guess it feels like the past coming back to ambush you in a quiet moment. He likes it. They need a single for *Southern Accents*. So Mike plays this chord circle for Tom, along with some other ideas. It is rejected because—and get *this*—it doesn't sound like the other stuff on the album. It doesn't *feel* right. We'll come back to that.

Mike says fine. He never was one to quarrel or quibble. Jimmy Iovine, the producer of their current project, says to Mike that Don Henley is looking for material for his current album project, *Building the Perfect Beast*. Can he play that track for Henley? Sure, says Mike. Henley listens, immediately writes the words to "The Boys of Summer" and we have a monster hit. Irony. Tom needs a single, passes over a monster hit because it doesn't feel right, still needs a single.

Later he meets Dave Stewart (Eurythmics dude) and they write two songs ("Don't Come around Here No More" and "Make It Better") that definitely don't feel like the rest of the stuff on *Southern Accents* (even has a drum machine, like "Boys of Summer"), but by now Petty has given up on the concept of his concept album and puts these two misfits on the album anyway and then releases them as the first two singles. Yes, it does work. He has hits—one does way better than the other, but hey, that's the biz. The summer's out of reach, but everybody wins.

I Should Just Let It Go

If you're Mike Campbell, do you get pissed off? Your inconstant bandleader has dismissed something he ought to have recognized. He gives a lame reason—as a matter of fact, the song sounds *not all that far* from other stuff on the project. He gets it too late. You've presented your friend and your boss with a great gift. He's got his head up his ass. Then he goes and does an exaggerated version of the same thing he rejected. If "Boys of Summer" doesn't fit, how about a little sitar and synth to go with that drum machine?

Of course, Tom didn't hear what Don Henley heard. And I don't see how Henley's words could be improved on. That is not what Tom would have written, even if I am dying to know what his take would have been. In a moment of hearing, Henley heard "This is the pain of the past, and I must reject this self-destroying nostalgia." And having heard it, he was able to write it. He could *see* her. And having written it, he brings one of the best rock voices in rock history, and he belted it right into our amygdalae. No, I wouldn't change a thing about this. I loved that song too much. It feels like dreaming too, doesn't it? Tom didn't really do nostalgia, so he wouldn't have made that mistake. But he wasn't much for even reflecting on the pain of the past. Maybe that's why the song didn't speak to him. Tom was a present-tense kind of guy, and Mike Campbell knew that. His composition didn't feel like the present, except maybe as resolution that takes hold when you see that Dead Head sticker.

Those Days Are Gone Forever

Now, that is a case study that'll help us make our way through the boys in the band, in greater detail. But we don't have to.

You've seen my names and how I got there. Yours will be different, but I'll bet you can see mine, if I named them right. So much of what Tom Petty did was done by "feel," getting something to *feel right* was his criterion for everything. He did everything that way, as far as I can tell. Creatives often work that way. They can't really tell you why they do what they do. You just have to trust them.

And they can be wrong. Tom said he had missed this song, but I think it was just humility in the face of the unknowable. I'm quite sure he would stand by what the thing felt like when he heard it. His failure was in not seeing the future in that present moment, but not in *mis*reading the present.

And maybe it really wasn't for him anyway. Maybe it was just destined for Don. The Sun always goes down alone, you know?

PART II

Girl Trouble

6

A Lover's Delusion

MARY L. EDWARDS

Something about the melancholic beauty of Tom Petty's vocals mingling with Stevie Nicks's, singing sad lines like "I'm the lonely silent one," really resonated with me when I was an angst-ridden teenager harboring a secret crush. This meant that "Insider," from the 1981 album *Hard Promises*, became one of the most-played tracks on what I pretentiously liked to call the soundtrack to my life.

As "Insider" is famously one of Petty's most sorrowful tracks, I couldn't have been the only lovesick teen that felt drawn to it. Indeed, anyone who has ever been heartbroken can surely relate to its forsaken lover-narrator and the negative emotions he communicates, such as abandonment, anger, loneliness, despair, and low self-esteem.

Beyond its great artistic achievements and cathartic potential though, what distinguishes "Insider" from other songs about unrequited love out there is that its lover-narrator doesn't direct his anger toward his beloved for her betrayal, but toward *himself* for being surprised by this betrayal. What "Insider" provides us with, then, is a first-person account of a lover wrestling with the question of why he failed to foresee that his beloved would abandon him. For this reason, the song calls one of our most common assumptions about love into question: namely, it undercuts the idea that lovers have privileged access to the mind of the beloved. It also shows how making this assumption may lead us to view our beloved with an arrogant eye, rather than a loving one.

I Need to Know

Lovers often purport to know what the beloved thinks, desires, or needs, without having to ask. Exactly why lovers feel justified in making such claims is unclear. The most obvious explanations seem to be either 1. that a telepathic relation obtains between lovers, or 2. that lovers acquire a heightened sensitivity to the meanings of the beloved's bodily movements in a way that enables them to know how the beloved feels just at a glance.

But neither of these stories seems likely. Even if you think that the latter is plausible, the fact that lovers can be—and frequently are—duped by their loved ones suggests that their capacity to read the beloved's mind—by whatever means—is fallible. A lover's ideas about what goes on in the mind of a beloved don't have what it takes to count as knowledge; they definitely lack certainty. So here we have a puzzle: if lovers cannot read the minds of the persons they love, why won't they back down? Why do they insist that they can mind-read? "Insider" speaks directly to this puzzle.

The song's lover wrecks himself for not foreseeing that his beloved would leave him in the dust, since—presumably—he's the one who "oughta know" her best. But he also realizes that he has been misled about the extent of what he can know about her. Because his consciousness is isolated from others in a fundamental way, he has never escaped from what he calls the "hall of strangers," not even when he was with his beloved. The isolation of each human consciousness then, turns out to be a cage without a key. This means that lovers never cease to be strangers in an important sense, no matter how intimate their relationship is, because each lover continues to have his or her own, private thoughts and intentions, which are invisible to the other.

The Beaver Monologues

The "Insider" narrative is in accord with what Simone de Beauvoir (1908–1986) contended: there is a dangerous tendency among lovers to delude themselves into thinking that they can merge their consciousness with that of their beloved. The mere fact that one person loves another is frequently—and mistakenly—taken to justify the belief that she can also know what he thinks and see the world through his eyes. In her chapter on "The Woman in Love" in *The Second Sex*, Beauvoir tries to figure out the reasons behind this common lovers' delusion. She connects it to the ultimate goal of love, which, she believes, is to identify with the beloved.

Now, it's important to remember that we are hearing the identification rap from one of the most kick-ass feminist philosophers of all time. Her college friends called her *Castor*, or "Beaver," because she was always working, which is how you get to be so kick-ass. These ideas about love appear in a book aimed at explaining how women's oppression inflects almost every aspect of their experience. The focus on women's oppression leads Beauvoir to believe that the desire to fuse your consciousness with that of the beloved is much stronger for female, heterosexual lovers in sexist societies. It's a perverse consequence of women's oppression. Beauvoir is certainly right to say that women in sexist societies are likely to be more invested in their romantic relationships, but lovers of all genders and sexual orientations seem to share the desire to identify with the beloved, to some degree. What's up with this?

So we admit this much: we often desire to be able to think 'the same' as the person we love. It's apparent in stereotypical "lover behavior," like reading the same books, rockin' to the same Petty tunes (maybe not quite hearing the words and taking the advice), adopting the same friends, and so on. When we act that way, the goal seems to be *insider knowledge:* knowledge of how our loved one ticks. But the "Insider" lover has fallen afoul of the idea that you can *know* another just by loving that person and doing the things lovers do. Why is it that lovers don't stop to consider whether their strategies for gaining insider knowledge actually work? Unless something (usually bad) happens to catalyze such consideration, thoughtfulness on the question is not the norm.

Beauvoir's answer has two parts. First, lovers often buy into the notion that their romantic relationship gives them some kind of magical insight into the beloved's mental states. That's because it's scary to be in love and it hurts to accept when something that's so close is still so far out of reach, so accepting this little delusion helps lovers feel secure in their relationship. After all, if they can know how the beloved thinks, they will also be able to accurately predict what choices he will make, including whether or not to give love in return. Lovers can, therefore, take great comfort in their faith that the beloved's thoughts are neither independent nor invisible, but on full display for the lover alone. This is why we can easily imagine a lover being alarmed and upset when she finds out that her beloved likes "Mary Jane's Last Dance" more than "Runnin' Down a Dream," which she likes best.

Second, if lovers can convince themselves that their consciousness is connected in some fundamental way to the beloved's consciousness, they don't have to work so hard. If you seriously believe you can read your loved one's mind, you have a great excuse for ditching the difficult, ongoing project of *getting to know* him. You can simply assume that he likes "Runnin' Down a Dream" just as much as you do (because you can make believe that you 'see' he has the same taste in music as you), which is way easier than figuring out what his favorite Tom Petty and the Heartbreakers song really is.

As Beauvoir sees it, though, lovers who think they can read the beloved's mind don't just lie to themselves, they also forfeit all the rewards that could be reaped from persevering with the project of getting to know the beloved (assuming he's worth knowing, of course).

So, basically, lovers who pretend to have insider knowledge do so because it is pleasant and because it makes it easier for them to wriggle out of the work involved in getting to know her. But we know, and the lover in "Insider" learns the hard way, that there ain't no easy way out.

An Arrogant Eye for Love

To explore the implications of lovers' deluded ideas about their capacity for insider knowledge, we can turn to the work of another celebrated feminist philosopher, Marilyn Frye. In *Politics of Reality*, Frye argues that lovers' delusory ideas about the reach of their knowledge disposes them to adopt an arrogant attitude toward their beloved, which has a lot of negative implications for the dynamic of the relationship. What's more, she contends that seeing your loved one with this arrogant eye is not really seeing them at all. If you want to really see your loved one, Frye recommends looking at them with a loving eye.

A loving eye is opposed to an arrogant eye. It is one that continually looks and searches, checks and questions. It is "one that pays a certain sort of attention." This sort of attention, in Frye's view, requires a discipline. Surprisingly, this discipline turns out to be one of *self-knowledge* and, specifically, "knowledge of the scope and boundary of the self." This is because I need to have knowledge of my own ambitions, fears, likes, dislikes, needs, and so on, to prevent myself from projecting thoughts that are really my own into my idea of my beloved's mind.

If I know that my favorite song is "Runnin' Down a Dream" and that that's just about the extent of my knowledge on song preferences, I also know that I can't presume that that's my beloved's favorite song too. Of course, having self-knowledge won't enlighten me about how it feels to be inside my beloved's head and it won't give me any clues about what my beloved's favorite song is. But, if I know where boundaries of my self lie, of where I end, I will have a clearer idea of where my beloved begins. This will allow me to look at her with a loving eye, one that sensitively appreciates the separateness of the two lovers and acknowledges that their interests are not neatly identical.

It's telling that it's feminist philosophers who have paid the most attention to love in recent times. In *The Second Sex*, Beauvoir makes the point that a heterosexual woman will typically pay more attention to her beloved than he will pay to her, for the simple reason that in patriarchal society there is more pressure on women to be successful in love. Consider for instance how unmarried women beyond a certain age are regarded as failures in our society as evidenced by the derogatory terms used to refer to them—such as 'spinster,' 'old maid,' 'crazy cat lady'—in a way that unmarried men—'bachelors'—aren't. Frye echoes this idea in her insistence that the arrogant way of seeing she describes is prevalent among men in heterosexual relationships. This is important to bear in mind when thinking about "Insider" because Petty initially wrote this song for Nicks, but Nicks refused it on the grounds that it's not a woman's song (she was much happier with "Stop Draggin' My Heart Around" in this respect).

Nicks seems to be right about this. "Insider," as I interpret it, is a (heterosexual) man's song in the same way that "Breakdown" is, although it's easier to see why in the case of "Breakdown," where the lover-narrator thinks he knows that "something inside you is feeling like I do"—which seems to entitle him to make the demand that you go ahead and give it to him! A woman is way less likely to speak to a man like this, since more is at stake for her in such a situation. *He* would still be considered a good guy if he attempted to seduce a woman this way and it backfired, whereas *she* is likely to face shame and ridicule as a 'ho', a 'skank', or a 'loose' (and, therefore, bad) woman if she did the same thing. A consequence of this double standard is that the heterosexual woman will usually proceed with caution—she'll look and listen, check and question—when she's forming ideas about her love interest. So, she is a lot less likely to be surprised in the way that the lover in "Insider" is. (She is also a lot less prone to the mistakes of an arrogant eye in general, which may be considered an "epistemic upside" of gender oppression.)

Nevertheless, the lover's admission in the song, that "it don't show when you break up," signals he has been on a journey of self-discovery, which eventually enabled him to see his beloved with a loving eye. And yet, it is only after the love affair has ended that he can start to see why his beloved rejected him for another. It's only by critically reflecting on what he presumed to know about her that he seems to achieve real insight into her motives for betraying him. But could it be possible for him to turn what he now sees with his new, loving eye into genuine insider knowledge?

How to Cry over Spilled Wine

The fact that the song's lover only starts to glean insights into his beloved's mindset once he starts checking and questioning what he previously took to be insider knowledge, arguably, betrays a view about how we really can gain knowledge of others. It's a view that, I believe, is in accordance with Matthew Ratcliffe's ideas about how 'radical empathy' is achieved.

In his essay, "Phenomenology as a Form of Empathy," Ratcliffe characterizes radical empathy as an intellectual tool that expands the range of what we can understand about the experiences of other people. Ordinarily, empathy takes the assumption of a shared world as its starting point. This is why you can understand how another feels when you see someone spill red wine all down the front of her *Full Moon Fever* t-shirt, and you can feel something of her sense of anger and frustration (although you do not feel quite the same as you would if it were your own t-shirt).

Ratcliffe highlights how experiences of everyday empathy like this occur "against a shared backdrop." In this instance, the backdrop is a shared world that incorporates certain values (*Full Moon Fever* t-shirts are cool) and certain facts (red wine stains clothes). But this shared world backdrop is simply—and some such as Frye might add, *arrogantly*—presupposed.

What distinguishes radical empathy from everyday empathy, according to Ratcliffe, is its refusal to take too much for granted as shared. In everyday empathy, the separation between my conscious experience and the other's is incomplete, since the same world, with the same meanings and values, is presumed to be the basis for both of our interpretations of events, which informs both our emotional responses to them in the same way. This is why everyday empathy has a potluck quality to it; it only hits its target if both parties are the same in the relevant ways. So, you will only feel something like what the person who gets red wine spilled on her t-shirt feels like *if* she is also a Tom Petty and the Heartbreakers fan, not somebody who really hates rock music and is only wearing that t-shirt because she lost a bet.

While everyday empathy—as a sort of gut reaction to what we perceive to be another's emotional state (which tacitly assumes that she shares our world)—is quite a crude tool for understanding others, radical empathy—which involves a great deal more thought—is much more sophisticated. In order to radically empathize with another, I must appreciate that the degree to which she and I belong to a shared world is variable and, crucially, acknowledge that my conscious experience is completely separate from hers. This is essential because certain experiences, such as those consistent with periods of intense grief, or psychological conditions like deep depression or schizophrenia, may not only have different contents (such as sadness versus indifference about getting wine spilled on your t-shirt), they may also take on an entirely different *form* to other experiences. In particular, the form of experience may change with regard to what possibilities appear on the surface of the world for the subject of that experience.

Ratcliffe notes how deep depression is often reported to coincide with "a loss of tangible possibilities." A person who cannot see many possibilities for action as being available to her is going to feel limited in her capacity as an agent. She is also not going to interpret events in the same way that she would if more possibilities were visible to her. If the person who gets the red wine spilled on her *Full Moon Fever* t-shirt is a Tom Petty and the Heartbreakers fan *and* deeply depressed, the form of her experience may differ from that of the non-depressed fan in the sense that this event may be experienced as taking place in a world in which there is no possibility of remedying the sadness it triggers, because things only ever go from bad to worse in that world. It follows that the same event will be more devastating for the depressed fan, as it might seem to her that her favorite t-shirt—perhaps the only one she feels comfortable going to gigs in—is simply ruined, FOREVER and no other t-shirt will ever be as good. Since the possibilities that are visible on the surface of the world for us—like that of finding new favorite t-shirts—may not look like possibilities to a deeply depressed person, this will change the shape the world takes for her; rather than being one that is filled with possibilities for improvement (and many potential new favorite t-shirts), it may be one where all action appears hopeless.

Radical empathy allows us to acknowledge how the form of experience can vary from one person to another, as well as the content. For this reason, it is a much more reliable tool for helping us to understand how others—who may occupy very different worlds to us—feel and think because it doesn't presuppose that the other person shares our world. It is also hard work. It involves paying close attention to the other and using our imagination to construct a picture of what her world might be like.

The Road to Authentic Love

In "Insider," the lover had presumed that he and his beloved occupied the same world, and he pays the price for being mistaken in this presumption. The metaphors he draws on to convey his feelings—those of being "burned by the fire" and "left to rust"—suggest that when his 'lover's delusion' is shattered, he experiences disappointment at the deepest level, that of existential feelings; background emotions that dictate the way we experience the world. Ratcliffe argues that those feelings contribute to the structure of our world and the possibilities that appear to be available within it.

The sorrow of "Insider," arguably, has an existential edge, as the rejected lover's melancholy appears to be intensified by his realization that he never really *knew* his beloved. This realization is likely to be experienced at the level of existential feeling because it drives him to question the extent of his possibilities in the world, and specifically, whether knowing another through love is a possibility. When he sees that his dream of insider-knowledge is impossible to achieve through love alone, he demonstrates an almost stubborn determination to fight till he gets it right, even if this means getting it when it's too late to salvage his relationship.

"Insider" is a song about progress. Its lover transitions from seeing his beloved with an arrogant eye to seeing her with a loving eye. Early on in the song, the lover states that he's "the one who oughta know" (we don't know what yet). It soon becomes apparent the reason *why* he thinks he oughta know is because he's an "insider," which permits us to deduce that *what* he was supposed to know is that his beloved was going to leave him for another. Then, he explains that he's "crawled through the briars" and come to the realization that when he was in love, he was trapped in "a circle of deception."

Finally, in the last verse, the lover no longer presumes to "know" anything about his beloved; he merely makes hypotheses (or, more precisely, 'bets') about her situation and her relationship with her new partner. He even attempts to radically empathize with her by imagining her inhabiting a different world, "a quiet world of white and gold," with her new lover.

This new, loving perspective is one that is conducive to the flourishing of what Beauvoir calls "authentic love." Toward the end of her chapter on "The Woman in Love," she describes this kind of love as predicated on the lovers' reciprocal recognition of each other's freedom to have differing morals and goals. Anything they choose to reveal of their separate selves, and anything they come to share, is a gift that constitutes their mutual love. Authentic love results from seeing your beloved with a loving eye. It's also, evidently, the kind of love that is worth working for.

Unfortunately for the lover in "Insider," the catalyst for his transition from arrogant blindness to loving clear-sightedness is being scorned by the one he loves, meaning that his potential to love authentically seems to be redundant before it's even been realized. Would the song's beloved still have abandoned him if he had learned to see her with a loving eye at an earlier stage in their relationship? Obviously, we would not be so arrogant as to presume to know, although we can imagine that the lover might have a better idea after questioning and checking what he thought he knew (and of course what he learned by writing "Insider").

Maybe his loving eye allows him to see that he's got a shot at winning her back. If so, he's probably prepared to do what it takes to do so and then to persevere with the difficult, ongoing project of getting to know her. Perhaps we can imagine this kind of happily-ever-after for the broken-up couple in "Insider." Perhaps not. Only one thing's certain and that's the lesson that this song teaches us: that getting to know another person is a long, long road!

7
She Went Down Swingin'

MEGAN VOLPERT

Rock'n'roll music was invented by women. Big Mama Thornton had already sold over two million copies of "Hound Dog" by the time Elvis turned a sweet little sixteen. Without Sister Rosetta Tharpe's 1938 single "Rock Me," there is no Little Richard, no Jerry Lee Lewis, no Chuck Berry, no Johnny Cash. Each of these men admitted it.

This might be my all-time favorite rock'n'roll history moment: Bob Dylan proposed to Mavis Staples in 1963 and she said no. He would go on to win a Nobel Prize for Literature (don't even get me started on that), and she would end up, well, without one—that is, after she was finished providing the soundtrack to the Civil Rights Movement. Although, arguably, having the pleasure of saying no to Dylan is quite a prize in itself.

And these godmothers of rock did not sit quietly in the discounted album dustbin. They instead begat many daughters. Let me remind you of: Dusty, Aretha, Joni, Janis, Donna, Carole, Joan, Yoko, Patti, Marianne, Stevie, Debbie, Chrissie, Madonna, Cyndi, Bonnie, Whitney, Tina, Sinead, k.d., Janet, Liz, Courtney, Tori, P.J., Alanis, Lucinda, and—fuck it, why not—Britney.

That's just a handful of the ones everybody can recognize by first name only. So women continue to be influential in the making of rock music, yet for generations they have nevertheless barely registered as mattering to it. Historians and critics invested in classic rock of the Sixties and Seventies have been particularly shortsighted—they can spot a pair of boobs sitting alone on a barstool at a distance of a hundred yards, yet even from the VIP section at a Heart concert they somehow cannot see Nancy Wilson cranking it up to eleven.

But let me put down this joint and get on to the point of this chapter: Tom Petty is a feminist.

Word to Your Mother

What is a feminist? A person who gets shit on a lot of the time—kidding (not kidding). Haters hate feminists because they believe in something that the haters do not. In the most basic sense, any person who believes that women should be treated equally to men can be defined as a feminist. Now we can quibble for a few millennia about the meaning of the words "women," "treated," and "equally," if you're into that. But what we cannot argue about is whether Tom Petty is a feminist. He was, and now that it's over, that means he *is*.

His life was proof. Ask the two daughters he raised, or the mother and aunties that raised him. Ask the charitable causes to which he contributed or the people with whom he toured across four decades. His songs are also proof because they consistently maintain feminist ideals. Some of these ideals include: that women are rational to the same extent as men, that women are equal partners in heterosexual relationships, that women are able to fight and to work just like men do, and that women should receive the same rights and respect as men.

Duh, right? Pretty tame and even obvious stuff to believe in, is it? Then why doesn't any other classic rock outfit have a catalog of songs to rival Petty's when it comes to high regard for women? Amongst bands comprised entirely of heterosexual, white males—Beatles and Stones, Zepp and Floyd, Steely and Doobie, Dead and Doors, Who and Tull, Eagles and Aerosmith, and any band ever named for a city like Boston or state like Kansas—no rock band can go toe to toe with Petty in this matter.

I'm giving a pass to Queen because if you get me going on the LGBTQ+ community's contributions to rock music, we'll have to shift gears into queer feminism and indeed start quibbling about what a "woman" is. On the chance that my definition is far more expansively permissive than yours, we're skipping it in order to provide a relatively safe space for grizzled rock dudes to dip a toe in at the shallow end of this pool.

If you are said dude, and you decide to dive, please don't pee in here like a neanderthal. So for the record, I'm here to discuss the most Basic Becky type of white bread feminism because that is really a very high-brow bar for most classic rockers to visit with any constancy, even though the world has continued to spin well beyond such simplicities to a more nuanced neighborhood pub where gender can intersect with racial, socioeconomic, and many other facets of identity (see also: Prince).

Where My Bitches At

There are as many feminist theorists as there are songs by Tom Petty. So that's a two-fold problem: which theorists should apply for this position, and which songs will they sing? Let's start by narrowing the field of theorists in the most obvious way by focusing on those who actually talked about music. There were a couple of feminists in the Eighties who were pioneers of New Musicology, a scholarly discipline that was critical of positivism. Up until that point, positivists studied music as if all songs worldwide operated on the same generic principles, so that just listening to the song itself was enough to interpret its meaning. Then feminists came along and asked rudimentary questions, like: Does it matter what culture this song is sprung from, or how that culture later responded to it?

Nowadays, the entirely uncontroversial answer to that question is yes. Music is not sublimely meaningless. Yes, we should bring cultural studies, social sciences, and philosophy into our understanding of music. You obviously agree with this point, or you wouldn't have wanted to crack open a book on Tom Petty and philosophy in the first place. So musical analysis has come to take on a variety of social meanings, but in the beginning, New Musicology was just a couple women holding it down. Chief among these is Susan McClary, who covers everything from seventeenth-century operas to Laurie Anderson's twentieth-century performance art in *Feminine Endings: Music, Gender, and Sexuality*. This book f-bombed the study of music wide open by examining how music constructs gender through both lyrics and composition, as well as how analysis of music has itself been gendered.

So Tom Petty is our cart and Susan McClary is our horse. Her project is the continual analysis of music through a

feminist lens, searching out the ways that sexism and patri-
archy continue to insinuate themselves in song. We're looking
to understand Petty's view of women, to analyze his body of
work and arrive at an understanding of how this work is feminist. So what songs do we want to put in the cart? I would be
glad to do literally all of them, but that's a six-volume magnum
opus instead of the six thousand words I'm allotted here (give
or take).

We'll take the lane of least resistance: *Greatest Hits*. Can we
agree that this 1993 compilation album, certified twelve times
platinum, is a representative sample of Tom Petty's catalog? It
includes a majority of the hit singles he had with the
Heartbreakers for their first twenty years together and even
stuff from *Full Moon Fever*, his one solo album by then.
Excluding work with Mudcrutch and the Traveling Wilburys,
Petty's name is on the cover of sixteen albums. Eight of those
albums are showcased on *Greatest Hits*. The compilation thus
covers fifty percent of his *oeuvre*, as well as one hundred percent of songs he ever wrote that charted in the top ten. So if we
agree that this is the least rocky road, let's begin the breakdown. Ready? Even if not, you're gonna get it.

"American Girl"

It's fair to say that, in a pinch, this doubles as our national
anthem. All of America (and well beyond) has been drawn in to
a state of empathy with this girl, this wholly relatable arche-
type of the dream where we can make it if we only try. When
the single was released in the UK the record company put a pic
of a Lolita-looking girl in heart-shaped sunglasses. Petty told
them to take it off.

And that was before he was famous—most people would
just roll with it, but not Petty. That wasn't the girl he was
thinking of, at all. His AG was raised on some bullshit and kept
in a small, narrow avenue of existence. Yet she instinctually
resolved that the world has more and bigger things to offer,
even if her efforts were to meet with the cold desperation of
highway traffic and the ocean of other people equally striving,
each in her loneliness.

This girl plans to be keeping her faith in the idea of
America—even when that idea is painful and the promised

success never quite arrives. What she ain't doing is throwing herself off the balcony. Petty vehemently denied apocryphal rumors that the song depicted a suicide, and even shrugged off the secondary speculation that the song was somehow inspired by a news item about a girl who jumped back in Gainesville. The American Girl is not a tragedy or a cautionary tale. Her sadness has been rather ordinary, and as the chorus makes clear, Petty wishes three things upon her: approval, relaxation, and longevity.

With all that healthy, wealthy and wise stuff he's reading in her tea leaves, Petty turns the American Girl into our hero. The *girl* is the hero. So who's the villain? Maybe those little promises, or maybe the cars rolling by, or maybe the dude in the second verse that popped into her mind for a minute. Who was that guy? What did he do? Nobody knows, because it doesn't matter. You're a flat character, bro, already faded away to memory and put far out of reach, not even given a chance at our attention, let alone our sympathy. We wish nothing but the best for the American Girl and hope to live by her fine example. I guess Petty could've written it as "American Guy," with the same number of syllables and the rhyme would even be a bit more on point that way. But he didn't. It would suck. It just would. Unless the line was "Bruce crept back into his memory," but I promised I wouldn't go there. But that line of imagining works pretty well with "girl" too, don't it?

Now, the horse almost bolted there and maybe you're reading a little defensively and working up your objection to this line of reasoning, which goes: nothing about the main character in the song is especially ladylike! The American Girl doesn't have a single characteristic about her that of necessity makes her a female. There's no inherent femininity to any of her thoughts or feelings at all. Yessir, that's my point. She's a human being. Ain't nothing gendered about it, except a pronoun that has been kicked around some since '76. That one *does* have to live like a refugee, until we can work it out, but life is very short.

"Breakdown"

This is one of those songs that'll help you decide if you're a glass half empty or half full type of person. It's not clear whether the two people in the song are on the verge of finally hooking up or on the verge of finally breaking up. Either way, Petty's cool with it. He says it's alright. Or it will be alright at least, if he can get his love interest here to break down. In its context, this is a feminist request.

First of all, they're on an even playing field because he has noted that they feel the same way inside. Once the eyes are already giving away that something's up and then they've run out of stuff to say about it, some type of action is required. Is she slamming the door, or falling into his arms? Breaking down is an action in either case, but these lyrics treat it as a noun. He wants her to go ahead and give him the breakdown. "Give" is the verb. To give: to freely transfer, cause, or allow. Permission. Consent. Gift. She's not going to get bulldozed; she'll give her breakdown. That is, she might or she might not. The song continues and concludes with his asking. We don't know if she did give him a breakdown, which deprives the dude of "winning" a situation by preserving its suspense.

Of all the cover versions of this tune, Petty really liked two of them—those belonging to Grace Jones and Suzy Quatro. Jones actually called him up and asked him to write a third verse because the original song was barely two and a half minutes. Petty obliged, and moreover, made clear in these additional lyrics that there was no need to drag out the end of the affair because the singer will survive it (see also: Gloria Gaynor, because "I Will Survive" debuted in '78 and then Jones recorded her cover of "Breakdown" in '80). That extra verse is the most insistent portion of the monologue, meaning that when gifted the opportunity to conclude the conflict in this song and to write it expressly for a female singer, Petty chose to construct a position of strength rather than perpetuate additional uncertainty.

"Listen to Her Heart"

It's a little-known fact that this song was inspired by a story Petty was told by his first wife. She and Shelter Records producer Denny Cordell had gone out on the town and ended up at Ike Turner's place. Crazy Ike locked up the mansion and wouldn't let anybody leave—then out came the trays of cocaine. This would have been in '77, shortly after Tina Turner finally bailed and exposed Ike as the wife-beating asshole that he was.

"Listen to Her Heart" is thus Petty's quiet way of confidently sucking his teeth at Ike from the moral high ground.

In the first place, this really took place. Petty listened to his wife's story and was so compelled by it that he memorialized it in song. He valued her experience enough to preserve it for the both of them. And then, of course, she's the hero. She can listen to her heart and he believes it'll tell her the right thing to do. No chivalrous rescue required. Even in a case where she might be a kind of high maintenance lady, Petty still trusts that he's not being used. Their relationship is okay, buddy, and she can't be taken away from it.

Certainly not by money or cocaine. The "cocaine" thing is one of the smaller record company skirmishes Petty faced that deserves more attention. They wanted him to change the line from "cocaine" to "champagne" because it was a more tolerable word to hear on the radio. Hey, decent rhyme substitution, too! But Petty didn't budge, the reason being that he didn't think it fit with the character. That's right: Petty waged war against the music industry to protect the idea that no woman gives a shit about the price of champagne. He was willing to risk airplay just to keep true to the fact that some assholes think you can win over a girl by shoveling coke at her. So you can roll up that Benjamin and stick it, well, let's just say it ain't where the blow goes. But if we hear a strange sucking sound, we'll know you got your bump.

That asshole doesn't know her, or really any woman for that matter. Even a high-class lady who might like to get high is still going to listen to her heart. And ask any of Ike's thirteen wives whether their hearts said they needed him. My apologies, that's a disputable claim—Ike definitely had at least eight wives; the other five may or may not be unproven hyperbole, because that what trays of cocaine will do to a man's mind. Not a woman's mind though, according to Petty. This is a portrait of a female who won't be addled.

"Anything that's Rock'n'Roll"

If you're confused about the inclusion of this song on the list, it's included on the version of *Greatest Hits* that was released in the United Kingdom, since it was a huge number one hit there. (You need to know they left off "I Need to Know," but I

won't do you like that.) The UK's favorite little ditty has two
ladies in it—the singer's girlfriend and the girlfriend's mother.
The portrayal of each is highly satisfying.

Even though the singer is partying with all his friends until
the sun comes back up, he isn't addressing this song to them.
He addresses only the particular party animal of his girlfriend.
She gets it. She's a rock'n'roller who's ready to grab hold of an
electric guitar the same as he is. She can't stand her daddy's
rules. The father and the boss—identified by a male pronoun in
the lyrics—are both jerks. Her mother, by comparison, may
ultimately be able to get hip to the notion that her little girl
should live freely. Her mama's open-minded about things in a
way that daddy and the boss just ain't.

Petty says that everybody has got to know that rock'n'roll is
fine, but it's only the women whom he credits as being able to
really jump on board with turning the music up. Petty gets the
feeling these women can understand him better than other
men do. He prefers to talk to women about the things that matter most to him. If you never saw the band crank out this tune
on *Top of the Pops*, you should YouTube it. Lynch is all the way
stage left and Campbell is back center (where Campbell should
be), while Tench is where Campbell should be and Blair is, well,
where he always was. Maybe not a gender bender, but a move
that surely says, "Don't put us in a boy box."

"I Need to Know"

This song puts power in the hands of women in three different ways. Most obviously, its addressee already knows the
thing Petty needs to know, and it's up to her to let him in on
it. She's got her own agency with that knowledge. Moreover,
it's up to her to pull the trigger on their relationship. Petty
doesn't know how long he can hold on while stuck in the
dark, but he's definitely trying. The song doesn't declare that
if she's leading him on, then he's going to bail. There's no
threat from his side. He might very well stick around if she
admits she was making him wait. And if she goes, she goes
solo. She isn't checkin' the back door to go off with another
guy (or gal), and, well, after all, it's a great big world. Maybe
he just wants to claim one of those slots on her dance card.
There doesn't seem to be any moralizing or pressure for

monogamy in the lyrics. The guy is in epistemic crisis, not jealousy hell.

But it's the underrated second verse that really does the heavy lifting here, where Petty expresses shock that his love interest could fall for the line of that other dude. His girl might be a bit sneaky and withholding, but that all means she's quite savvy. After all, as I said, the word was "solo." How could she fall for some cheesy line? The possibly spurned lover thinks his lady should know better. He thinks she's a smart girl and needs to know why she'd do such a dumb thing. His love affair is only a letdown if it proceeds from that initial acknowledgment of his girl's sagacity.

It's also worth noting that Petty says he based the rhythm for this track on Wilson Pickett's version of "Land of 1,000 Dances." This was Pickett's first recording session in Muscle Shoals and the biggest hit he ever had on the pop charts. The lyrics are pretty much just a list of popular dances that one ought to be familiar with in 1966. In the long list of silly dance names like the watusi and the Bony Maronie, plus an endless string of na-na-na-nas, Pickett sings that you've simply got to know these dances and that he needs somebody to help him. The verbiage clearly stood out to Petty, but so did that imagery of a chaotic dance hall. Lots of switching partners going on and sometimes all of a sudden one gets left on the outside. Here again, the boys apply and the girls have their pick.

"Refugee"

By all accounts, the lyrics for this classic hit were written in less than a half hour, with Petty improvising both words and melody as he paced around listening to a cassette of riffs that guitarist Mike Campbell had given him. The gist of it is that these two lovers are facing the same fights as everybody else. They're not the first to encounter whatever pain they're suffering. Throughout each verse, Petty not only sands down their issues so they are equal to every other couple on Earth, but ensures that each of the two people in this relationship are equals. It's about everybody's fight, not mine, not yours. Everybody.

The tone is consistently one of encouragement above judgment. No pressure, just an option. Believe what you want, fight what you fight. If not for repeated "honeys" and "babies," this might actually be advice of a close friend. And it is a close friend. Our lovers are our friends, too, right? So it doesn't make a difference to him, and he's willing to blot out any sense of past wrongdoings because they both know they have something worthwhile. She's got her own opinions and feelings, and deals with her past in whatever way she needs. There's not usually any need to talk about it, but it's gotten the better of her now.

It's an intimate moment. He has been looking for this chance to tell her. The singer is neither dismissive of nor annoyed by the pain his love interest is going through. He is supportive without casting himself in the role of her savior. She's not fleeing *to* him like a refugee. He expects that she can be free just like anybody else, but she's got to feel it to be true in her own gut first.

"Don't Do Me Like That"

Alright, now we're getting into the thick of it. When people accuse Petty of being a jerk to women, this is usually the second track they cite (and we'll deal with "You Got Lucky" in a few minutes here). These people interpret the lyrics in a literal way that devalues Petty's history and his sense of humor. On its face, sure, the song is about a guy threatening a gal that she better not dump him because what goes around comes around. But Petty himself is not that guy and he expressly doesn't endorse the thinking of that guy.

The song's opening line states that Petty is talking to a friend of his and then the song continues to report on what this other man said about the gal who dumped him. It's explicitly stated that this is some other guy's opinion, but moreover, the tone of Petty's singing implies that he is making fun of that opinion. He does this thing where he pulls a vocal from way up high in his nose, often accompanied by the addition of a little extra Gainesville twang. In this case, he's dropping the T at the end of "don't" and running out some very long vowel sounds. When he sings like this, he is basically doing his impression of the rednecks he grew up with. It undermines the idea that they know what they're talking about. The trope is irony.

And on this track, Petty has a highly particular redneck in mind. "Don't do me like that" is something his father used to say all the time. As everyone knows, Earl Petty was an abuser and a drunkard. He was a real hard man to love and our hero got out from under that man's roof as quick as he could. Every time Earl would be yelling at little Tommy not to do him like that, our hero just tried to sit there and not crack up. Any laughter would mean he was gonna get it much worse. But he filed the line away and here it is popping up when Petty needs a refrain that will convey how much of a dumb ass the dude in the song is. It's a knock at machismo.

"Even the Losers"

This is just your basic Danny and Sandy summer love affair, except Danny thinks of himself as a loser. Sandy cracked him wide open, made him feel. There's a whiff of destiny about it and it meant so much to him that he simply hopes it meant a little something to her, too. Compared to *Grease* though, there's no sex appeal in this tune. Petty says they sat on the roof and smoked, threw rocks off the overpass, and so on. Fiery kisses aside, there is no mention of getting friendly down in the sand or making out under the dock. Petty offers a paean to summer flings without ever calling attention to the gal's body or even really talking about sex. The rest of the title itself is a pun that references sex, but it equally refers to the singer's hope that he's lucky enough to be remembered by this gal who he remembers so fondly.

Beyond the lyrics, there's a good little nugget to think about in the song's intro. Before the band sounds even one note, some lady opens the track by hollering that it's just the normal noises in there. Mike Campbell had been noodling around on the guitar at home and was ready to get down to properly recording a demo track, but he was worried that the cassette deck was going to pick up sounds from a nearby washing machine. His wife, Marcie, stuck her head in while the tape was rolling to protest to her husband that it was just the normal noises in there.

Unbelievably, they added it to the final mix. Why? It's a headline that reads: "Lead guitarist's leading lady brings grumpy band back from brink of despair." This was in the midst of a hundred studio takes of "Refugee" for a *Damn the Torpedoes* album that they were unsure would ever see the light of day thanks to the MCA contract dispute. Nothing at that point felt normal. Obviously, they all needed a good laugh and this slightly surreal intrusion into their sacred band space turned out to be just the right tension breaker. In homage to the good sense of Marcie, to whom Mike has been happily married since 1974, they included it.

"Here Comes My Girl"

This girl is a lot like Marcie Campbell, similarly reassuring that things will turn out fine because their relationship will last forever. Petty was stuck on how best to write lyrics for this Campbell riff, but the story eventually opened up to him when he hit upon the idea of writing it as a kind of narration. He credits Blondie and The Shangri-Las, two wildly successfully female pop groups, for showing him how to narrate. The Heartbreakers had been playing gigs with Blondie, who frequently embraced a sort of talky monologue instead of singing something all the way through.

The partnership with this girl is characterized as good, free, and right. Far from being a throwaway object, she's the only person who helps him rise above his worries and stand up for himself. She's all he needs. Perhaps calling her "my" girl in the hook line is a little on the possessive side, but this is arguably counterbalanced with the opening line of the chorus where she looks him in the eye. That is something equals do. In fact, if she's the one coaching him to regain his sense of self, to stop wondering and waiting so much, she's risen a bit above him.

The other bit that sticks in the craw is that tossed off phrase to introduce the bridge of the song, where Petty asks the audience to watch his girl walk. Yes, to watch a girl walk at some basic level uses the gaze to objectify her. On the other hand, which way is the girl walking? If you're just watching a girl's butt as she walks away, do not pass go or collect two hundred bucks. But if a girl's walking toward you and you're admiring her confident approach more than her features, that's another ball of wax. After all, it ain't called "There Goes My Girl," or "I Wish I Had a Girl (Who Walks Like That)." Petty doesn't say she looks good or fine—she looks *right*. His lady is formidable, not necessarily beautiful.

He could've given us an image of her wrapping her legs around his velvet rims, but he chose to put her arms around him instead. He could've made this music video into a pretty hot little story in the vein of ZZ Top, but instead he turned in footage of the band just playing it, with no girls present whatsoever. In fact, if you watch this video closely, you'll see that it starts off straight enough, but then Petty takes turns singing quite intimately to each of the Heartbreakers, one by one. Those smiles are a bit more than guys having fun playing music together. These are homoerotic knowing glances. They build, as Petty flings himself across Tench's piano like every torch singer who ever darkened a lounge. If you still doubt it, watch the action build to the last such object of Petty's affection, Ron Blair. He embraces Blair and as the camera swings around, it frames them in a virtualized kiss. Then Petty and Lynch are outright leering at each other. Bedroom eyes.

From the start of the torch-singing, Lynch isn't even doing a good job of pretending he hasn't been instructed to flirt with Petty—I mean, *c'mon*, he does the *double eyebrow* thing. I admit there may be some sex implied here, but it isn't exactly straight up . . . and so I promised I would *not* do this. But watch it yourself. You tell me. I don't know what it is, but I know what it is not. It may be objectifying something, but it isn't a "girl" in the usual sense.

"The Waiting"

One interpretation of these lyrics is that they're about getting laid, and yet again, the video simply features the band in performance with nary a lady in sight. He had the chorus first and struggled to write verses around it. The chorus itself neither addresses the woman from the verses nor contains any mention of romance whatsoever. Also yet again, Petty's inspiration comes from a female musician he admired. In this case it was Janis Joplin, who famously said, "I love being onstage and everything else is just waiting."

The love story he then wrote into the verses showcases another strong woman, one who can help him to live the way he wants to now. Though he admits to having chased skirts in the past, all it ever did was bum him out. Petty says quite directly that there is not much glory or fulfillment in womanizing. He'd rather wait for the woman who can make him a better man, and urges the woman to wait for his more sensible self, too. They're waiting together.

"You Got Lucky"

This is the real sore spot here. Petty says "You Got Lucky" is the most misunderstood song he ever wrote because it is so widely believed to be rude to a woman. The lyrics are basically admonishing a love interest that she's welcome to bail out if she thinks she can do better than their relationship. The idea is that the speaker is such a good catch she better not leave him. It sounds cocky. But there's no story and no real personality given to either of these two characters—because the lyrics are not what matters about this song. Petty himself thought of it as just a little love song that wasn't really about anything at all.

In interviews, the majority of his thinking about this song is always anchored to the way it was made. It was bizarre for two reasons. First, Campbell made the foundational riff for it using a drum loop, not a guitar. In the studio, Lynch recorded a second drum loop and additionally played over both loops. Second, Tench plays a synthesizer instead of proper keys of any kind. Boy, was he pissed about it, too. The Heartbreakers almost never used a synthesizer even at the height of Eighties techno madness. Still, this track is unique for the ways it showcases the band's ability to play with technology.

That helps explains why they seldom played it live, and perhaps more usefully, it reveals why they did such a weird music video for this song. The "You Got Lucky" video was a truly pioneering endeavor for MTV, both for its space cowboy (*Mad Max*-ish) setting and for its little bit of introductory business before the song kicks in. After that video, tons of bands lugged their gear out to the desert and even Michael Jackson was inspired to do long story intro work before beginning to sing. In the video, the Petty and Campbell emerge from a space-car (some step-child of a DeLorean), followed by the arrival of Lynch, Tench, and Epstein (sounds like a shift law firm) on a moto and sidecar outfit. They discover a tent filled with technology. They find televisions, radios, pinball machines, and of course, a guitar.

Petty's whole concept for this video is about what kinds of technology to embrace. Some of it—the tape-player and the guitar are well treated—the guitar even makes it back to the space-car in the keeping of Mike Campbell. But they dump the tape player, finally. They listen to recorded music, but it's about playing live for them. Some of the gadgets they lose interest in quickly. Hilariously, the televisions are playing their own previous music videos, alongside game shows and beauty pageants. The bandmates don't appear to recognize themselves in these videos and quickly move on to other pieces of tech. This is astute social commentary on Petty's part, taking an early, understated stab at what MTV has done to them, in the same vein as his interest in covering The Byrd's "So You Want to Be a Rock'n'Roll Star."

"You Got Lucky" isn't conceited as much as it's a conceit. It uses the bare bones of a romantic relationship as a slightly more specific and relatable stand-in for the generic problem of how to know when we've bitten off more than we can ethically chew. That tape-player got lucky when he found it. Petty was thinking about the way these new technologies were shaping their work as a band. In 1982, the synthesizer was pretty cockily marketed as the absolute best thing to happen to music, and at less than a year old, the fledging MTV network was obviously the absolute biggest thing to happen to bands. Or not.

Petty was still a decade away from calling out these industry confrontations directly in the lyrics with the likes of *The Last DJ*. His audience didn't really get it, so he let "You Got Lucky" slip away into the rarities bin—a sure sign that he did not approve of or even acquiesce to the mainstream interpretation of his song as simply some vulgar dude lording it over his less than adequate girlfriend. And he was, after all, in the throes of a protracted battle with the record company which, frankly, got lucky when he found them, too. Good songs are hard to find.

"Don't Come Around Here No More"

Here's another case of relatively empty lyrics, which could be more easily sung by a smallish woman looking to get a restraining order than by a heart-hurt man. But this time, the video gets us into trouble rather than out of it. To begin with, let's acknowledge that Dave Stewart, of the Eurythmics, takes much of the credit for both lyrical and video content on this one. Everyone knew the *Southern Accents* album was taking too long and not properly gelling, and Petty may indeed have ceded far more control than usual on what ultimately became the album's big single. Even so, Stewart got his inspiration from Stevie Nicks, the (smallish) female powerhouse at the front of Fleetwood Mac.

Stewart attended a party at her house. Nicks was trying to break up with guitarist Joe Walsh, of the Eagles, and kept yelling at him through the door that he shouldn't come around there anymore. Stewart ended up crashing in a spare bedroom and awoke to find Nicks trying on a bunch of Victorian clothing. Nicks's witchy ways and accompanying outfits are well known, but Stewart, who knew very little about her at that time, was struck by how much the whole scene was like something out of *Alice in Wonderland*. That vibe would go on to inform the video in an extremely literal way, and Petty ended up on Tipper Gore's shit list over it (although it didn't stop her from playing drums with Petty on a later occasion, so hanging chads and warning labels and other bygones must be left to dangle in the currents of history).

Back then, Gore was forming her censorious Parents Music Resource Center when the video debuted, and her six-year-old kid was having nightmares about Petty's Mad Hatter eating a cake made of Alice. So the Heartbreakers ended up briefly targeted by the PMRC clan, more for the violence of cannibalism than for any implication of sexism. Louise "Wish" Foley, the "kid" who played Alice in the video, was an unknown twenty-year-old at the time. I often wonder if the video would've garnered the same criticism had they asked Nicks herself to play Alice. Stewart had a role as Caterpillar in the video, so why not also Nicks? That Petty and Nicks shared a common orbit was well known by this time and it would've made a great cameo from a friendly face. Would the video read as sexist with somebody so powerful in the role of Alice?

She made it into the song in another way, too. Both she and Petty were recording at Sunset Sound at the time, and Nicks had booked some backup singers. She ended up canceling a session and Petty invited those singers to get into the mix of "Don't Come Around Here No More." The whole construction of the song was haphazard and spur of the moment like this, from doing weird experiments with roadie Bugs Weidel pulling the tape out of the deck to create sound effects, to trying to show an orchestral cellist who only knew how to play sheet music how to jam. And sitar!

Let's face it: everybody who touched this was addled extensively by cocaine. Petty would end up lamenting that the song never existed separately from its video in the minds of his listeners. It was lyrically vacant but sonically very exciting, and it helped the Heartbreakers turn a corner as a unit. Plus, Stan got a girlfriend, and that did every Heartbreaker a temporary favor. He and Wish Foley moved in and stayed with it for two some odd years, which for Stan was an increase of about 365 x 2 over his usual relationship. You do the math (don't forget leap year). The macabre humor of the video casts a shadow over a song that was not at all sexist. Wish Foley just thought it was funny. On the other hand, it won best special effects at the second annual MTV Music Video Awards that year, so the kids obviously thought it was alright. If you want to argue that the video ruins the song completely, you've got to be willing to side with Tipper and the PMRC—and that's one hell of an icky slippery slope.

"I Won't Back Down"

There's no gendered content here whatsoever, and thus nothing to discuss. So let's instead pause to appreciate the fact that "I Won't Back Down" was written collaboratively with Jeff Lynne and also included a healthy dose of input from George Harrison. Petty was consistently able to form strong bromances, even with other superstars whose egos were equally massive. He was personally uninterested in macho bullshit and games of one-upmanship (see also: The Traveling Wilburys, and revisit the flirtations in "Here Comes My Girl"—not the work of insecure men).

"Runnin' Down a Dream"

This is another testament to Petty's faith in his musical relationships. Campbell got the solo on the first take and Petty loved it so much he let the song run out over four minutes rather than cut or fade any of that wicked guitar part. The only gendered content in the song is a reference to Del Shannon's "Runaway." Shannon was one of the many rock elders who sought to collaborate with Petty, eventually resulting in the production of his 1981 comeback album *Drop Down and Get Me*. They were still hanging out a few years later (even though Petty had stolen Howie Epstein from him) and Petty's inclusion of the "Runaway" reference got a big smile out of Shannon.

"Runaway" is itself well in line with Petty's view of women. The singer is miserable after the dissolution of his relationship and he wonders what when wrong. Never does he blame the woman or demonize her as cold or capricious or cheating. He still wishes she was there by his side, and his wondering has a quality parallel to the open-ended potential for forgiveness in "I Need to Know." Indeed, the remainder of "Runnin' Down a Dream" is willing to go with the flow of whatever is down the road. The rain soaks through both Shannon's and Petty's lyrics, and Petty ends on an optimistic note that he's willing to go where the mystery leads him. If it's his lady who's run away, he's willing to run after her.

Free Fallin'

This three-chord song that was written in just a half hour for his first solo album became the first ballad Petty ever released as a single and was ultimately the longest-charting hit of his entire career. His description of the stereotypical good California girl was improvised on the spot just to get a chuckle out of Jeff Lynne. She's an extension of the American girl—she loves her mom, her boyfriend, horses, Jesus, Elvis, and America. What else in life is there, really? And the force in opposition to this good girl is the bad boy—the boyfriend she loves—because he broke her heart and doesn't even miss her.

Oh, but he does miss her. He's sulking around in the shadows (and the mall!) proclaiming how free he is, even though he's attached himself to a bunch of vampires and really he's more fallen than free. As he feels himself falling, she creeps back into his memory and he wants to enact the grand gesture of writing her name in the sky. But his days living in Reseda are just so long and there's that freeway intruding on his yard. He's steering toward an escape into nothingness, wants to leave this world for a while.

The record company execs didn't want to get on board for this song as the big single because they thought the references wouldn't be appreciated outside the confines of Los Angeles. What do Mulholland Drive and Ventura Boulevard mean to the rest of America? They underestimate us, don't they? We all understand malaise. The American girl has a case of it, too, even though her boyfriend here is only reporting on her positive qualities. Both the good girl and the bad boy are actually suffering in the same flat way—stagnating in their sparkle, falling in their freedom.

At concerts, this was always a main staple for singing along. There's a joyous crowd surge, the flicker of lighters held high or arms waving in unison. It really is something to behold, the togetherness in an audience brought on by this tune. Yet it is a ballad and there is a clear melancholy there, everybody feeling the awful and predictable weight of a million individual situations as they strain gloriously to be *freeeeeeee* and then sink inevitably down into the open mouth of *fallllllin'*. The existential tension of this position is given equally to the good girl and the bad boy. She may be at home with a broken heart right now, if the bad boy's conjecture is to be believed, but we all know she'll soon be heading out in hopes of finding a little more to life somewhere else.

"Learning to Fly"

Although the song itself has no gendered content, the storyline of its video turns learning to fly into a metaphor for growing to understand women. It features several different types of women and their varying influence on a wide-eyed young man. At first, he's just a tiny toddler having a picnic with his mom and dad in picturesque Fifties style, albeit in the surreal scene of a desert. Then, like a mirage, three scantily clad go-go dancers appear. The boy wanders toward them, careful not to get too close to their high kicks, drinking them in with unblinking eyes, mesmerized until shaken out of it by his mother's hand jerking him back by the shoulders to rejoin their picnic.

This first glimpse of the sirens is echoed in his adolescent years. There he is, innocently cleaning the pool when a somewhat older and clearly more mature young lady hops out of the water and begins to walk toward him with seduction in her eyes. He tries to ignore it and carry on with his work, but she grabs him by the shoulders—an echo of his mother in the previous scene—and kisses him forcefully amidst Campbell's soaring slide guitar solo. The young man doesn't know what he's doing, but he closes his eyes and tries to be in the moment. We don't get to see who pulled away first or what happened next, but the scene ends just as Petty sings that the world may break your heart.

We next see the young man, hair a little longer and acting very much like a wise guy, carrying on backstage at a club where he becomes entranced into following a nearly naked waitress. He watches as she puts something in his drink, then he picks it up and downs it willingly. He's tripping out and watching her dance, while Petty again acts as harbinger of doom, reminding us that coming down is the hardest thing. All three of these archetypical femme fatales are presented as the necessary evils of this young man's education about life. Even his mother comes off like a scolding prude, equally as damaging as those women from which she aims to protect him. Freud be damned. Or at least darned. Where's the feminism? Guess you'll know when we get there.

None of these little vignettes really gets a proper ending, until the last woman in the video shuts it all down with a firm happily ever after. We're back in the desert once again as the young man literally crashes right into her on the highway. They emerge from their flaming automobiles, the woman clad in a simple black dress that is the most conservative attire on any woman in this video. We don't even see her face, just a mass of blonde curls—a very different view compared to the bodies that have been very much on display so far. This isn't a good-time scene with women for bad influences, it's a horrible accident with a woman who's his equal match.

She's neither hunting him down nor in need of being saved by him. They are both a mess and have been literally driven into each other's arms. They reach for each other at the same time and fall into the kiss that concludes the video. He's had quite a few rocky comedowns in this video, and knows when he gets to the crash at the end that he has rather ironically arrived at just where he ought to be. After the shallow sexiness and outright manipulation present in each preceding scene, the young man has learned that flying requires a proper copilot.

"Into the Great Wide Open"

This song contains two very fierce broads, and there's a third one added in the video. Most obviously, Eddie learned everything he knows from a girl who happened to have the same tattoo as he did. She's played by Gabrielle Anwar in the video, perhaps best known for dancing the tango with Al Pacino in *Scent of a Woman*. They both have a heart with a dagger through it on their right forearm. She taught him some chords on her guitar after they moved into an apartment that they could both afford—equals all the way. Though Eddie's future may have been wide open when he first arrived in Hollywood, it was only after he got together with this girl that the sky would prove to be the limit.

But he pretty well torched his own chances, clueless rebel that he was, and this line in the chorus is a hat tip to a rockin' Welsh woman who deserves to be more widely known. Two years earlier, The Replacements used the same line in "I'll Be You." Paul Westerberg himself in turn had cribbed it from Jim Steinman's "Rebel Without a Clue," which was written for Bonnie Tyler's *Secret Dreams and Forbidden Fire* album five years before Petty nicked it from The Replacements while on tour with them.

You may know Bonnie Tyler best for "Holding Out for a Hero," the soundtrack to Kevin Bacon's famous game of tractor chicken in *Footloose*. Or for the "Here She Comes" collaboration with Giorgio Moroder that is widely accepted as the best thing about the 1984 film restoration of *Metropolis*. Or for "Total Eclipse of the Heart," subsequently made more famous in 1995 thanks to the Hi-NRG version by Nicki French. Or for her decades of philanthropic work on behalf of children, animals, and breast cancer charities. Or for her three Grammy nominations. And she's still going strong today. She also does a great cover of "Learning to Fly." But Petty covered her first— "Louisiana Rain" on *Damn the Torpedoes*.

In the video, there's another woman who isn't mentioned in the lyrics—Faye freaking Dunaway, who was already in the midst of her second big career revival by 1991, after breaking out in the late Sixties and then coming back full force in the late Seventies. Among the finest actresses of her generation, she lent her talent to Petty's video first as Eddie's landlady, then as his savvy manager. Unlike Petty's later industry depictions like Joe the CEO on *The Last DJ*, Dunaway's character is highly respectable and credited with much of Eddie's ability to succeed. Unfortunately, he doesn't give as good as he gets. When he snubs her by blocking her entry at an awards after party, she waves her cigarette like a fairy godmother with a magic wand, lightning strikes in the background and suddenly Eddie's career begins to go down the toilet.

At the end of the video, with Eddie broken and beaten by his own ego, Dunaway smiles and walks away clean. So does Eddie's girlfriend. After she throws his awards at his head while he stands confused in their swimming pool, she ends up sitting alone in their mansion on the hill, shaking her head as he runs away with roadie Bart. The heart on their mutual tattoo has faded and all that's left is the dagger. Anwar and Dunaway are free to carry on as they were, but Eddie's future is wide open in the queasiest sort of way at the end. The cautionary tale of Tyler's original song strikes true here, as Eddie is clueless without the aid of his better lady angels. The song alone wouldn't give you Petty's viewpoint, but the video couldn't be clearer.

"Mary Jane's Last Dance"

When this song was first written during the *Full Moon Fever* sessions, it was titled "Indiana Girl" and the chorus went "Hey, Indiana girl, go out and find the world." Strong echoes of the American girl and the California girl we already know well, but something about it didn't sit right and he left it on the shelf for several years. During the solo *Wildflowers* sessions, Petty was forced to offer up a new Heartbreakers track to fulfill the tail-end of his greatest hits agreement with MCA, and Rick Rubin got him to dig up this one. Petty began to rework the chorus that had never felt like a good fit, and this track turned out to be his last dance with drummer Stan Lynch, which may explain the resigned break-up vibe present in the newly rewritten chorus.

Some people think that Mary Jane is a marijuana reference, but let's take the lyrics at face value and examine this character. She seems to take after her mother, both of them good looking and neither ever slowing down or sticking around much. Yet she grew up right, and remains in charge of her own good times. She was unashamed to stand around in her underwear in the hotel window, and leaves her lover to wake up alone. She tells him point blank from the beginning that she's got to keep moving on and she won't stay long. She wears her party dress as a kind of armor.

Petty's lyrics are reverential, and his video concept is no less so. Whereas Mary Jane in the lyrics may be just a bit dead inside from trying to kill her pain, the video asks Kim Basinger to play her as a literal corpse. Undertaker assistant Petty steals her from the morgue, puts her in a wedding dress for one last dance, then gently floats her body out to sea. The final shot is Mary Jane floating just beneath the surface of the water, eyes just opened as if she is receiving new life. Although there is not much hint of necrophilia in the video, the creepiness of it is undeniable. However, in a deeper analysis of the two main texts to which this video has been compared, it is evident that Petty's version is a feminist redemption story.

The video is sometimes compared to *Great Expectations* by Charles Dickens, mainly for its rather shallow and literal connection to Miss Havisham's wedding dress. In the novel, Havisham was jilted by a con man who left her at the altar, which she commemorates by constantly wearing her wedding dress and using her adopted daughter to exact revenge on innocent men. Havisham herself is a formidable woman who let her life go further to shambles as a twisted form of justice. Mostly terrifying and unloved, this woman doesn't bear much resemblance to Mary Jane—Havisham fidgets with her pain like a loose tooth, keeping her agony alive, instead of dulling it like Mary Jane does. Many a dissertation has been written on the feminism of Dickens's portrayal, but suffice it to say that more than a wedding dress in common should be required to make this analogy stick. There is no shortage of artwork featuring women who wear wedding dresses in unusual situations.

The video is more closely tied to "The Copulating Mermaid of Venice," a short story by Charles Bukowski. It's a vulgar piece of work, just like its writer. Nobody would ever accuse him of being a feminist. In this one, two drunks steal a corpse just for laughs, each have sex with it after they discover it's a beautiful young woman, then they float her out to sea. Bill is a callous jerk and Tony falls slightly in love with her, crying in the car on their way back from the beach sendoff. The two plots clearly have some things in common, but tonally, they could not be more different. The slight whiff of Tony's more sensitive and haunted connection to the corpse becomes the whole emotional landscape of Petty's video.

Why does Kim Basinger float back to the surface and open her eyes? As a bit of mythic magic during a full moon, perhaps Petty's care and attention were able to revive her into a new life. Or as a metaphor with the sunrise coming soon, perhaps she'll continue to live on through his memory. Any way you slice it, there's agency embedded there. Her face remains placid, no hint that she will rise up to avenge herself like Dickens's Havisham, but certainly she is not fading namelessly away with little consequence like Bukowski's mermaid. Though she's given neither backstory nor clear future, neither is Petty's character. And lest we forget, he put on a suit to match her wedding dress. In reducing the horrifying grotesquerie of its influences to the merely somewhat macabre, Petty's video ends up giving Mary Jane quite an equal footing alongside his morgue assistant.

"Something in the Air"

This is a cover of an original Thunderclap Newman song with no gendered content to consider. It's all peace, love, and understanding stuff. The British band featured Pete Townshend, of The Who, on bass and his chauffeur was its writer. It knocked "Ballad of John and Yoko" out of the number one slot and sat there for three weeks, also keeping Elvis's 1969 comeback hit "In the Ghetto" stuck at number two. Two groups with fierce female leads have each done a great cover of this tune: Labelle (as in Patti plus three others) in 1973 and then the Eurythmics in 1985—which would have been at the height of Dave Stewart's collaboration with Petty on the *Southern Accents* sessions. When the remastered version of *Greatest Hits* was issued in 2008, "Something in the Air" was replaced by his "Stop Draggin' My Heart Around" duet with Stevie Nicks.

"Stop Draggin' My Heart Around"

Petty has called Nicks an honorary Heartbreaker. They share a love of top hats and have shared several duets together, this one most prominently. "Stop Draggin' My Heart Around" was the first single from her 1981 solo debut, *Bella Donna*. When Petty gifted it to her by way of their mutual producer, Jimmy Iovine, he didn't know what he was getting into. That song would end up competing with his own next single, "A Woman in Love." Radio stations weren't willing to put two Petty songs into heavy rotation at the same time. She kept him off the top of the charts with his own music!

Nicks gets to sing most lines in the verses, but their simultaneous chorus makes clear that they've each been dragging around the other's heart. Petty gets only two lines to himself, which he uses to acknowledge that Nicks wants to be her own girl. He can appreciate her independent streak, but she retorts in the next verse that he needs someone to look after him. She's says he's a bright-eyed kid who would make a good meal if she were to leave him unprotected. They each suffer and neither can look the other in the eye, but Nicks comes away seeming slightly sturdier simply for carrying most of the message in the verses herself. His lifelong personal affection for Nicks as well as his professional generosity with her in this song are evidence of Petty's interest in keeping strong women front and center.

1994–2017

In the two-plus decades after *Greatest Hits*, Petty continued to write lyrics that empowered women. On the 1994 *Wildflowers* outtake that he gave to Rod Stewart, "Leave Virginia Alone," Petty envisioned a brainy, bejeweled charmer who breaks all the rules. She finds the good and can forgive where others wouldn't. Some think of her as a loser, but Petty says she's worth more than rusty Cadillacs and diamonds that turn to dust. He thinks she deserves to be left alone because though it appears she's worse than most, she is also somehow better— she has a kind of magic that is really a sight to see, powerful.

The very last track on the last disc of 1995's *Playback* is "Up in Mississippi Tonight," an old Mudcrutch outtake in which Petty truly wishes Sally all the happiness in the world when she leaves him for a rich guy and the big city, searching for something more stable and perhaps less simple than her mountain boy could offer. On the *She's the One* soundtrack in 1996, he composed "Angel Dream" in praise of his future wife Dana's extraordinary ability to save him from himself.

His 1999 divorce album, *Echo*, was seldom played live due to Petty wanting to put its nasty feelings about this private trauma behind him. Yet the album itself hardly denigrates his first wife, Jane. In fact, *Echo* contains two of his most feminist songs, "Free Girl Now" and "Swingin'." "Free Girl Now" celebrates the liberation of a woman who used to have to keep her mouth shut while under the harassing thumb of her boss. She's no longer his slave, no longer bowing down. The song joyously affirms her freedom and looks forward to a time in the near future when she'll be far away with fresh purpose in life.

"Swingin'" is likewise a tale of a girl who makes good. She'd gotten in some trouble with the authorities, but in the end, her mother-in-law helped her out and she knew her own mother would've been proud of how she's managed to overcome the challenges in her life. Petty sings that she was feeling great and she put up as much of a fight as any man, ticking off the names of famed jazz bandleaders like Benny Goodman and Tommy Dorsey, as well as prizefighter Sonny Liston. These women are heroic figures.

Even 2002's *The Last DJ* takes a break from the main body of music industry criticism to offer up "The Man Who Loves Women," a cautionary tale about a womanizer who will face a big comeuppance and end up paying for the women he's mistreated. The 2006 *Highway Companion* outtake "Home" features a beleaguered and addled man whose only place of peace is found when he settles down in his lover's arms. On 2009's *The Live Anthology*, he's scraping up four hundred bucks in single-minded pursuit of a trip to see his love, "Melinda." For 2010's *Mojo*, Petty saw "Something Good Coming" for his luckless girl, who might have driven her mama crazy but was also "Good Enough" for him. "U Get Me High" and "Red River," on 2014's *Hypnotic Eye* feature deep, mystical connections between himself and powerful women.

Mic Drop

I could go on, but there's no need. Should we talk about how his daughter, Adria, grew up to direct music videos for Beyoncé?

PART III

Uncertainty

8
Tom Petty Didn't Really Need to Know

DANIEL ZELINSKI AND DON FALLIS

As Aristotle pointed out, it's human nature to desire knowledge. Tom Petty had an obsessive interest in this basic desire. Such an intense focus on knowledge is rare among American rock musicians. Although Bruce Springsteen did want to know whether love is real in "Born to Run," you don't see Bruce consistently yearning to know stuff! But Petty's obsession is a large part of what made him one of the most down-to-earth and accessible rockers of his generation.

Many of Petty's early songs are explicitly about knowledge. Several of them exhibit a deep anxiety about lacking knowledge and the possibility of being deceived. Petty frequently, both implicitly and explicitly, implores that he *needs* to know something. While uncommon among modern rockers, this intense need to know is typical of modern philosophers, beginning with René Descartes (1596–1650).

Later in his career, though, Petty clearly learned to accept the uncertainty of human life. He is content to acknowledge that he's still learning to fly—no particular destination for landing, just guessing he'll know it when he gets there. In fact, Petty seems to embrace the freedom of not knowing. This acceptance of uncertainty as a path to inner peace harkens back to popular philosophical views from ancient Greece, India, and China.

Shadow of a Doubt

In his early music, Petty's need to know was intense, but it was also specific. He was obsessed with relationships. Within the lyrics of many of his songs, he confidently asserts knowledge of his own strong feelings for another, but he also expresses doubt concerning others' feelings towards him. Most often, this centers on a fear that his passion for someone may be unrequited.

In "I Need to Know," he worries about whether a love interest has been leading him on, and in "Fooled Again," he fears that his love interest has been fooling around behind his back. He seems to be obsessively worried about being played, lied to, or fooled. In "Don't Do Me Like That," he fears that lies will cut him down to size. And, in "Shadow of a Doubt," Petty *thinks* she loves him, but laments that his love interest has been difficult to figure out. He even suspects she likes to deliberately leave him in the dark. Petty hated not knowing and craved certainty that was beyond a shadow of doubt.

At first glance, Petty's need is reminiscent of René Descartes, whose own obsession with knowing resulted in his recognition as the Father of Modern Philosophy. Descartes was, among other things, a brilliant mathematician, and he attempted to provide a foundation for all knowledge that was as firm as the absolute certainty he saw in math. He meant *certainty beyond any conceivable doubt*, which is an extremely stringent standard. It's a much higher standard than is required for a criminal conviction, where guilt must only be demonstrated *beyond a reasonable doubt*. Descartes pursued this quest for absolute certainty by entertaining bizarre scenarios under which it seemed all his beliefs might be false. For example, he imagined that an all-powerful malicious demon was hell-bent on deceiving him about everything.

Descartes's stringent standard forced him to consider the unsettling prospect that he didn't truly know anything, since through these fantastic scenarios it seemed conceivable that every one of his most cherished beliefs could possibly be false. Nevertheless, he held fast to his program of doubt until he settled on a claim which passed the test, which he could not conceive of as false in any way—his famous, "I think, therefore I am." In his *Meditations on First Philosophy* (1641), Descartes elucidated his epistemic insight, explaining that the claim "I exist" is necessarily true whenever it is conceived. It was a "Eureka!" moment in the history of philosophy.

Descartes's "I think, therefore I am" is widely regarded as an important epistemological insight at least as much for what it placed beyond the bounds of knowledge as for what it identified as absolutely certain. While Descartes confidently asserted knowledge of his own existence as "a thing that thinks," he struggled immensely in attempting to demonstrate that he could be as certain of the nature of the world outside of his own mind. He could, for example, be absolutely certain that he was currently having a perceptual experience of seeming to be sitting at his desk, but he worried it was conceivable that he was having this experience while he was in fact lying in bed sleeping and merely dreaming that he was at his desk.

Epistemologists refer to this as the Problem of the External World, where the external world consists of everything outside of one's own current mental states, including other people. In fact, other people were doubly problematic for Descartes, since even setting aside their physical existence, there's the problem of getting inside their heads. My knowing that you exist is one thing; my knowing what you are thinking and feeling (or even that you are thinking and feeling anything at all) is something else.

Epistemologists refer to this additional challenge as the Problem of Other Minds. And, there's no need of illusory dreams or malicious demons here either. Humans are more than capable of keeping their true thoughts and feelings hidden and deceiving others themselves; as Petty laments in "Shadow of a Doubt," it's simply a complex kid who keeps him guessing.

Only a Broken Heart

Although they both shared a desire for certainty and worried about vanquishing doubt, the parallel between Petty and Descartes isn't as close as it might appear. Petty had his doubts, but they weren't nearly as pervasive as Descartes's. Setting aside a few brilliant, surreal videos (including the amazing *Alice in Wonderland* interpretation in "Don't Come around Here No More"), nowhere in his music does Petty directly challenge the fundamental reality of the physical world. He seemed to have no concern for entertaining the possibility that nothing is real. Petty worried about cheating lovers, not malicious demons; he worried if his relationships were real, not if the world was.

In this respect, Petty's epistemological views are closer to G.E. Moore (1873–1958) than Descartes. In his 1939 book *Proof of an External World*, Moore famously responded to the problem of the external world by raising his hands and affirming, "Here is one hand. And here is another . . . Therefore, an external world exists." This was just *common sense*, according to Moore. Our senses give us direct access to the external world and the mere conceptual possibility that our senses could go awry (if we are dreaming while asleep or tripping while on LSD, for example) is not enough reason to doubt them. Claims based on one's own direct perception are, Moore maintained, inherently credible. As the saying goes, "Seeing is believing." And more to the point: unless credible grounds for doubt are present, seeing *justifies* believing.

Petty was clearly ensconced in this common sense camp; we don't see him questioning what he senses or feels. He had no concern for the problem of the external world. But, he was deeply obsessed with the problem of other minds. He needed to know what others were thinking and feeling, and he doubted he could truly access it. Moreover, his lyrics suggest an interesting response to this problem.

While perception gives us access to the external world, it doesn't seem to give us direct access to the thoughts and feelings of others. I can directly see what you look like and what you do, but I can't see "inside you." I can't see your inner thoughts or feelings. At least, that's a popular epistemological position ever since Descartes and the common-sense valuing of external perception didn't seem to help. But, Petty rejected this claim. He thought that he could know how others thought and felt; he thought that we all could.

So, how do you see what someone else is thinking and feeling? It's simple: look into their eyes (they are, after all, "the windows to soul"). Just as Moore felt that he knew he had a hand because he could see it and feel it, Petty frequently affirmed that he knew how someone truly felt because he could see it (and feel it) in their eyes. In "Breakdown," Petty informs his would-be lover that her eyes give her feelings for him away, so there's no reason to pretend otherwise. Similarly, in "The Wild One, Forever," the eyes tell of an instant love connection. And, in "Only a Broken Heart," the eyes reveal that old amorous feelings are still present.

Whether or not the eyes are in fact "windows to the soul," Petty seems to have been right in asserting that the eyes are an excellent sign of an individual's feelings. Many philosophers and psychologists have attempted to provide theoretical analyses of the mechanisms involved in the sort of empathetic connection which Petty describes. But, experientially, it is not a reflective judgment or an act of imagination; it is a direct perception. I can see how you are feeling, at least if I'm in tune with you and know how to look. Moreover, psychologists have recently connected a whole host of involuntary and semi-voluntary behaviors, centering on the eyes, to emotions. For example, research suggests that whenever anyone is looking at someone they're attracted to, their pupils dilate. Your eyes really do give you away.

Will You (Still) Love Me Tomorrow?

So, through empathic perception, Petty maintained we could know the feelings of others. But, how far does this certainty extend? I might be able to look into your eyes and tell that you love me, maybe even that you love *only* me. But, can I look into your eyes and see that you will *always* love me? And, even if I could see that *you feel* you will always love me, couldn't you be mistaken? After all, many couples have felt they have had a love that would last forever only to find out later, often painfully, that this wasn't true. To paraphrase the words of Carole King and Gerry Goffin, famously sung by The Shirelles, the challenge is that the light of love is in your eyes tonight—but will it still be there tomorrow?

In his early songs, Petty occasionally suggests that we *can* know when we've found a love that will last forever. In "Here Comes My Girl," for example, the love interest confirms that they will last forever, which is believable beyond doubt because they are looking each other in the eyes when it's said. He affirms that this shared passion can transport lovers to an epistemic state where they can confidently exclaim, as in "Refugee," that they don't need to talk much about how they've got something, because they both just know it. This state conveys a sense of unshakable certainty so strong that it can lead you, as in "Listen to Her Heart," to admonish a would-be new guy that it doesn't matter what he does to try to woo away the love interest, because Petty knows everything is okay while this other guy doesn't have a clue. Petty appears absolutely certain here, suggesting *it's impossible she'll ever leave me*. But, is it really?

We wonders whether, in addition to attempting to convince the other guy to back off, he isn't also trying to convince himself. He says he can't begin to doubt the relationship, but as we've seen time and time again, he does doubt it. Petty could not seem to fully convince himself that knowledge of an *eternal* love was possible. As Descartes would remind him, it isn't inconceivable that anyone's feelings might change one day, no matter how deep and how sincere they are today. Moreover, this doubt doesn't rest on the crazy Cartesian worries that your whole life might be a dream or that you may be under the spell of a malicious demon. It simply rests on the knowledge that people can change. In the words of the existentialist philosopher Jean-Paul Sartre (1905–1980), it rests on the recognition that *Hell is other people*, the recognition that others are free to disappoint us and thwart our hopes and expectations.

As Heraclitus (who famously said, "you can't step into the same river twice") and the Buddha both taught, the one constant in life is change. The possibility that your love may fade or that someone new may come along can't be completely ruled out with absolute certainty or even with the common-sense certainty that accompanies direct perception. The sparkle in your eye—telling me you love me and you never want to leave me—may not be there tomorrow, let alone ten years from now. How can I *know* it will?

This philosophical question is also a deeply personal one which cuts many of us to the core, especially those who have loved and lost. In his early music, Petty was obsessed with this question, searching for certainty, but persistently plagued with doubt. Then, he seemed to strike upon another response.

Into the Great Wide Open

In the second half of his career, arguably beginning with his first solo album—*Full Moon Fever,* in 1989—there's a marked shift in Petty's approach to knowledge and certainty. Instead of pining for certainty, we now hear him comfortably affirming that has no way of knowing what lies ahead in "Time To Move On," and confidently proclaiming that he is clueless in "Into the Great Wide Open." His motivations for this shift may be debated by biographers, but it suggests a radically different approach to the epistemic challenge of Descartes's insistence on absolute certainty. Later in life, Petty seemed to come to accept and reconcile himself to the fact that absolute certainty regarding the future is unattainable.

This approach of accepting uncertainty has a rich tradition in philosophy too, dating back well before Descartes to the Pyrrhonian skeptics of Ancient Greece (the founder of this school, Pyrrho, was a fourth century B.C.E. Greek philosopher). These philosophers affirmed an attitude of skepticism towards claims of knowledge, with the primary aim of attaining a strong and enduring tranquility in the face of all life's uncertainties. Most of what we know of the skeptics' method and teachings we owe to Sextus Empiricus, a Greek philosopher from the second century C.E. (primarily through his work, *Outlines of Pyrhonism*). In contrast to Descartes, Sextus held that the doubt inherent in the quest for epistemic certainty inevitably leads to anxiety, frustration, and disappointment. Hence, he instructed that in order to find tranquility one must learn to be fine with uncertainty and suspend judgment on doubtable claims.

This didn't mean that there were no claims the skeptics were willing to affirm. In particular, the skeptics did not deny the certainty of their own feelings. Sextus clarifies that the skeptic merely won't assent to anything that is not evident. One's own perceptions and feelings are directly evident, but claims about the future, especially ones that involve human decisions, are not. According to Sextus, this suspension of assent extends beyond claims about the future to claims concerning whether or not anything was essentially good or bad. These judgments depend in part on future consequences, which are not evident. Moreover, such judgments cause individuals needless frustration when they fail to attain what they deem to be good or when what they deem to be bad comes to pass.

So, Sextus wouldn't take issue with Petty's assertion of knowing that "Anything that's Rock and Roll" is fine. But, he would challenge younger Petty's claim in "Here Comes My Girl" that the two lovers will never change their mind about what they've found together, and even his claim in "The Wild One, Forever" that he'd experienced a moment of passion he'll never regret. For Sextus and the older Petty, one's *present* feelings are evident, but any *future* feelings are wide open.

A similar pragmatic skepticism is found in ancient Asian philosophy, including Buddhism and Daoism. Buddhism originated with the teachings of Siddhartha Gautama ("the Buddha") in the fifth century B.C.E. and Daoism arose around the same time in ancient China. The Buddha is said to have instructed his followers that speculation concerning abstract issues, including claims about the past and future, was idle and counter-productive to the central concern of alleviating suffering. He compared such speculation to being shot by a poison arrow and focusing on factual questions about who shot you and why, rather than addressing the suffering caused by the arrow and the poison.

Moreover, the Buddha contended that this sort of speculation isn't merely irrelevant to alleviating suffering. Such pursuits are themselves often a *cause* of suffering, since our knowledge is constrained by our perceptual experiences, which are fallible and limited in scope. Hence, the wise course is to adopt agnosticism and learn to be fine with not knowing. Jack Kornfield, a contemporary American Buddhist teacher, described the Buddhist practice of acknowledging this "don't know mind" quite similarly to Petty's approach to learning to fly. He advises us to learn to admit that we don't really know whether a "bad" thing might lead us to something better. And, he recommends that we find ways to be able to rest in uncertainty and even to be able to laugh about it.

The virtue of not knowing is also reflected in the ancient Daoist parable of a farmer who responds to his horse running away without grief, explaining, "Who knows what's good or bad?—we'll see." The next day, the horse returns bringing with it several wild horses, but the farmer tempers any excitement with, "Who knows what's good or bad?—we'll see." While this appears to be a stroke of good fortune, the farmer's son breaks his leg attempting to ride one of the wild horses; again, the farmer responds, "Who knows what's good or bad?—we'll see." The next week, a general comes to town and conscripts all the young men into military service, but, seeing his broken leg, passes the farmer's son by. However, when the farmer's friends congratulate him on his good fortune, once again he merely responds, "We'll see."

"We'll see," indeed. Things aren't always as they seem and the future doesn't always unfold as planned or expected. It's a simple and universal truth. The story admonishes us against judging our current circumstances as absolutely good or bad, since these judgments depend, in part, on a future which is uncertain. This attitude was an anathema to the young Petty. But with the wisdom of age, he seems to have come to accept that the future is uncertain and to enjoy the journey, as in "Runnin' Down a Dream" where he's working on a mystery, wherever it leads.

(Beyond the) Need to Know

Not all philosophers are convinced that "not knowing" is a virtuous state, however. In fact, it seems antithetical to the nature and etymology of philosophy as the "love of wisdom." In particular, being fine with not knowing would seem to dampen any motivation to *find out* and hence suppress human inquiry. But, would it really?

Neither the Pyrrhonian skeptics nor the Buddhists nor the Daoists objected to the *desire* to know. In fact, Sextus insisted that acknowledging one's own ignorance was a prerequisite for inquiry and claimed that Skeptics remain open to the possibility of knowledge. He contrasted Pyrrhonian skepticism both with philosophers who claim to have found absolute truths and with those who claim such knowledge is unattainable. The skeptic achieves tranquility by taking no position on what's good or bad and subsequently neither avoiding nor pursuing anything *intensely*. "Intensely" is important here; it's not that the skeptic doesn't have interests or preferences, but she does not pursue these *intensely*. Similarly, in Buddhist and Daoist philosophy, a distinction is made between desire and craving. Fundamental to Buddhist teaching is the claim that craving, not mere desiring, is the root cause of suffering. Desiring to know only becomes a problem when it becomes obsessive; *needing* to know is the issue, not desiring to know.

In Petty's early music, we've seen that knowing was often a craving; he *needed* to know. In particular, in these early lyrics, he frequently needed to know that his love was requited and his lover was faithful. Recall the deep anxiety Petty conveys over the possibility that his love might be leading him on and about to leave him for another guy. In "I Need to Know," he's unsure of how long he can hold on in the face of this uncertainty. In "Fooled Again," he's pissed that he might be being played for a fool and nobody will tell him what's going on. This need is a deep and nearly universal one, which is part of what makes Petty's music so powerful and popular. It's firmly embedded in human experience and appears over and over across cultures and throughout popular culture.

The universality of this particular need to know, and the longing and heartache which accompanies it, also makes purported remedies for it popular. The essence of the remedies forged by these ancient philosophies, and rediscovered by Petty, involves the recognition that you don't *really* need to know. You need food; you need water; you need shelter; maybe you need *Damn the Torpedoes* remastered on vinyl. But, no one really needs to know the future will work out "perfectly" and they'll live "happily ever after." Believing you do need this is a recipe for anxiety and disappointment. And, ironically, those who overcome this obsession are arguably happier than those who don't.

Have Love, Will Travel

There's one final criticism worth considering: the need to know seems clearly tied to passion. The need with which young Petty was most obsessed seems tied to romantic passion: the yearning to find "true love," including the feeling of absolute dependence on your beloved. Being fine with not knowing whether or not you've found your soulmate requires being fine with the possibility that you have *not* found your eternal soulmate. But, should we be fine with this prospect? Romeo and Juliet didn't have this inner tranquility; the kids had a burning passion for each other, so much so that they chose death over life without their beloved. And, if the alternative involves not caring, why would that alternative be any better? Is it really worth cultivating Petty's attitude in "Breakdown," where it's alright if you love me but also fine if you don't? Is it really love if you are fine with breaking her heart and you don't even miss her, as in "Free Fallin'"?

The ideal perspective on love and life may be in the eye of the beholder, but here are a couple of points. Crucially, there's a fine line between passion and obsession. While passion takes place in the present moment, obsession is concerned with the future. And, here's the irony: needing to know that what you are sharing with another will last forever can prevent you from fully enjoying the present. For an "enlightened" soul, every moment (including moments of love and passion) is a gift, it is enough, and its value is not diminished come what may. To paraphrase a popular Daoist saying, "Love's more about the journey than the destination."

Moreover, obsession can have the tragic consequence of driving away the very person with whom you are hoping to share your future. After all, Elvis warned that we cannot carry on together with suspicious minds. Finally, the type of openness and equanimity that these philosophers are advocating arguably promotes a deeper love where we're free of preconceptions of a future we're "supposed to" share and in which the well-being of the other (and ourself) is paramount. This type of deep love stands in contrast with the obsessive passion often associated with true love, where we can't live if living is without our beloved. But, the older Petty suggests this deeper love in songs like "A Wasted Life" and "Have Love, Will Travel," where the quality of a relationship is not dependent on how long it lasts and we recognize that life and love will endure even if our lover leaves.

Romantic, all-consuming love is definitely idealized in our culture. But we must be careful not to create a straw-man of the alternative. Neither the mature Petty nor any of the philosophies we've considered are suggesting that there's anything wrong with love, even passionate love. The issues they all have are with *needing* to know if these feelings are requited, and if they are, needing to know that this love *will continue forever*. A person may feel they've found their soulmate with whom they'll share a lifetime, but whether or not this is in fact the case only time will tell.

This realization doesn't preclude you from loving, but it enables you to love with your eyes wide open about the uncertainty and mystery of it all. At least, this is the view of several ancient schools of philosophy and it seems to be an attitude that Petty came to embrace. As he learns to fly, he may take a beating or get his heart broken, but he realizes that what goes up tends to also come down. Petty's response, which echoes those of the Pyrrhonian skeptics, Buddhists, and Daoists, is to fly amongst the clouds of uncertainty with their potential for loss and heartache.

After all, what if the worst is true? It's "Only a Broken Heart," so we can follow our feelings and dreams even though none of us knows what awaits us when it's "Wake Up Time."

9
Wherever the Road Leads

ASHLEY WATKINS

One of the recurring images we see as we listen to Tom Petty's music is that of life as a road to be traveled: a familiar motif in literature, art, and even common parlance.

Not only is the road image rich in philosophical implications, it has an unexpected and intimate connection with one of Petty's most central nuggets of wisdom: that we have to wake up every morning and climb the hill again. The road ahead can make each of us doubt and fear, but if we allow Petty's words and example to take us through an examination of the uncertainty of our possibilities, we'll find that we always land on solid ground. Every road leads to the virtue of persistence or, if you like, the duty to kick ass.

We find the road in glimpses and brief mentions in songs such as "Learning to Fly" and "Running Man's Bible," and at the very center of others like "Runnin' Down a Dream," "Kings Highway," and "Love Is a Long Road." The idea that time, life, and its constituents like love and success are paths of some sort—journeys from wherever we start to, as Petty says, God knows where—isn't new to any of us. We talk about life paths, religious paths, paths to freedom, and all the roads and routes we take through our time on earth. Taking a path sounds like a choice, but only if we think there's more than one before us.

What did Tom Petty think? Well, I can't begin to know. But the imagery we find in Petty's lyrics can help us think about the nature of time, our future possibilities, crippling uncertainties, faith in the good ahead, and how the nature of these things leads us to a doctrine of dogged persistence that Petty practiced unflinchingly in his life and career. Because here's the thing about roads: they're not roads if they're never traveled.

Flirting with Time

Imagining life as a road brings up a lot of what philosophers call *metaphysical* questions: questions about the nature of the world that are beyond or above the physical, or about the so-called first principles of things. By 'life,' we obviously don't mean general definitions of living things—that it's these kinds of molecules as opposed to those, that it's what engages in Darwinian evolution, that it's bacteria but not viruses. When we talk about our lives, we mean our existence. It's whatever starts with our birth and ends with our death.

In this sense, even non-living things have a kind of life. The life of Petty's Danelectro Longhorn bass began sometime in the 1960s and will end on whatever sad day it's destroyed. This is why life and time are so intimately connected and are both often conceived as a road. We measure our lives by points in time. If our road through life begins at a point in time and ends at another, it makes sense to think that the road of our life is our road through time.

Now we come to our first important Petty-guided distinction. It's tempting to move from this image to the idea that *all* of time is represented by a road, and while the journey down that particular rabbit hole is fascinating, it's very, very long. It's also not quite where the music leads us. The picture is of a more personal road, the one on which we start out all alone. What matters is what we find along it and where it ends. In other words, the road is characterized by the events that make it up, like that moment we saw a coyote run across it. So, while there are plenty of important questions about the nature of time—whether it's linear, if it really passes as we think it does, if it merely contains events or is identical with events—these would take us too far from our purpose.

Think of it this way: we can't change our perception that time passes in a linear way. If the passage of time is an illusion, as some philosophers suspect, it's not the kind we can shake off or see through. Inevitably, we'll behave as if it passes even if we believe for philosophical reasons that it doesn't. It's hard even to imagine what it would look like to behave as if time is an illusion that never catches up with us. What's important for how we live our lives is what we think about the events that are in store.

To work within the spirit of Tom Petty and his music, we have to take the practical as our true aim. Petty's music is earthy and meaty, having everything to do with the day-to-day reality of being in the world as a feeling, acting person. So when it comes to the metaphysical questions, we ought to judge their importance by how they bear on the way we live our lives. What we want to know is, where does our road lead? Is our future really open?

Going Wherever It Leads

When we ask if the future is open, we're generally asking whether or not future events are determined, or possibly fated. Though there are theological versions of similar ideas, such as predestination, it's not necessary that there's any conscious being who made the decisions that determine how every event will go. All that's needed is the existence of some natural law, or a set of natural laws, that govern cause and effect. Once we have some state of affairs, or some way that the world is at a given time, those natural laws mean that there is only one way that things could have been before and only one way things can go after.

Fatalism doesn't necessarily depend on causation or natural laws. Some versions of fatalism are indeed religious, involving the machinations of some higher being. Others, like Aristotle's (384–322 B.C.E.), are argued for using only logical principles and truths. The basic idea is that since every proposition is either true or false, any propositions about the future are either true or false right now, making the future described by those true propositions unavoidable. We just don't happen to know which ones are true right now. But, like Petty, we need to know, don't we? Or maybe we can't know, but it doesn't matter to determinists and fatalists since some of those propositions will be true and the rest false.

Though they're subtly different positions, the general outcome of fatalism and determinism for us is the same. In a determined or fated world, there's only one road to take, one series of events that will happen. If this is the case, then none of us can do anything other than what we're determined to do. We may *feel* as though we're walking around deciding how we'll behave, but it's just an illusion: it was never really possible that we'd do other than what we've done. Thus, free will is only illusory. So, maybe it's just not true that everybody's had to fight to be free. We all just get kicked around by the universe and there aren't lots of places to run to.

Like any philosophical position, this isn't universally agreed upon. The position that a determined world excludes free will is known as "incompatibilism"—that freedom and the way the world *is* are not compatible ideas or assertions. Compatibilists, on the other hand, believe that some reconciliation can be achieved between determinism and free will. It seems to me that the disagreement comes down to our intuitions about what a choice is. Some of us just can't conceive of a genuine choice that's determined or fated to happen, while others can. Free will or not, the fact remains that in a determined world our future is anything but wide open.

Such a worldview may offer both anxieties and comforts. Maybe we're not free falling at all, but we can't see it doesn't matter what we do. The idea that we might not have free will is disturbing, especially since so much of our identity is tied up with the choices we make and how they affect the world around us. It seems that in the absence of free will, we're not really morally responsible for hitting cruise control or putting the pedal down. If we've lived pretty stellar lives, this can take the wind out of our sails to say the least. Conversely, if we've been fairly deplorable it might be a comfort to think that none of that heinous stuff we did was really our fault. Perhaps the view that none of us is acting of our own free will can make it easier for us to forgive others as well as ourselves.

It's also easy to see how determinism and fatalism might give way to defeatism: a resignation in the face of our powerlessness to affect a determined world. Some may find this depressing and wonder what the point of getting out of bed is when the rain is unstoppable. Why do anything at all, if everything is already determined or fated to happen? But also there's a kind of weird peace that comes with a road that's set in stone. After all, if you're just following an itinerary made by a (hopefully decent) cosmic travel agent, walking toward a determined set of events rather than a chaotic mass of decision points, can't you stride forward with more confidence without the dread of responsibilities like so many stones in your shoes?

Refugee from Responsibility

Is it this determined world that we see in Petty's music? I don't think so. Everywhere we see that the future is wide open. "A Woman in Love" laments that anything can happen, and even that anything can end, while "Learning to Fly" tells of frightening possibilities of melting rocks and burning trees at the end of a road that leads to God knows where. Futures are open and possibilities are real in our Tom Petty world. But is Tom right? Are we?

There are plenty of arguments out there to support such a view, so we shouldn't back down. The element of chance in quantum mechanics dooms causal determinism with the very scientific thinking that lent it plausibility. But these arguments aren't necessary for us. The Petty spirit demands attention to *lived* experience, in which what is knowable from first-hand experience holds far more weight that what *might* be true. We can't solve all the metaphysical puzzles with certainty before we go on living.

Let's look again at the comfort provided by walking along a determined road toward events over which we have no real influence. Even if we're convinced for philosophical reasons that that's what we're walking toward, like the story of Eddie rebel, we still don't know what the events ahead of us will be. A determined world is not necessarily a *predictable* world. The world might be determined even if no one, not even a perfect intelligence, could actually use natural laws to predict the future. We certainly don't have the knowledge or time to make such minute predictions.

Perhaps those predictions aren't even possible in principle. So from our perspective, we're walking straight into darkness. We often think we can see some way ahead; we make plans, setting down our paving stones for a smooth ride. In reality, we're fumbling ahead through the fog of external influences, hoping our house doesn't burn to ruins, or in a fit we punch a wall for no reason we can name. Maybe we get lucky and a tree doesn't crash down in front of us, cracking our pavement and forcing us down a detour we never wanted to take. What good is a determined future if uncertainty prevails?

Another anxiety lurks. Like our perception of time passing, we can't make ourselves feel as if we don't *really* have any free will, any responsibility for what we find along our road, even if we're convinced intellectually that we don't. We can't make our voluntary actions feel involuntary through the force of our belief that we can't act otherwise. Our experience overcomes the metaphysical possibilities again, and we end up with an anxiety much discussed by existentialists: the dread of responsibility.

At every step, we decide to take the actions that make us who we are. Our freedom can have unforeseeable consequences, consequences that we're nevertheless responsible for. This dread is general and ever-present. It's not the fear of any particular consequence of any particular action but the general fear that always accompanies our sense of free will. Like other great responsibilities we feel ill-equipped to handle, such a huge weight can cause us to dig in our heels against the forward motion of time.

It'll All Work Out

In the face of such uncertainty and responsibility, Petty clearly advocates an attitude of optimism. It's not naive cheerfulness or the muffled commentary of one whose head's in the sand, nor is it the tooth-grinding grin of a person who takes pains to rationalize and polish the ugliness of the world around us. "It'll All Work Out" expresses this optimism in the simple and gut-wrenching way that only Tom Petty could do.

Melancholy and honest, there's certainly no rose-colored hue to the lyrics, no self-help silver-lining talk in the discussion of failings and mistakes. Yet there's also nothing disingenuous or self-pitying about the simple repeated line, like a mantra: it'll all work out. What grounds this optimism—what does 'working out' amount to?

It's reasonable to suppose at first that faith is involved. Specifically, faith that there's something good waiting down this road. Why else suppose that it'll all work out? Why else think that even when everything feels so not alright there's no reason to cry? There must be something to look forward to, some reward at the end of a harrowing journey or at least a few oases along the way. If we take it on faith and take it to the heart, all we have to do is wait for that good outcome. But that's the hardest part, isn't it?

I don't think this is all there is to it. Remember that the future is open: anything can happen. (Well, almost anything.) That means that a supremely negative future is among the cards for each of us, and you only see one more each day. We know just from looking around that sometimes incredibly bad things happen to good people, and they always seem to happen to *some* people. To have faith that we'll be able to say we got lucky seems inexplicable and indefensible. Petty's brand of optimism doesn't require faith in the good ahead, nor is it inconsistent with the possibility that no such future good exists. In fact, the optimism and the faith are happy side effects of something more fundamental. To understand it, really, we need to look back at our sense of the passage of time.

Time to Move On

"Time to Move On" says it all. As we've seen, we have no way of knowing what lies ahead. We want to make it better, but we don't know which way to go to get there. The dread weighs on us physically, like a nauseous malaise. We stand in front of the darkness of uncertainty, frozen like a deer in the headlights.

The message is ultimately positive, but not because the tension is resolved with sappiness or silver linings. The motivation for moving on is that there is *grass growing under our feet*. Time passes with or without our co-operation, and that it does so is the reason to keep walking. We don't overcome the dread by waving it away with consolations or even with a positive attitude. We overcome it by fully embracing our responsibility to keep moving. We don't have to live that way, like . . . well, you know.

In other words, it's built into the nature of the road that we must travel it. There are a few ways to cash this idea out. One is to "go Aristotelian," or at least "neo-Aristotelian." It's a virtue to maintain the disposition to keep moving despite our feelings of dread. This virtue is a special type of persistence; not just the persistence needed to achieve specific goals when faced with specific obstacles, but the general persistence required for a life lived fully despite uncertainty and dread. So the world may be ever so big, but we have a promise, however little, to keep, even if we have to die trying.

If we count persistence among the virtues, it'll be necessary for full human flourishing, or what the ancient Greeks called *eudaimonia*. To live a good life, we must be persistent in this way. To be persistent, we have to practice. According to Aristotle, the way to gain a virtue of character is to behave in accordance with that virtue until a habit is formed. Essentially, fake it till you make it.

We can also think of this in terms of duties. It sounds like no fun at all, but hold on. We have a duty to walk down the road of our own free will rather than let ourselves be dragged around by the relentless passage of time. This duty arises from the kind of beings we are. We're the kind of being that perceives time linearly, that cannot predict our future regardless of whether it's predetermined, and that feels a robust sense of control over our decisions. It would be a sort of violation of our dignity, as the type of beings we are, to fail to fulfill this duty. We persist not because we think it will necessarily contribute to any flourishing or happiness, but because it's a sort of natural law of our being. The nature of the road demands that we walk along it. Because we are what we are, we have a duty to kick ass until the bitter end.

There's undeniably a flavor of the existential idea of authenticity in this as well. Generally, we think of authenticity as something like being your true self, especially if it means defying norms or expectations. An existentialist such as Jean-Paul Sartre (1905–1980), however, emphasizes not only being your true self but *making* your true self via your actions. For Sartre, doing is everything. Freedom feels like a burden and causes us incredible dread, which he also likens to nausea in his famous work, aptly titled *Nausea*.

Nevertheless, we have to embrace that freedom to be truly authentic. To deny our freedom is to make ourselves into passive objects rather than the active subjects that we are. The existentialist hero is one who takes on the full weight of freedom and persists in the creation of his or her life, in the pursuit of a project and in accordance with the most basic values. Such a hero carves out a road actively, step by step.

He's the One

Each possible view, virtue or duty, provides a conceptual framework to answer the same question: How do we best survive in the great wide open? On this, Tom Petty was an expert and one of our best examples. As our Aristotelian hero, he embodied the virtue of persistence throughout his life and career, overcoming the disapproval of his father, early musical failures, and the break-up of his first band, Mudcrutch.

Persistence was just a part of Petty's virtuous character, which included honesty, integrity, generosity, and temperance (except when a wall got in his way). In fulfilling duties, too, he showed us the way. Undoubtedly he fulfilled any duty to persist, and took seriously his duties to fans, bandmates, and the young musicians who came after him. He never shied away from the duties he gained not just as a human being, but as a human being with influence. Perhaps most clearly, he showed us what authenticity looks like. He made himself, creating his life in the pursuit of his project: rock'n'roll music.

As we stand at this point on our road that we call the present and look out toward a horizon of ultimate uncertainty, we might have complete faith that there's something good waiting, or we might not. We will certainly feel the weight of responsibility and the sickening dread of the next step's consequences. But the road must be traveled and the hill must be climbed, day after day.

Whether we think the ultimate purpose is our own happiness, or fulfilling our duties, or authenticity, in the end the only way to carry on is to keep kicking ass and go down swingin' just like the man himself.

10
Change of Heart

RANDALL E. AUXIER

You already know this: There's an indescribable moment when you suddenly see something for what it really is. It was there before, but you didn't want to see it, or you just couldn't, and then a line is crossed. Others saw it before you did, but you couldn't quite bring yourself to it. And then, well, there it is. He was cheating on you. Your friends all knew it. Some part of you knew it too, but until you found the lacy underwear in his shoe after the business trip, and it wasn't yours . . . and now where are you?

Let's call this sort of realization the "liminal moment." It's not a word you hear every day, although we are all used to "*sub*liminal advertising" and Freudian "sublimation." My handy e-dictionary tells me that "limen" is Latin for "threshold." That's a significant crossing, from inside to outside, or vice versa. You have to carry the bride over that line or she might get away from you later. The valley vampires can't cross that line without an invite. So if that's liminal, then I guess all the stuff that gathers on the doorstep of the mind beforehand is sub-liminal. And when your actions derive from a fear of that crowd at the doorstep, you're sublimating.

Tom Petty was a master of the liminal moment. He could read it in himself and he could see it in others. He was a great believer in everyone's power to choose what we get, and he always thought we should accept responsibility for the fallout. The misery (or bliss) you live with is your own creation, with your choices. Some of it is foreseeable, some isn't. But when the truth dawns on you, you ought to face it, own it, and have the courage to do what's necessary.

Phenomenology

Philosophers invented a kind of description they call "phenomenology." It's a fancy word for a simple thing: the description of what it's like to be conscious of something, like swimming or free falling or feeling like heaven right now, or something from a dream, or changing your heart.

Most philosophers would rather argue about the *theory* of phenomenology than actually *do* any describing. The reason is that it's hard to do it, and it's more of a talent than a skill. Poets are more likely to be good at this kind of description than philosophers are. So, some philosophers like Ernst Cassirer (1874–1945) and Martin Heidegger (1889–1977) will turn to poets to get some words they can use for things like, oh, for example, liminal moments. Cassirer liked to quote Goethe when he needed some insight into the most basic experiences we have (he called these experiences the "Basisphenomena"). Heidegger preferred the romantic and lyric poet Friedrich Hölderlin.

So what is phenomenology and how can *you* get some for yourself? Well, if you're a poet, you probably already know how to do the trick. But if not, you need to find yourself a poet and borrow some words, but put 'em in prose. I found myself a pretty good poet for this little exercise here. Here's an example: So let's say you've got this relationship, and you fought hard for it to work, maybe you fought too hard, beyond what it was worth. And then one day that asshole you were living with slipped and said something, and all at once you realize you were never really needed, just a piece of comfortable furniture in that asshole's emotional world. He never needed you, he only wanted you around, to walk on and sit on and lie on—and lie to.

Brings on a change, doesn't it? That asshole pushed just a smidgeon too far, made you fight just a tad more than you sincerely could. And now you see it for what it always had been. You were doing all the work, weren't you? Well, there's no going back now, is there? Don't fret. It won't take long to get over this, now that you crossed the threshold. Somebody should write a song about this, this, what? Change of heart? Yeah. That's the ticket. If you could find yourself a poet, you could do some phenomenology, say what it's like to reach a turning point like that.

You Got Lucky

Part of the problem with phenomenology is that your job is to describe the most indescribable, intimate, embarrassing, even shameful stuff. You have to do that in a way that everybody can relate to it. It ain't good phenomenology unless it's common to *the* human experience. So maybe *you* didn't actually ever live with that asshole I just described (I did, back when I was young and very stupid—now I'm not young). But we all know someone who did time in a relationship like that. We've all seen it, we all know it, and that's why the song resonates. Thanks, Tom. I really needed that. And as usual, you said it better than I ever could have.

If you were spared the first-person version of that change, congratulations. Either you got lucky, or maybe *you* were the asshole. In my case, I got the apology from her years later, so I'm pretty sure I was on the receiving end of that one. But for all I know, I owe someone an apology, too. I'm trying to learn to see when I'm the asshole, but it's so hard, you know? You might want to do a quick survey of your own wreckage just to be sure. If there is one moral lesson I take from observing Tom Petty's life, it is: try not to be an asshole, and when you discover you have been one, try to set it right.

How about his brave apology for displaying the Confederate battle flag in concert? That sort of self-honesty must be one of the most admirable traits anybody can cultivate. And to be straight, it's the reason we don't just like Tom, we love Tom. He gives us the courage to try to find the liminal area between standing our ground and being an asshole. The hell if anybody is going to back me down, but there is also that moment when I cringe. I crossed the threshold and said what shouldn't have been said. Sometimes you're the Dark Angel.

Like you (I'm sure), I have wanted to say out loud that several somebodies got lucky when I found them, but that's the pain talking, isn't it? Does Tom *really* want her to just go if he doesn't take her all the way there? If so, why is he warning her about the genuine scarcity of good love? No, he wants her to stay. But he's hurt. He sees. He's on his way to a change of heart, but it hasn't happened just yet. She still has a chance.

Let Me Get to the Point

So there's the moment before the limen, and the moment after, and they are as different as Gainesville and LA. It's funny.

When people speak of the continental divide, everyone pictures the Rocky Mountains. There we all are, sitting on our Harleys with Bob Seger (he's sort of a Yankee version of Tom Petty, isn't he?), looking east, looking west, trying to decide from the summit. But in the part of the country Tom comes from, you might be standing on that divide without even knowing it.

Once I was riding on a tour bus in Colorado, up Pike's Peak, and the guide (who was a bit too perky for my curmudgeonly soul) announced that we were crossing the divide and that the water going east was destined for the Atlantic Ocean. Later I said quietly to her that she should correct her spiel. That water is headed for the Gulf of Mexico. Taken aback, she informed me that the Gulf of Mexico *is* the Atlantic Ocean. I think Tom would know the difference.

I just let it go, but I have been on the *other* continental divide. Peachtree Street, in Atlanta. The water going off into the east ditch goes to the actual Atlantic Ocean. The west ditch is headed for a very different body of water, namely that Gulf. But the crown in the center of Peachtree Street sits there, subliminally being the difference that makes the greatest difference if you're a raindrop. And you're a raindrop.

Most of us fall comfortably on one side or the other of Peachtree Street, but a few of us pause on the crown, and the slightest quantum nudge makes all the difference as to whether those wave-cars out on 441 take us to a bigger world, or whether we stagnate in the same brackish swamp until a merciful cloud absorbs us and drops us someplace better. Maybe Ventura Boulevard. It's pretty painful when something is that close and still out of reach. I know you've been there.

Continental Divide

A political scientist named Sayre once said that academic disputes are so bitter because the stakes are so low. He managed to get himself a Wikipedia article for that one. The trouble is that once in a great while the stakes are high. You wouldn't think that an argument over the right way to do phenomenology could possibly rise to "high" in the stakes department. But history is stranger than fiction sometimes. I mentioned those two philosophers, Cassirer and Heidegger, and their favorite poets. They differed on more than just favorite poets.

But your choice of a favorite poet is pretty revealing. More on that later.

In 1929 these two phenomenologists met in Switzerland (always the neutral territory) to debate the future of philosophical research. Both were inheritors of a tradition in philosophy that descended from Immanuel Kant (1724–1804) and Georg Hegel (1770–1831). These old dudes were the fathers of "phenomenology," and Cassirer and Heidegger were their great-grandsons. The favored poets were of the same generation. Goethe emerged into his fame at the same time as Kant, and the poet Hölderlin was Hegel's college roommate. Cassirer was fifteen years older than Heidegger, tall and stately, and he stood for the tradition of humanism, internationalism and liberal values. Heidegger was a Napoleonesque young turk, with his snickering, disrespectful followers in his train.

Germany's a big place compared to, say, Belgium, but not as big as Texas. In the universities in Germany, everybody knows everybody, pretty much. Cassirer had published two of his three-volume masterwork *The Philosophy of Symbolic Forms.* Heidegger had published Part I of his planned three-volume study, calling it *Being and Time.* (He never finished it, but it didn't matter.) When heavy hitters of this sort are on the same fight card, Germans start murmuring about how many rounds and who's going down. They knew it was a big deal, but as time has gone by, it turned out to be even bigger than they thought.

Very soon the Germany they knew would exist no more, replaced by the regime of thugs in brown shirts, and an unbridled militarism. People like Cassirer—Jewish, urbane, morally decent and cosmopolitan—would be murdered by the millions. People like Heidegger—smug, anti-Semitic, hate-mongering nationalists—would be murdering them. But in 1929, they could still talk about how people should do phenomenology. It was a liminal moment.

God, It's so Painful

One of the secrets of a great song is knowing what to leave out. If you can say less and say it simpler, but without losing the emotional punch, you'll let more people in. They'll identify with your characters. No one in the history of songwriting (or even poetry) was better at this combination of simple economy and emotional power than Tom Petty. Some of the impact surely had to do with the way he delivered the goods vocally—the strained, thin, almost sneering punch in the snout. Some part of it was those ringy, droning guitar sounds. But most of it was in how he condensed and concentrated the whole story into the one desperate moment when everything came clear.

Has it ever occurred to you that you have no idea what the American girl's pain was about? Abusive father? Unfaithful husband? Unrequited love? Ungrateful son? And you don't know what she did about it. And you don't even know what was supposed to last all night. And you don't know what the little promise was that she'd rather die than not keep. Come to think of it, you don't know shit about this girl. And you certainly don't know how it feels to be her. All you know, and all you *need* to know (as some poet once said, almost) is three chords and the truth (well, four chords in this case). But I know you see her, shivering on her balcony, and you see cars rolling by like waves, and you *do* feel her pain. And you say to her, from the depths, "forget about that bastard and his promises."

You can tell she'll get through it and he's gonna get it. How did Tom and the boys do that? It's a superpower, isn't it? Tom reaches out and reaches in and poof!, you have his fever, or her pain, or anyone's mood or emotions he wants you to share. It floats straight from the Rickenbacker to hammer and anvil in your head, shoots from the cardioid to the cardio, and there it breaks you into the great wide open. That's no private image of a girl on *her* balcony—not "the" balcony, *her* balcony. I'll be damned. It's Juliet, and by the way, Romeo is an asshole these days. Wherefore? (That's Elizabethan slang for WTF.)

And here's another thing you know, just below your conscious thoughts. She might jump. Listen to how Tom delivers the line about the pain. To run or to jump? To be or not? And that is where the feeling of the song, that drive toward an open future, helps us know what to make of her choice. She won't jump. Mike Campbell is going to crank the guitar to crunchy fuzz and dance her away from that cliff until she dissolves into that sea of cars heading north on 441, to Atlanta, maybe even Peachtree Street. Otherwise, that asshole wins. Tom and the boys never let the asshole win. Well, almost never.

Free Falling

Heidegger wrote in 1927 that we experience two things when we stare over a precipice (or a balcony, I suppose). The first is fear that we might fall. The second he calls "Angst," which is deeper. It is a matter of pondering our freedom to jump. He says we can follow that moment, in a phenomenology, to some pretty powerful and dark places. Down deep, we aren't men and women any more, we're just existences that will, sooner or later, *not* exist. And by some cosmic irony, we are the existences doomed to awareness of our ultimate end. And in some very twisted (but all too human) way, we *want* to die, to orient ourselves on that vanishing point. It's not just to have it all over with, but rather to be what we *are, now*, without kidding ourselves about the meaning of it all.

At this moment, in 1929, people were still trying to get their minds around the slaughter of the First World War. It was something approaching twenty million deaths. Granted, soon enough the humans were going to raise the stakes by a factor of five, but nobody could have imagined that in the innocence of the Roaring Twenties. Freud himself revised his big ole theory to make room for something other than sex—namely death. He called the new drive "thanatos" (just Greek for death) and decided it was a basic impulse in our damned and doomed race. And there were others who decided to tell us about ourselves and this odd obsession with death, but no one, not even Freud himself, could hold a candle to Heidegger.

Petty-ness: Shadow People in Shadow Land

The bad news is that Heidegger has his finger on something. There's a part of us that's just so bad (and not in the good sense of bad). I am naming it "Petty-ness," and it's the Dark Angel, and it's the beasty that crouches at the door of our damaged hearts and makes us feel things like "You got lucky" and "I'm the one who ought to know" and "I don't feel you anymore" and, "I don't even miss her" and . . . well, you fill it in.

The songs don't lack for the sentiment. There's a version of "The Damage You've Done" up on YouTube that just shows pictures of the mess left by the 9/11 attack in Manhattan. Pretty hard to watch, pretty angry, and it's not like the song doesn't fit. In Petty's world, sometimes we have to give voice to that sort of feeling. One great big pile of death. That's what this life is. Never gonna clean this up.

Tom Petty was very brave. He would have made a fine officer, in the worst sense of those words. He was a leader who led by example, and he preferred to be honest—Heidegger calls it "authentic"—rather than concealing the darkdeepdown, the violence that overruns justifications and revels in revenge, served frozen. But it is *always* re-venge. It is never unprovoked ultraviolence (as Anthony Burgess named it). So Petty knows how it feels, and, *with us*, he puts on a sneer and lets us sing along. I hate how much I love that sneer. Petty gives us permission to see the world in terms of assholes and dreamers, and he invites us to flip a bird to the former and guard the latter. But there's an asshole of a beasty in the darkdeepdown of some dreamers, and they have to let it out sometimes to protect the gentle ones.

But our *Tom* isn't Petty. I feel pretty sure that Tom would think Heidegger was an asshole, and he would let the Pettybeast out of his crouch. It's not that the Nazi dude said nothing true. The problem is that Heidegger *became* a Nazi, and didn't turn in his party credentials until 1945. It was a choice. As time goes by, it gets clearer and clearer that the boy didn't keep his alter-ego in the corner, where our hateful side ought to be stowed. Somehow, somewhere, maybe somebody kicked him around some, but it's no excuse.

Heidegger's mentor had been a Jew, Edmund Husserl (1859–1938), although the mentor had become a Lutheran in early adulthood. That masterwork of 1927 was dedicated to the converted Jew, although the dedication was deleted in 1941 (under pressure, but Heidegger went along with it). Here is what that mentor said in a letter:

> The perfect conclusion to this supposed bosom friendship of two philosophers was [Heidegger's] very public, very theatrical entrance into the Nazi Party on May 1st. Prior to that there was his self-initiated break in relations with me—in fact, soon after his appointment at Freiburg [Husserl's chair]—and, over the last few years, his anti-Semitism, which he came to express with increasing vigor—even against the coterie of his most enthusiastic students, as well as around the department.

Husserl had helped the boy into his own esteemed chair at the university. The boy took it and shat on the old man. In the aftermath of the Second World War, Heidegger didn't pass the de-Nazification tests and was banned from teaching, and when he eventually won his appeal, the government force-retired him rather than letting him teach. And Heidegger never renounced the Nazis, never apologized, not one hint of remorse.

Compare that to Tom's feeling and public statements about his use of the Confederate battle flag. We all make mistakes. But assholes are Petty, and Tom is not. So, in Davos, 1929, the announcers really must say: "In this corner, we have Martin-the-Asshole Heidegger, and his phenomenology of death and anxiety." He comes out swinging, says we're all fallen, all find ourselves thrown into a world we never made (Yes, Jim Morrison swiped that line from Heidegger), trapped in a language and a history that send us reeling into the abyss, and only the Führer can redeem us.

He said, and I quote: "Let not propositions and 'ideas' be the rules of your being. The Führer alone is the present and future German reality and its law. Learn to know ever more deeply: that from now on every single thing demands decision, and every action responsibility. Heil Hitler!" (Yes, he said it, and he never took it back.) It's quite beyond Petty-ness. It's nearer to Satanic. But of course, it might also be the truth about our worthless hides, God help us all.

Tom's World

Unlike the darkdeepdown, Tom's world always makes a strange kind of sense, given the circumstances, and so it pulls back from the precipice. This isn't World War. It's post-apocalyptic and oddly peaceable, like the city he leads in *The Postman*. I *love* his city. I don't want the world that *gives* him that city, but if that was my world, I want to live in Tom's city. First rule, no guns.

Now, what else do we have? It's a refuge from the damage they've done, but it's not for self-pitying refugees. Tom knows that everybody's had to fight to be free and he knows that everyone believes what they want to believe. It's not about dreaming, it's about running one down, at 120 mph if need be. (I choose that speed because it's the fastest I ever drove, and it was in Germany, on the Autobahn, and I got a ticket, which was supposed to be impossible—I didn't dream of that little fine, but it's all I ran down that day . . .) My point: It's alright, at the end of the line, if you live the life that you please.

There's this quasi-libertarian anarcho-syndicalist *choice* thing in Tom's world. Yeah, maybe you got dealt a shitty hand. And maybe you've a got a right to bitch about it. But it's not what you're dealt, it's how you play it. If you've got a phenomenological eye, you know that every asshole has a tell. They've all got weaknesses. That's *why* they're assholes (more on this in a moment). In a tough hour, or two, or five, they *chose* it. They're no less free than you or me, and you really have to remember that, if you want to live in Tom's world. Nobody absolutely *has* to be an asshole.

Tom made no secret about his abuse as a child, even while his father was still alive. That couldn't have been easy for anyone. But it was important. It helps us understand where Tom's insight and his anger come from. According to his brother in the documentary they made (thank God), it's like Tom's father singled him out and made him into an alien being. (He really always was interestingly weird-looking.) The more Tom was abused, the more Tom rebelled. It might have been possible to kill him, but in a contest of wills, it wasn't possible to break him. Lots of other people tried, and sure, they got their blows in. But no way do the assholes win in Tom's world. And that's all of us, isn't it? In Tom's world, I mean. Aren't we all a little braver there? Not that it's equally bad for *me* personally (it wasn't and isn't), but if you're *not* finding this beasty in yourself (and I see mine), it's like I said before, you're probably an asshole, or a saint. I am here to protect and serve.

Assholes

I have been using that word a good bit. We're reminded of Tom's nice cover of the Beck song by that title. But that word is doing some real work by this point. I know you get it, but I'm starting to have an academic's conscience about it. I guess I should define it. Fortunately, the spade work got done by somebody else before I got there.

A philosopher named Aaron James published a book a few years back called *Assholes: A Theory*. It's actually a big book, and semi-serious. I'll boil it down to a sentence. An asshole is someone who consciously and self-servingly excuses himself/herself from the rules he/she knows (very well) apply to everyone else. That is pretty ept (the opposite of inept, right?). It covers everything from cutting in line to cheating on your taxes.

Further (I now pontificate, inspired by Aaron James), assholes count on non-assholes to be non-assholish so that they can slide by on their assholeness. Some non-assholes are afraid of assholes, while some will pick their battles with assholes pretty carefully, often after losing a few rounds to an asshole who was willing to raise the stakes until we have to choose between becoming assholes to *beat* the assholes, or letting the assholes win. In that second group are people, like Tom Petty (and me on my best days), who say, in effect, "you can stand me up before the Gates of Hell, but . . ." well, you know the rest. I would rather burn in hell than see an asshole win, where it was in my power to resist. If all of us who felt that way joined together . . . well, never mind. It won't happen.

It's not reasonable to ask everyone to stand up to the assholes, and those who do have their own reasons and have to accept the consequences. One consequence is that people may call you an asshole. But they'll be wrong, and that has to be good enough. But there's a painful truth. That choice to *not* be an asshole is as thin as Tom at twenty-five. You have to keep making it better, and every day you get one more card, because it's *in you*. That's the Dark Angel beasty crouching by the door. It fucks with your mind, makes you into someone else's masterpiece. It tells you, "they all do it, what does it mean anyway?" If you ward off this Petty-ness, your feeling of absurdity becomes a phenomenological insight into others. And that's how you recognize assholes. Something familiar here. Hmmmmm.

But there's a secret too. Assholes don't care about *other* assholes or protect them, and in fact may pile on when another asshole is going down, having tested the patience of non-assholes beyond their liberal forbearance. No, assholes only care about Number One. But a damaged non-asshole is forever on the lookout. The searchlight shines within and without, and it never settles for what comes under the beam. For every feeling that gets lit up, there are twenty-five more hiding behind it, too clever, too ashamed, or too paralyzed to take a step forward. But the phenomenologist in Tom's world has to feel them there, fool the clever, comfort the ashamed, and provoke the paralyzed.

I'm Too Alone to Be Proud

And that's what the songs do. The asshole scrambles like a cockroach for the darkness. The non-asshole placates the petty beast in the corner: "Here's a bone for you; it came from an asshole, so chew on it good." I wonder what kind of laugh they had at Tom's house after sending a cease and desist order to George W. Bush's campaign headquarters saying, basically, "You can't play my song, asshole." What song? Well which song would a true asshole want for his own, without earning it? You know, the kind of asshole who wants people to believe that his opponents, who actually *went* to war, were cowards, while he partied and drank and defiled women on his daddy's dime? That kind of asshole might have the blood of a million people on his hands one day. I'm supposing he's too alone to be proud, at this late date.

But assholes can be (and often are) charming, when they *want* to be. Assholes are sometimes very smart. Assholes are always crafty. They have to be. Assholes learn where your weaknesses are, in case you need to be controlled later. Assholes are often patient, but when their moment arrives, you'll see them for what they are. And they are, one hundred percent of them, cowards. Their deepest fear is that you'll know them for what they are. It's a moment of vision. And you won't have to say a word. They'll know that you know, even if the gun is in *their* hands. You'll stand your ground because you're not an asshole. And so, assholes take from themselves what they can never take from you, which is the choice to be with others, authentically. Even that self-depriving act is a twisted sort of freedom, but you'll have to leave them to it. You can't save an asshole.

The Moment of Vision

It's Heidegger's phrase, this "moment," printed in double bold type in *Being and Time*. In the midst of the bleak and despairing tale he spun, he found a ray of light. But if the light within you is darkness, how dark is that darkness? I read that somewhere. For Martin Heidegger the moment came along in 1933, when Hitler took power.

It wasn't just that he took his old professor's chair and then started talking shit about Jews, it was that he missed not a second in getting himself elected Rector (President) of the University and implementing the policies of Hitler in removing Jews and Marxists from their positions and depriving them of their privileges. How far would he go? Not that far, it's true. He wasn't a brave man. He resigned before things got pogrom-like. Reasons unclear. But he also didn't apologize, let alone take up for anyone. He let 'em die and uttered not a word of protest or remorse. Asshole. His favorite poet Hölderlin said:

> A place to rest
> isn't given to us.
> Suffering humans
> decline and blindly fall
> from one hour to the next,
> like water thrown
> from cliff to cliff,
> year after year,
> down into the Unknown.

That's just where Heidegger was, and what he saw. I have a perfectly clear intuition that if he had been a German citizen, Tom Petty wouldn't have survived the Second World War, and not because he would have got sent to the Eastern Front. Like him, I'm not on the Left or Right, and I try to imagine myself in the circumstances of being German in 1933 (and beyond). I hope they would have had to kill me to shut me up. I'm not sure. But I feel certain that they would have had to kill Tom Petty, even if he didn't have a dog in the fight. And maybe the Heartbreakers, too. And probably Bruce Springsteen and the whole E Street Band. It's the beginnings of a partisan cell, isn't it? Put that in your phenomenological pipe and smoke it, Professor Doctor Heidegger. Call it a moment of vision.

Now, for all his gleanings of apocalypse, Heidegger had managed, almost miraculously, to avoid military service in the First World War. Not many German men in their twenties could say *that* in 1914, or '15, or '16, or '17. About two million of his countrymen didn't live to see 1919. He claimed he wanted to be a priest. Heidegger's aspiration to God's service, in celibacy, poverty, and obedience, somehow vanished in, oh, about

November of 1918. But hey, that war sucked and was evil. Maybe he didn't have a dog in the fight? Maybe I would have wanted to be a priest, too. I'm really *trying* here, okay? I'm not judging.

I Catch Myself Wondering, Waiting, Worrying

Okay, I am so totally judging, but hear me out. Maybe Heidegger was damaged. He was about five feet tall, in elevator shoes. Maybe he felt like he had something to prove. But that's all of us, too, right? Maybe it tempts the asshole in you. But you have to find the resources to climb out of this well, and maybe they're in the darkdeepdown, to *not* become an asshole. How does it work?

Tom describes it a few times. It's almost as if we have to face ourselves like two gunslingers, right on the verge of ultimacy and then it dawns on us, what are we fighting for? Whatever that "choice" is, it goes all the way down. It's a mystery, but I think I see the sign of it, if not the thing itself. Have you ever seen, like in the middle of an interview, when Tom Petty breaks into a smile, without *saying* anything? *That's it*. That's what it looks like, even if I don't know where it comes from. He had gigantic teeth and a huge mouth, so it may not be as affecting when *your* skinny ass does it, but non-assholes (by grace and by choice) all have that capacity. Assholes do not, at least not while they are assholing, which slowly, sadly becomes a way of life for them.

Don't feel sorry for them. You can't live their lives for them. And, on the side of humility, you don't exactly choose the joy; it chooses you. You know the moment I'm going on about. I will give it a name. I shall call it: "Here Comes My Girl." (Certainly make that "Boy" if the shoe fits.) Now you can repeat it under your breath because it's the sort of thing you say twice.

I think that the smile I'm describing has a structure. It is always a gift given to us by someone else, arriving when we never saw it on the horizon. We're surprised by the joy of something unanticipated, and this smile starts in the darkdeepdown and rises almost against our will until it emerges right out onto our faces and spreads our lips until our teeth are bare. I hope we brushed them, but it's too late now. Then our teeth part, we throw our heads back, and we let out just exactly the laugh that made her fall for us. It is the sign of deep vulnerability, that someone else can bring this out of you. It is momentary, but it is real. You'll be on your guard again in three or four seconds, but we saw you.

Actually, it's more than that. We saw you *see* someone *else*, and lose yourself in the moment of it. That smile only shows up when, well, when the phenomenological equivalent of "Here Comes My Girl" advents. It isn't an event, it's an advent, when an incarnational, soteriological second coming of the possibility of happiness takes us from within. I'll bet my ass . . . no, yours . . . I'll bet your ass that Jesus had a smile like that . . . and Buddha and Muhammed and Confucius and Lao Tzu. I know Gandhi had it because I saw it in the films. It came from anyone who told you that the light is eternal within us and that love is more powerful than assholes, and, if we listened at all, it probably grew from an experience like this one. Cassirer's favorite poet, Goethe, wrote this:

When embodied there I meet
All I lost as soon as dead,
Happy as before am I.
Him she clasps with silent smile,
And his mouth the hour improves,
Sent by kindly Deities;
First from breast to mouth it roves,
Then from mouth to hands it flies.

In short, this says "Here Comes My Girl." Goethe called this poem "Mischievous Joy." This little exercise in smiling, by the way, is phenomenology. It isn't a theory, it's a description of something you have experienced. Remember what I said about liminal moments? Maybe one of those is now stuck between your teeth like the last bit of corn on the cob, and I imagine you smiling, hominy caught between incisor and eyetooth.

Now, the question is, what do you do with these moments? They aren't that rare. But do you give them the power they should have over your consciousness? Its habits? Its very structure? If you do, the beast crouching pettily in the corner won't ever get control of you. It has the same bit of corn residue caught in its teeth, too. Looks ridiculous. It isn't the beast that makes you an asshole. It's the fear that others will *see* it that might make you an asshole. Relax. Everybody sees it anyway. What are we supposed to be, more than human? We don't have to live like refugees.

Damn the Torpedoes

The day Hitler came to power, Ernst Cassirer said to his wife: "It is all in vain. I shall never write a word again." By the estimate of the critics of the time, Cassirer had lost the match with Heidegger at Davos. "And in this corner, Ernst the-Ernest-Gentleman Cassirer," who will never stoop to being an asshole in order to defeat one. He was a better man than I am, as I have more or less proved in this little inquiry. Cassirer always thought the best of people, even when they were misbehaving. Oh, to be so decent!

Heidegger and the ill-mannered entourage of young men who followed him everywhere sat in the audience, whispering and snickering as Cassirer, in the most erudite and humane language, explained that the future did not lie in in the destruction of the history of ontology, as Heidegger insisted, but in the project of human self-liberation. He didn't say self-knowledge would be good news. He was no innocent, as his critics claimed. But he also didn't seem to have a darkdeepdown, and he didn't know the Dark Angel, and so he didn't seem cool. Heidegger, with all his brooding ominosity, seemed the picture of self-possessed futurity. But all that bravado left its cowardice on display within five years, and then he spent thirty more hiding from what was plain enough to those who know the beast in the corner.

So maybe if Cassirer won't defend himself, he needs someone with a darkdeepdown and a deal with the beasty to launch a few waterspinners at the fleet of Heideggerian assholes who cruise the troubled seas of academia? Damn the depth charges. I'll surface and empty a few tubes in their smug direction.

Between You, Me, and the MF Lamppost

So Heidegger has thousands of followers—mostly frustrated, cowardly academic crypto-Nazis who are still trying to excuse their little Führer for his (now) more than obvious status as The Biggest Asshole of Twentieth-Century Philosophy. And he has some competition there, but apart from Bertrand Russell, no genuine rivals. (And Bertrand Russell wasn't really a coward of any kind.

There is a special kind of British personage whose transcendent superiority actually comes from a bizarre, reckless courage, which, in perfected stupidity, can be pressed to the very ruin of the Empire. On this heading, one might consider Field Marshall Douglas Haig, for instance. After sending about 800,000 British lads to their senseless deaths, the assholes made him an Earl. One supposes he died believing it was a worthy sacrifice, if not quite *his* sacrifice.)

This category of cold-blooded arrogance, peculiar to the British, whose language we all speak (or, as Heidegger would say, whose language speaks *us*), must await its own new nomenclature. Even Tom Petty might be at a loss for words, but, the word "motherfuckers" recommends itself . . . except that it impugns mothers and you can't sing it on the radio (Tom's tune "Spike" wasn't aimed at radio, I suppose). I invoke it because it's the worst word I know (proving that I'm not hip *or* hip-hop). I may be sheltered. So this notion about the new nomenclature has to be between me, you, and the lamppost.

To his credit, Lord Russell thought Field Marshall Haig was an asshole, along with the horse he rode in on. *And* Russell went to prison over it, for a pretty long stay. He didn't back down. There's something in that, although I'm damned if I have a phenomenology of it. I'll ask a British friend, one who has a beasty in the corner but isn't an asshole, or a Lord or an Earl.

Okay, so the beast just got the better of me. I may delete all that, or maybe I'll wait for someone else to suggest it. Maybe I'll ask my girl. Here she comes. But *she* would understand, which is why she is all I need. I certainly never used the "MF" word in print before, and I don't speak it either. Except when the beast is loose, which has happened more since the election of 2016, but it's my responsibility and I'm owning it. Aaron James wrote a follow-up book to *Assholes* specifically dedicated to our forty-fifth president (may he not be the last). I'll try to get this into print before I get Mr. Hyde Pettyfog (my Dark Angel's name) back into his corner, but I don't want my friends from church reading this. They might decide I'm an asshole, even though I praised Jesus a minute ago.

Refugees: The Story of the Moral

Ernst Cassirer managed to get out of Dodge before they came for him. First to England, then Sweden. Still not safe. He alighted in New York in 1940. He continued writing wise and erudite books. Everything he said was true and much of it profound. None of it was cool. Tom Petty is cool. I have promised myself I would do a phenomenology of coolness someday (not that I'm cool, but you can hope). Coolness has a fun twist: If you're trying to be cool, you automatically aren't. But *not* trying doesn't do the trick either. A promising paradox, but hard.

Cassirer didn't try to be cool, he tried to be honest, and to be himself. That's cool, in a way. He was intense. That's cool, too. I wish I had known him. Tom Petty was intense. I would have been afraid to know him. What if he didn't like me? Jesus, what if he thought I was an asshole? No. Banish that accursed thought. Cassirer, save me, okay? You're the phenomenologist. Tell me Tom would like me, okay?

As I scan the past in my imagination, I'm sort of relieved that Cassirer was spared the full truth about the Holocaust. He died suddenly of a heart attack one month before the Second World War ended. He was seventy-four. He lived longer than Tom, but not as long as Heidegger. Don't look for justice in longevity. But something inside me is feeling protective of Cassirer. He deserves more than history gave him.

Cassirer has, optimistically, a hundred or so people who faithfully read and teach and write about his books. I'm one of them. The reason his following is so small is that he got stomped on by an asshole in 1929—there are several important books about this liminal moment—and no one wants to back a loser. Well, almost no one. There are always a few rebels. But Cassirer didn't really *lose* because you can't defeat a decent person with bullshit. Yes, a Nazi might say something true, but its truth is spoiled by the source. What Cassirer needs is a philosophically minded, Tom-like (maybe even Pettyish) defender to extend to the Heideggerian assholes the middle finger of truth. As far as I can tell, or anyone else can, Cassirer didn't have even a nodding acquaintance with that beast in the corner and he had the decency to think no one was truly made of darkness. I think otherwise. And Cassirer, who dismissed his own darkdeepdown so easily, wouldn't understand Tom Petty's music full of liminal moments either.

We Tom Petty fans, we are finite and flawed, but we own a beast and we know an asshole when we see one. It's a phenomenological act of self-recognition, and it's painful. But we also know "Here Comes My Girl," which the phenomenologists call "authentic being with others."

Heidegger said it was impossible. I've never seen a picture of Heidegger smiling. Maybe he was never authentically with anyone else, but that doesn't give him an excuse for saying *we* can't do it. And Tom Petty disproved it with every silent (mischievous) smile.

Tom never claimed to be a genius or a hero, and maybe he knew better than we do. But I would put him ahead of pretty much any rock star as a phenomenologist of our finitude and our beasts. At the risk of verging on the para-social, I miss him very much.

I'll keep his example in mind and try not to be an asshole. Even when it's justified. Unless I have a change of heart.

PART IV

Corporate Machine

11
Forever the Wild One

S. KELLER ANDERS

"When it's all over," Tom Petty told Steve Pond at *Rolling Stone* in July of 1981, "all you're gonna leave behind is the records. That's all the fuck you're doing."

That's it: that's Tom Petty in a nutshell. A whole philosophy in an offhand quote to a reporter that somehow defines Petty, his career, and his love of rock'n'roll. When you listen to "Runnin' Down a Dream," or the pervasive classic "I Won't Back Down," you can hear his commitment to the music—plus his stubborn demand for freedom. He wanted freedom to pursue a dream, to live fully, to make art on his own terms.

Though he might not have put it in these words, Tom Petty was an uncompromising defender of his artistic freedom. As a songwriter and musician, whether solo or as part of the Heartbreakers, Petty fought—to the brink of personal ruin, to protect his work, and to protect the ability of his audience to access his music. Risking his career and those of his bandmates in the Heartbreakers several times over the course of his long career, Petty made it clear that he valued his freedom as an artist more highly than he valued commercial success.

In philosophy, when we talk about artistic freedom, we're usually thinking about the creator of art—whatever kind of art it is— and the art that is being created. Art is a form of expression, a creation that is subjective, emanating from the point of view of the person creating it. "I never paint dreams or nightmares. I paint my own reality," as Frida Kahlo put it. But the artist doesn't act in isolation. There's a third component to artistic freedom: the observation of the art by a person other than the artist.

When we have the artist, the art, and the audience in relation to one another, we can start to poke at the tension between them. Can the artist creating the art define what that art looks like to the audience? Does the art stand alone, once it has been created? What does the audience see when they look at the artwork? This is the framework under which we can consider "artistic freedom" as an idea worth considering. And with the set-up in place, artistic freedom can go in some interesting directions.

Genius at Play

You'd never find Tom Petty calling himself a genius. In interviews, he was always more likely to throw a sardonic quip at a nosy question, or say something so flippant—including that bit from '81 mentioned above—that it begged more questions than it answered.

It's not that Petty wasn't aware of his talent, or the way his thoughtful lyrics appealed to a broad, appreciative audience. Take "Free Fallin'," for example. This is a song that ranked at #7 on the *Billboard* "Hot 100" in 1990, was certified silver in the United Kingdom, and remains one of his most recognizable tunes. Petty told *Esquire* in 2006 that while he was grateful to audiences for making it a hit and he thought it was a good song, its commercial success as an anthem kept it from being one of his own favorite tunes.

The man wasn't inclined to claim his own accolades, despite more than twenty albums, dozens of singles, the Radio Music Awards Legend Award in 2003, and the Billboard Century Award in 2005. But for Petty, commercial and critical success wasn't the measure of his creative achievement. It always came back to the music: Petty's love for rock'n'roll and creating songs to honor that devotion.

We get our contemporary idea of a genius—the fantastic physics of Albert Einstein or the deep grace of Maya Angelou—from the Enlightenment in the seventeenth and eighteenth centuries. In the centuries before the Enlightenment, "artists" were primarily if not exclusively considered to be masters of the fine arts—painters, sculptors, poets, musicians. The work of artists was commissioned by the church, the state, or private patrons, and created to the standards and whims of those in a position to pay for it. Such authority and control over the production of art didn't entirely preclude artists from creating works of their own inspiration, but it definitely restricted the means by which artists could produce their own art, uninfluenced by the demands of those holding the purse. They were more *artisan* than artist.

As political systems in Europe and the West shifted and reformed during the Enlightenment period, these patronage structures began to fall apart. The Enlightenment fostered the notion of the individual as an independent actor, a person, separate and singular from collective society, empowered with human reason and logic. Furthermore, such an individual person held certain natural rights, simply by virtue of being a rational human being. (During the Enlightenment, a "rational human being" was equated to a "male human being," but for our purposes we'll consider all humans to be humans, with or without gender applied.) And with the notion of the individual, along came the concept of a genius: an individual, rational person who innately bore the talent and ability to create. More specifically, to create art.

Genius at Work

This was the perspective of the philosopher Immanuel Kant (1724–1804), with whom I have spent more time than is really comfortable over the years. His 1790 work, the *Critique of Judgment*, wrestled with understanding how our newly individualized, rational selves might generate beauty and create the sublime through the vector of free will, released from the constraints of overbearing authority. It takes a third of the book, but Kant finally lands on assigning the category of *genius* to those artists capable of producing works of evident beauty.

The nature of genius, according to Kant's discourse on the fine arts, is that the artist is running down a dream and going wherever the mystery leads. At the heart of it, "aesthetics" is the philosophy of subjective feeling, and we engage with aesthetics when we think about art, and think about the creation of art, and think about how to observe and appreciate art. For Kant, a genius is someone with the talent for fine art, and the possession and application of such a talent leads to art's own beauty—for which a creator's genius is required.

Our Mr. Petty, possessing such a talent that his songs are in every jukebox and digital playlist, can certainly live up to this standard of genius. Genius, in Kant's aesthetics, is the very embodiment of artistic freedom because originality is a primary cornerstone of genius. Petty agreed with this in a 1999 interview with *Billboard*. He said that the band needed freedom to explore on stage each night; they avoided routine and tried to keep things feeling fresh when they performed.

Freedom, freedom, freedom. It's so deeply woven into Tom Petty's artistry and philosophy that it becomes the significant characteristic of his genius. For Petty, artistic freedom is both the means and the method. There is the freedom of the artist creating art through the method of genius, and there is freedom as inspiration that becomes the means by which artistry—beauty—is revealed.

Getting All They Can Get

By the 1970s, the American record industry had shifted from a multitude of small independent labels to large conglomerates. Usually started by musicians passionate about their work, record labels became huge corporations motivated more by the profit to be made off contracted musicians than by any concern for the music itself. For Tom Petty, who by 1981 had been around the block a few times with record companies, this conception went against the very ethos of rock'n'roll music, which valued originality, accessibility, and artistic freedom.

Back in the days when he was just getting started, saying you wanted to be a musician was basically admitting a willingness to go broke and never have a career. Petty told *Billboard* in 1991 that he was doing it for the love of rock'n'roll, because a professional musician could never expect to be so wildly successful. It was all about the music, and the record label was the vehicle for getting the music recorded and out to the public.

Today, musicians and musical artists have general access to high-quality devices and materials on which to record their music. Once recorded, there are a variety of tools to promote and distribute these works to a worldwide audience, using web-based services and social media. But this is a quite recent situation. Until the early 2000s, with the launch of MySpace and YouTube, musicians aspiring to professional success trod much the same path as their counterparts some fifty years earlier, with limited access to high-quality recording tools and inadequate means to distribute their music without corporate backing.

For Petty and the Heartbreakers, their relationship with MCA Records had started off rocky and never really settled. Following the tumultuous production and success of their third album, *Damn the Torpedoes,* the band regrouped a year later to begin work on *Hard Promises*. After *Torpedoes* hit as the #2 record for seven straight weeks on the *Billboard* album chart upon its release in 1979, Petty found himself in a far better negotiating position during the production of *Hard Promises* a little over a year later. By all accounts, *Hard Promises* came together more swiftly and with greater ease than *Torpedoes*, which was beleaguered by the demands of new producer Jimmy Iovine, Petty's ongoing lawsuit against MCA, and a shift in the band's sound from a garage-rock feel to the more sophisticated and smooth tone we usually think of as Petty's signature today.

Hard Promises had gotten to the all-important "masters" stage of approval, when the band, the producers, and the label have all signed off on the tracks and structure of a record before beginning manufacture of the record itself for distribution. On the heels of the sales of *Damn the Torpedoes*, which has to date been certified three times platinum in the United States (that is, sales of over three million records), MCA Records elected to give *Hard Promises* the VIP treatment by applying "super-star pricing" to the forthcoming album.

In the early Eighties, the typical record price was $8.98. A consumer could pick up just about any new release for that price, from the terrific *Autoamerican* by Blondie to The Pretenders's self-titled debut. "Super-star pricing" was MCA's gimmick to up-sell records it was confident would succeed by pricing them at one dollar more, banking that customers would buy a super-star record despite the price hike because it was too hot not to buy. MCA tried this tack with Steely Dan's seventh record *Gaucho*, as well as the *Xanadu* soundtrack, which became far more popular than its movie counterpart. Both records found commercial success despite the increase in price, and MCA had a solid bet that *Hard Promises* would perform similarly.

To say that Tom Petty was not pleased with this decision—made unilaterally by the record company—understates the depth of his commitment to the ethic of artistic freedom.

Overdeveloped Morals

When it comes to thinking about the reasons why we do the things we do, we land in the study of ethics. Why do we obey laws, care for others, share resources, protect that which we consider important? Ethical thought attempts to answer these questions. Ethics represent the "codes of conduct" of the people in a society, or a community, or a workplace. This is distinct from *morals*, which reflect an individual's personal beliefs about what is right or wrong.

The contemporary ethicist Peter Singer describes the consideration of ethics in his 1999 book, *Practical Ethics,* as choosing paths of action based on which ones have the best outcomes, on the whole, for all those who are affected by those actions. While there are several different ways of conceptualizing ethical behavior, Singer's definition neatly summarizes the type of ethics called "practical" or "applied" ethics. This terminology refers to thinking about ethics in terms of real-world issues, such as animal rights or disparities between the wealthy and the poor.

We can take this idea of practical ethics and examine Tom Petty's professional decisions. When MCA Records informed Petty and the Heartbreakers that *Hard Promises* would be priced in their "super-star" model, Petty immediately protested. Biographer Warren Zanes speculated that Petty was remembering what it was like to be a teenager—one who would be pissed off about having to scrape together that extra dollar for his record—instead of thinking like the commercially successful rock star he was, who only cared about his own cut of that extra dollar.

For Petty, price-jacking for no reason other than to turn a higher profit was a threat to the audience he and the Heartbreakers had built over the course of five years, touring the country and connecting with fans. It was a direct blow to the artistic freedom he continually defended from the influence of the record label. Though a higher price point would conceivably make the members of the band wealthier, it ran counter to ethical behavior. If, as Singer puts it, ethics demands the action with the best outcome for all involved, Petty was behaving ethically by taking into consideration the impact of a price hike on consumers, who would be more significantly affected by the increase compared to the record label or the band.

Petty used interviews with the media, of which there were several, as a way to make sure his point of view was widely known. The negative publicity garnered by revealing MCA's pricing decision before the record was released gained Petty's protest traction with the label's executives. Yet when the price remained unchanged, Petty adhered more deeply to his ethical perspective. He and the band threatened to withhold the masters of the record, the finalized version of *Hard Promises*, refusing to allow it to go to production unless the price remained at the standard level. If that wasn't sufficient to induce a change at the record label, Petty pointedly insisted that they would change the title of the record to "Eight Ninety-Eight," no matter its price. This was a true defense of artistic freedom as an ethic: better that the music not be released than be subjected to a compromise of its accessibility.

Of the many things to admire about Tom Petty, it's this story that I love best. There have been only a few musical artists over the years who have publicly advocated for the availability of their music to customers when it would reduce the artist's income to do so. It's a wonderfully ethical mindset, to care as much about the audience for your music as about the music itself, and in keeping with the highest ideals of artistic freedom, to value the art over the art's price.

Faced with significant negative publicity and the seriousness of Petty's intentions, MCA backed away from the superstarring of *Hard Promises* and released the record for $8.98. Yet Petty, never that far from tongue in cheek, couldn't resist taking one last jab at the situation. On the cover of the album, Petty is standing in a record store, idly looking off to the side at something unseen. Toward the lower right corner, a cardboard sign reads "$8.98," a sharp reminder to MCA and all who would go up against Petty, his ethics, and his determination to retain artistic freedom.

"God, I hope it ain't overdeveloped morals," Petty joked with Pond during that '81 interview for *Rolling Stone*. "I don't know. It ain't that big a deal . . . I hope we're not remembered as the band that fought the record company."

Raised on Promises

Tom Petty's early professional career was by turns lucky and unfortunate. Mudcrutch, the first of Petty's bands to be signed to a record label, fell apart following poor response to its one and only single. When he formed Tom Petty and the Heartbreakers with guitarist Mike Campbell in 1976, his initial contract with Shelter Records for Mudcrutch became the next contract for the Heartbreakers. While the Heartbreakers's self-titled first record was more of a hit in the United Kingdom than the United States, the band had better luck with sophomore album *You're Gonna Get It!* in 1978, which certified as gold.

But the consolidation of the record industry continued to swallow smaller record labels throughout the Sixties and Seventies, until only a handful of large, multi-national corporations represented the majority of commercial music. So it went with Shelter Records, who sold their interest in the Heartbreakers to its distributor ABC Records in 1978. ABC, whose roster included Ray Charles, The Four Tops, Dusty Springfield, and The Fifth Dimension, saw the Heartbreakers through *You're Gonna Get It!* before financial instability forced a sale of the company to MCA Records in early 1979.

The story goes that, shortly after the acquisition of ABC, MCA Records sent out a letter to the artists it acquired welcoming them to the label. For Tom Petty, this was the first he had heard of his record label folding, and upon learning that he wouldn't be offered the opportunity negotiate new contractual terms for the Heartbreakers with the move to MCA, it was clear that drastic action had to be taken to countermand this risk to his artistic freedom.

Consonant with Dignity

Of the many ideas Karl Marx and his collaborator Friedrich Engels introduced to the world, the concept of Marxian economics is perhaps the most enduring. The Marxist political experiments of the twentieth century owe their existence to Marx's perspective on economic thought. Today, economics as a discipline exists as a spectrum with capitalism at one end, and Marxism far at the other.

Two elements of Marx's vast, complicated system of thought remain useful tools for engaging in the philosophy of economics, or the thinking behind why and how goods and services are produced, distributed, and consumed. The first of these is the disparity between a worker who produces something, and the private owner who profits from that production. The second is the means by which the value of a product can be fed back into the worker's production to create further value, which accumulates to the private owner over time.

Like many ideas in philosophy, the Marxist system can get a little loopy. In fact, in his great work *Capital,* Marx himself called the process above a spiral, for the way the system feeds into itself. But we can see the relevance of Marx's theories about production and value to Tom Petty's 1979 defense of his economic interests and artistic freedom.

Petty Grievances

The contracts musical artists typically sign include provisions for *how* an artist's music will be produced such as studio time, how and when the artist's work will be distributed, how the work will be promoted, and how the artist and the record label will each be compensated for the sale of the album. For Petty and the Heartbreakers, the contract Petty originally signed with Shelter Records for the band Mudcrutch didn't reflect the interests of the far more successful Heartbreakers.

"It was the principle: the idea of being told to report to those guys really pissed me off," Petty told Mikal Gilmore for *Rolling Stone* in 1980. He didn't want to work his ass off to succeed with the Heartbreakers, only to have the old Mudcrutch deal hung around his neck. Effectively being "sold," without notice and without the opportunity to re-negotiate his contract, pinned Petty and the Heartbreakers under MCA's control—and it would give a dime to the band but a dollar to MCA no matter how much commercial success the band saw. Petty was outraged that MCA thought they had his number, banking a surefire hit record against a band's old paperwork.

MCA's unwillingness to renegotiate Petty's contract wasn't too surprising: they, in effect, "owned" the work the Heartbreakers would produce, both the two records that already existed and any records going forward. In the Marxist sense,

Tom Petty and the Heartbreakers were the workers, and what they produced was their record albums. Shelter Records, ABC Records, and then MCA Records were the private owners who received value—profit—from the albums the Heartbreakers produced.

By virtue of Petty's original Shelter Records contract, the distribution of the value from the record albums favored the record label over the artists who made the record. And as each record album gained more and more commercial success, further value of greater profit was gained by the record label, especially if the terms remained favorable to the label based on the first Shelter Records contract. No matter how much work the Heartbreakers put into their music or their touring, the record label would always gain greater profit than the band.

Thus the threat to Petty's artistic freedom was twofold: first, he and the band would never see the full value of the profit from their artistic works return to them monetarily. Second, Petty would never gain real ownership over the songs he wrote—every song on every album—or the completed albums.

When Petty wouldn't comply, MCA sued Petty for breach of contract. So Petty turned to the courts as well, countersuing in pursuit of the chance to negotiate a new contract. All the while, despite the legal battle, preparation for recording the third album *Damn the Torpedoes* was underway, with MCA record producer Jimmy Iovine coming on board. The tension was high.

Petty put his career, his future, and the potential of financial success on the line. He went up against a major record label, fighting for himself and his artistic freedom, which was unheard of at the time. Though he and the Heartbreakers had achieved some commercial success, Petty was not wealthy or powerful compared to the executives at MCA Records. His only real power was as an artist, using his refusal to create music as a tool to force MCA to negotiate. He was in the role of a Marxist worker, confronting a private owner to gain the real value of the work he produced.

When the case finally settled and Petty renegotiated his contract under MCA Records, he and the band were free to continue the production of *Damn the Torpedoes*, the album that would dramatically elevate the critical and commercial success of the band. Yet for Petty, it would have been worth it to give up all the fame and fortune to keep true to his artistic freedom, the necessary condition for him to create his music at all.

The Wild One

Tom Petty had the kind of musical career that any artist would dream of: multiple award-winning albums, sold-out touring spanning decades, critical acclaim, and commercial success. His unexpected death in 2017 rocked the music industry, the many artists he influenced, and his wide audience. Though he can rightly be remembered for his songwriting talent and musical artistry, I find myself reflecting on his lifelong commitment to artistic freedom.

The risks he was willing to take to stay true to his art floor me. His genius at work in crafting some of the most memorable songs of the twentieth century is evident in every karaoke jam of "Free Fallin'" and each time the radio plays "Mary Jane's Last Dance." "I don't see myself as the savior of anything," he told *Billboard* in 1982. "On the one hand I'm flattered; that's why it's so hard to complain. What we're really striving for is to inspire someone."

Tom Petty was a true artist, for whom music required freedom. His consistent defense of this freedom is an inspiration, just like his music is for audiences contemplating his musical genius.

12
When Money Shouldn't Be King

BRIAN BERKEY

Throughout his career, Tom Petty maintained a fairly adversarial stance toward the business side of the music industry. In the late 1970s, he voiced his dissatisfaction with the transfer of his contract that followed the sale of his record label, Shelter Records, to MCA, stating that he objected to being treated like a piece of meat to be bought and sold.

After MCA refused to give up its rights to the contract, which Petty had come to believe included terms that unfairly favored the company's interests over his own, he decided to finance the production of the next Tom Petty and the Heartbreakers album (which would become *Damn the Torpedoes*) himself. He took on over $500,000 in expenses and then refused to release the album.

In order to force MCA to void his contract, he declared bankruptcy. The company subsequently agreed to a new contract that included terms that were more favorable to Petty, and the album, which included the hits "Refugee," "Here Comes My Girl," and "Even the Losers," was released.

Shortly before the band's next album, *Hard Promises*, was scheduled to be released, Petty learned that MCA planned to sell it at its new "superstar artist" price of $9.98, instead of at the standard price of $8.98. In order to pressure the company to sell the album at the standard price, Petty threatened to prevent its release, or he would title the album $8.98 and organize a protest letter campaign among fans. After a standoff that lasted approximately a month, MCA relented, and the album was released at the $8.98 price.

In a 1981 interview, Petty said that his main objection to MCA's plan to sell *Hard Promises* at the superstar price was that he had been told previously that the album would be priced at the standard $8.98, and that the company had subsequently changed its mind. He insisted that MCA wasn't the enemy. At the same time, however, he made some more general comments that suggest that he had broader concerns about an emerging trend in the industry toward higher album prices that would make it more difficult for fans to afford to buy the music that he and other artists worked so hard to produce. He didn't want MCA singled out, since all the record companies would've liked to hike up their prices.

Petty even added that the company did a great job selling their albums, but just couldn't see that the reality on the street was that these price hikes weren't fair. Perhaps the clearest indication that his objection to the price increase was not merely that he had been misled by the company about the price that *Hard Promises* in particular would sell for, he worried that he'd better take a stand now, before albums ended up priced at twenty bucks. The *Hard Promises* album cover was also designed to make a statement about the pricing controversy; it depicts Petty standing in a record store near a crate of albums selling for $8.98.

These conflicts with his record companies earned Petty a reputation as someone who would fight for both his own interests as an artist and the interests of music fans. Articles at the time of the *Hard Promises* controversy discussed the cases in some detail, and the headlines described Petty as a rock'n'roll hero who was ready to fight the good fight and to keep on fighting it. When Petty died suddenly in October of 2017, many of the articles commemorating his life and impact on the music industry highlighted his early conflicts with his record companies. His willingness to take on powerful companies, and his ability to win those fights, are prominent among the things that he is remembered for by those who followed his career in the music industry.

More Money, More Problems

Despite the conflicts with his record companies in Tom Petty's early career, and his critical attitudes toward trends in the music industry (dating back at least to the time of *Damn the Torpedoes*), it was only twenty-one years after the *Hard Promises* controversy, on *The Last DJ* (2002), that Petty took up the state of the industry in his music. It's sometimes suggested that the *Full Moon Fever* (1989) hit "I Won't Back Down" reflects the stance that Petty adopted toward the industry throughout his career. While this seems true, the song itself doesn't directly address *issues* related to the music business, or the relations that artists or fans stand in to those on the business side of the industry. A slightly better place to look is the first few lines of the title track on 1987's *Let Me Up (I've Had Enough)*. But I will explore *The Last DJ*, and suggest that Petty held philosophically interesting and interconnected views about the value of music and the ethical obligations of those working on the business side of the music industry.

On the value of music, Petty seems to have believed that it isn't exclusively about whether people subjectively enjoy their experiences of listening to it. I think he held a view that is at least partially "objectivist," on which individuals can be mistaken about the value of their own musical experiences. They can, for example, enjoy music that is in fact of poor quality, believing it and their experience to be more valuable than it really is.

The belief that people can be mistaken about the value of their musical experiences helps to make sense of Petty's view, which comes through pretty clearly on *The Last DJ*, that those working on the business side of the music industry act wrongly when they make choices about which music to produce and market entirely on the basis of what will make the most money for their companies. If the most profitable business model for a record company is to produce and heavily market large amounts of "pop" music by artists that sound relatively similar, it's because many people are willing to pay for albums by such artists, for concert tickets, and for merchandise, but wouldn't be willing to pay (or to pay as much) for albums by or concert tickets for other kinds of artists. And if many people are willing to pay for a Heartbreakers album, but not a particular boy band offering, maybe they enjoy, and therefore value, listening to the Heartbreakers more than the boy band.

If the value of music consisted entirely in people's subjective enjoyment, then it's hard to see what could be wrong with making decisions about which music to produce entirely on the basis of which albums people are most willing to buy. After all, people's willingness to fork over the cash shows how much they expect to enjoy what they're buying. If we think, as Petty clearly did, that there's something objectionable about the trend toward producing only the music that will be easiest to sell to the public, then we must also think that there are values relevant to decisions about which music should be produced based in something other than listeners' subjective enjoyment.

It might be said that willingness to pay isn't a good predictor of how much enjoyment a piece of music could produce because people with a lot of money will tend to have different tastes in music than people who are broke. Thus, making album production decisions entirely on the basis of what will make the most money for one's company would tend to provide maximum subjective enjoyment of music only for the rich, while those with fewer resources will tend not to have their musical preferences satisfied.

Petty was concerned that access to valuable musical experiences was becoming more limited because of the increasing focus on profit-making within the industry, but it doesn't seem to me that his objection to the trend toward making recording choices based on their profit potential is based primarily on the concern that the poor won't get their preferences satisfied.

The Subjectivism Business

In addition to helping make sense of Petty's view about the ethics of deciding what music should be produced, several songs on *The Last DJ* support the view that Petty held at least a partially objectivist view about the value of music. Before looking at this evidence, what are subjectivist and objectivist views about the value of music?

Subjectivists think the value of a piece of music lies entirely in the subjective enjoyment that listening provides to people. So, if we want to know how "valuable" it would be to produce a particular album, we attempt to estimate how many people will listen, and how much each of them will enjoy the experience. We could also drill down deeper by attempting to estimate how many times each person will listen, and how much enjoyment each instance of listening would produce.

If something besides subjective enjoyment contributes to the value of artistic creations, such as albums, then we can't estimate the value of producing an album in this way. Views that are at least partially objectivist say there *are* additional factors. So, they say we need to assess how the album would embody whatever other values we think are relevant, and then weigh that alongside our subjective enjoyment. This means it's possible that an album generating less *overall* enjoyment might still be more valuable than one generating more enjoyment, as long as the album with fewer fans embodies enough of the other values to be more valuable *overall*.

It's not surprising that the suits on the business side of the music industry tend to operate as though they accept the subjectivist view. After all, people's willingness to pay for things like albums and concert tickets surely correlates with their expectations about enjoyment. So making decisions about what to produce on its profit-making potential treats the value of music as consisting in the enjoyment it provides. Some might dismiss the music industry execs as money-grubbing, but there's an argument that can be made in their defense that appeals to the subjectivist view.

Unlike arguments that managers of companies are obligated to maximize shareholder profits, the argument that appeals to the subjectivist view about the value of music gives weight to the interests of the *consumers* who will purchase the music. This makes the argument more plausible than the shareholder-focused arguments for profit maximizing. The argument goes like this:

1. **Record companies should aim to produce music with as much value as possible.**

2. **Music is valuable only to the extent that it will produce enjoyment in listeners.**

3. **Record companies should produce music that will generate as much enjoyment in listeners as possible.**

4. **People's willingness to pay for things like albums and concert tickets is the best indicator of how much enjoyment they will gain from musical experiences.**

5. **Therefore, record companies should aim to produce music that will maximize the amount of money that consumers will be willing to pay for what they produce.**

Proposition #1 is a plausible general premise that both proponents and critics of profit maximizing record companies can accept. I see no reason to think that Petty would have rejected it. #2 is a statement of the subjectivist view about the value of music. #3 follows directly from #1 and #2, so that anyone who accepts both #1 and #2 must accept #3. #4 is a plausible claim about the evidential relationship between willingness to pay and enjoyment, one I suspect few would want to deny. And #5 follows from #3 and #4, so that anyone who accepts both #3 and #4 must accept #5. So anyone who accepts #1, #2, and #4 must accept #5. And since #1 and #4 are both quite plausible and widely accepted, it seems as though those who reject #5 must reject #2.

Hello, Joe

Why should we think that Petty rejected #2, apart from the fact that it seems clear that he rejected #5? Perhaps the strongest evidence can be found in "Joe," a song that's direct in its criticism of how record company execs make decisions about which music to produce. The song is written in the voice of a record company CEO named Joe, although Joe's statements reflect Petty's views about how CEOs do their jobs, and not what "Joe" would actually say. Joe seeks out artists who will become famous and generate a lot of money for his company, and thereby for himself. Petty doesn't think Joe is mistaken about what will generate the most money for his company. So he also doesn't think Joe is mistaken about which music sells best. But Petty thinks Joe is deeply mistaken about the real value of the music he chooses to produce.

Joe wants to seek out attractive female artists willing to undress on stage, and who can look somewhat convincing holding a guitar. That strategy may be the most profitable one available to Joe, but Petty's delivery and the song itself demonstrate that he thinks CEOs who do this are acting wrongly. They're not producing music that's valuable in the relevant sense, even if they sell a lot of albums and concert tickets, and even if they generate as much subjective enjoyment among consumers as possible. Consumers who pay for music of this kind, but not for music that's objectively better, are simply mistaken about the value of their musical experiences.

CEOs like Joe take advantage of consumers' susceptibilities to these mistakes, rather than do what might help alleviate them. And record companies often shape consumers' preferences, exacerbating the tendency to overvalue music of some kinds and undervalue other kinds. By marketing certain artists more heavily than others, companies can generate the public perception that the promoted artists are producing better material, even if this isn't the case.

Goodbye, Johnny

Joe's attitude about sexy female artists is contrasted with his attitude toward fifty-year old Johnny, who is first mentioned on *The Last DJ* in "Money Becomes King." In that earlier track, Johnny's music is generally of high quality, although he struggles to maintain his motivation due to the changes in the industry that Petty criticizes throughout the album. Joe dismisses Johnny's claim that the company keeps shady books and advises that his music would sell better if he'd die a little faster. Petty suggests it's objectionable when record executives value artists and their music only insofar as they can be expected to generate profits for the company.

Petty's view that the industry's focus on profit-making fails to generate especially valuable music is clearest in *The Last DJ*'s title track, about a DJ who refuses to become a company man. He insists on playing music he believes is good, not what the upstairs suits tell him to play. Presumably, the DJ's bosses are instructing him to play music that attracts the largest number of listeners, generating the most money for the company. Petty thinks the most valuable music won't be played in that case. The insistence of the higher-ups on playing what sells is just a celebration of mediocrity, and Petty laments the DJ's termination as a loss of the last human voice. The DJ represents the kind of informed judgment about the quality of music that's lost when artistic decisions are made exclusively by businesspeople chasing the most profit. Such decisions are inhuman in a way that we should care about. Only resisters of the corporate logic of the fast buck dominating the industry can maintain what's left of the human element in music. And only securing that human element can protect our shot at producing for the public the most valuable kinds of music.

Upstairs versus Downstairs

Accepting Petty's partially objective view about the value of music doesn't necessarily commit one to agreeing that it's *unethical* for those on the business side to focus exclusively on making as much profit as possible. But it's a plausible basis for arguing against that exclusive focus. It goes like this: The role of businesspeople in the music industry is to ensure that valuable music is produced, and what makes music valuable is not merely (or maybe even primarily) its ability to generate enjoyment in listeners, so that they will pay for it.

As I said, Petty is pretty clearly committed to the view that the exclusive focus on profit-making in the music industry is ethically unacceptable. His rejection of subjectivism about the value of music helps make sense of this commitment. Still, it's worthwhile to look at the evidence in a few songs on *The Last DJ* that points to Petty's rejection of the exclusive focus on profits. This will help to clarify the connection between Petty's view about the value of music and his view about the ethics of the music industry more generally, with specific ethical commitments drawn from the songs.

Petty's critique of the music industry's trend toward an exclusive focus on profit appears in four songs on *The Last DJ*. We went over the title track already. One of the aims of the businesspeople that the song refers to, clearly derisively, is to find out what price can be charged for stuff that used to be free. We went over "Joe." The artists get fame while Joe gets profits. An additional ethical commitment highlighted in this song is that record companies should treat their *artists* fairly and with respect. After describing the kinds of artists that Joe seeks out, Petty has Joe describe these musicians as begging the company for money after their album sales begin to slump. Joe says they won't be able to get anything from the company, since the corporation is properly lawyered up in ways artists simply can't afford. The attitude that Joe expresses toward Johnny's eventual burn-out later in the song is intended as objectionable for similar reasons. It's clear that Petty disapproved of how record companies often treat their artists. It's plausible to think that Petty put this point in "Joe" at least partially motivated by his own experience, fighting legal battles with record companies.

The conflict between the business side of the industry and resisters of the trend toward thinking of music in purely economic terms is also featured in "Can't Stop the Sun," the final track on *The Last DJ*. This song is written in the voice of someone resisting the trends that Petty criticizes. It strikes a note of optimism about resistance to these trends, suggesting that the suits' efforts to transform the industry will always run up against those who oppose them. The businessman being spoken to by the song's protagonist only thinks he's in charge—but Petty wagers there will always be more artists who won't back down.

If Petty Became King

The album's most complex and philosophically interesting song about Petty's commitments on the ethics of the music industry is "Money Becomes King." Petty compares the experiences of a music fan over time, highlighting how things have deteriorated as making money has come to play a bigger role within a music world increasingly dominated by corporate interests. vIt's written in the voice of the fan who assures listeners in the song's opening lines that there was a time in the past when money wasn't the dominant force in the music world.

The fan then describes an artist named Johnny, who loved being a musician before money became king. Back in the day, fans could afford to go to concerts given by artists like Johnny without too much difficulty, and the music generated feelings akin to those experienced by religious believers. The fan even references the salvation of his soul, and also compares the quality of Johnny's lyrics to diamonds and gold. Petty surely viewed lyrics as an important element in the quality of songs. This clearly highlights another reason why Petty was frustrated with trends in the industry in recent years. Lyrics got buried in droning sounds.

The remainder of "Money Becomes King" describes the transformation of the fan's experience over time. First, the price of concert tickets was increased, so that it became harder for fans to afford to go—they had to pawn all their belongings and sell drugs to buy their tickets. When they arrive at the concert, Johnny is lip-synching to his new beer commercial. The crowd at the concert, unlike crowds at earlier shows, consists primarily of wealthy people who show little interest in Johnny's actual music. From the cheaper seats where the fan is sitting, it's hard to see the stage, so they watch Johnny on the big screens hung nearby. Obviously, the fan's experience has changed quite dramatically from the quasi-religious one described earlier in the song. In Petty's view, these changes are explained by the increased focus on making money.

The most interesting lines on the album come at the end of "Money Becomes King." After describing Johnny's music, now being routinely played for a tiresome circle of VIPs, the fan sees in Johnny's face on the screen that he still sometimes tries to give it everything he's got. But Johnny's eyes betray that he is sad about the whole effort. Here, Petty suggests that the trend toward a focus on money in the music industry not only negatively affects fans, but also undermines the motivation of artists who would otherwise produce valuable music and play the kinds of shows that the fan describes at the beginning of the song. Petty understands that pure profiteering in the industry can change the nature of the music itself. It can alter participants' motivations, sometimes in troubling ways, and undermine the value of the activity.

The closing verses of "Money Becomes King" suggest that Petty thought the emptiness described—in the artist, in the art itself, and in the fans—was the most troubling result of an increased focus on making money in the music industry. If the subjectivist view about the value of music is incorrect, and record companies should aim to produce music with the most value, then the increased emphasis on making money isn't only problematic because it leads to worse music. It's problematic because it undermines the motivation of artists to create good music in the first place. This isn't because artists will all be motivated to create music that will sell best, but because an industry so focused on making money may undermine the motivation of artists who do value good music to create anything at all.

We all want to avoid that. Petty certainly avoided it. *The Last DJ* didn't sell a lot of copies, but his fans surely appreciate the effort that went into creating this unique and thoughtful album.

13
We Stand a Chance

RAUL HAKLI

In the popular media Tom Petty has often been represented as a lonely hero fighting battles against corporate agents who try to benefit from him. While it has been a common practice in the music business for record companies to take advantage of young artists with little experience and legal understanding, Petty became famous for fighting and winning some legal battles against his record company. The main battles took place at the end of the 1970s and the beginning of the 1980s.

The first one started when Shelter Records, the record company that had signed Petty, was sold to ABC and then to MCA, and the band was denied a renegotiation of the bad deal they had in spite of the success of the first two albums and a clause in the contract forbidding such transfer without the consent of the band. The band argued that MCA would have to let them go, but the company had other plans and stated that the band wasn't making enough money to pay for the cost of the recordings.

MCA told Petty that he owed them $575,000 and that in order to cover it, he would have to make six additional albums with them. Petty declined, and famously hid the master tapes of their record in progress each night to prevent the company from publishing the songs before they were finished. MCA and Shelter Records both sued him for breaching the contract.

The second one took place when MCA was planning to raise the price of their fourth record by one dollar and Petty stood up to them, managing to postpone the price increase. Later in his career he continued to challenge corporations by publicly criticizing radio companies and the music industry more generally. Especially in the early Eighties, stories about Petty were titled along the lines of this one from the July 1981 issue of *Rolling Stone*: "Tom Petty: One Man's War Against High Record Prices."

Such an individualistic picture of Petty as a lonely hero is misleading. I think there's an alternative interpretation: Petty was not engaged in a one-man war, rather he was acting as a group member engaged in a joint project aiming at collective good.

Something Good Coming

My own interest in Tom Petty and the Heartbreakers and my love for their music date back for over thirty years, but it wasn't love at first sight. The first time I remember hearing them was in 1985 during the Live Aid concert that was broadcast live all over the world. My younger sister and I were watching it on TV, hoping to see some of the big pop stars of the day, such as Madonna or Prince. Instead, to us two teenagers most of the acts were unknown, boring, or strange. Or all of the above. We saw artists like Neil Young, Bob Dylan, and the Cars, and we didn't really get what they were about.

At one point came this goofy guy with square sunglasses and mutton chop sideburns; it was Tom Petty and the Heartbreakers. We didn't know whether to laugh or cry. To us, the guy looked like a horse and sounded like a sheep, and the other band members didn't exactly look like heartbreakers either. But little did we know rock'n'roll! Soon this guy would be our hero, as he was for so many others, and the music of this band would be deep in our hearts forever.

My second encounter with the music of Tom Petty and the Heartbreakers came a couple of years later. My older cousin had been studying in the US and had been exposed to a lot of music that was not well known in the northern outskirts of Europe. One summer when he was going to drive to another city to participate in a tennis competition, he invited me to be his racquet boy and a travel companion. I happily agreed. We set off for the trip and he put on the cassette that he had purchased before coming to Finland for the holidays. It was *Pack Up the Plantation*, the live tape by a band I didn't even remember hearing about before.

My musical taste hadn't developed very much yet, and my own records were a rather mixed bag from various artists like Paul Anka, Talking Heads, Commodores, and the Rolling Stones. Being used to studio recordings, the sound on this live tape didn't impress me and neither did the music, which somehow seemed to lack in groovy rhythms and catchy choruses. I was just hoping for the tape to come to an end so that we could switch to something else. But boy, this tape was long. And when it finally ended, I learned that it was actually the only tape he had taken for the whole three-hour drive—and back!

So there was not much to do but listen to the same tape over and over again. My cousin loved it and told me all kinds of stories about the songs and the band, and about why the singer's voice was as strange as it was. Gradually, I got to know the songs and learned to like them a little bit as well. Finally, after returning from our trip and listening to the *Pack Up the Plantation* for six hours in total, I had no choice but to walk to the record store and buy my own copy. And then every time I got some money to spare, I went to the record store and, one by one, bought each LP they had made, and I loved them all.

I Won't Back Down

And I wasn't alone,. even though Tom Petty wasn't really popular in Europe at the time. In Finland where I lived, pretty much no one knew about him before 1989, when the *Full Moon Fever* solo album finally started receiving radio play even there. In the US, however, he was a star. Still, he apparently had managed to retain some of his regular-guy style, and he was often characterized as "one of us," someone easy to relate to.

One reason for this was that he had received a lot of publicity from two legal battles against his record company and actually managed to force the corporation to withdraw their original demands. While the first battle concerned their contract, the second one was about record prices, which was something every music lover would have been hit by in their hearts and their wallets. The case got a lot of media attention and Petty gained a reputation for defending the guys on the street through his "one man's war against high record prices," as *Rolling Stone* described it.

In this narrative, Petty was seen as something like Robin Hood, taking from the rich corporate giants and giving to the poor. This line of thinking was fueled further by Petty's constant refusal to allow the use of his music in TV commercials and the stories of Petty forbidding concert promoters to sell exclusive ticket packages, even going so far as to personally move the fancy VIP tables aside from the front of the stage. In interviews, Petty himself has denied such interpretations of his actions as altruistic. According to him, there are no nobles amongst the thieves in the music business.

It is not easy to say how his actions should be interpreted, but this is the question I'm asking here. Someone might suggest a cynical interpretation according to which Petty's motives were ultimately selfish: In the record deal case he was just trying to get more money instead of their original "penny per record" deal, and in the price increase case he was worried about whether the extra dollar charged would have a chilling effect on record sales. There is a third alternative, which I think is more likely than either of the others.

My hypothesis is that instead of a lonely hero acting alone, he should be seen as a group member acting together with others for the benefit of his group. This kind of action is neither narrowly self-interested (aiming at my own benefit) nor altruistic (aiming at your benefit), but something that in the literature has been called "we-mode" action (aiming at our benefit). The relevant group that Petty has identified with may have varied across time, but it seems to have included his bandmates and maybe road managers, friends, and family members, plus in some cases also fans or even music lovers and music creators more generally. He seems to have been a person who cared more about maintenance of his artistic integrity than maximization of profit, and he identified with others who shared his appreciation of rock'n'roll music.

The Talk on the Street Says You Might Go Solo

How can we decide whether Petty's actions were individual actions or whether they were parts of joint actions or group actions? Just as individual human beings are agents who can act intentionally, sometimes groups of individuals can be intentional agents, too. One rather common way of thinking about agency in an abstract fashion is to say that an agent is something that has both beliefs and desires, and is somehow capable of figuring out what to do in order to satisfy its desires based on its beliefs. If I have a craving for beer (desire) and a vague recollection that there's still one bottle in the fridge (belief) I may be able to do what philosophers call practical reasoning and conclude that I'll have to get my butt off the couch and over to the fridge.

Some groups, for instance many companies, satisfy such conditions of agency as well as individuals. It's a common practice to say things like "MCA wants to find new acts" or "Time Warner believes the music industry will rebound," and we can easily understand what these kinds of claims mean. Companies like MCA and Time Warner have decision-making mechanisms that, on the basis of individual agents working within these companies, create these kinds of goals and beliefs that can be attributed to the company itself. Some MCA manager may be authorized by company execs to find new acts, and the Warner directors may agree on what they think is going on in the music industry.

In addition to having beliefs, desires, and a decision-making mechanism, agents also need a way of initiating actions. In the individual example of me and my beer, perhaps I just don't have enough agency to get my butt off the couch—but I have trained my dog to fetch me things from the fridge. In the case of group agents, this usually happens via individual agents, like those who work for the company and are authorized to act on its behalf. So something like this is going on when corporations act, as in when MCA sued Petty. There were managers and lawyers and assistants who were all doing their parts in pursuing the company's objectives.

But a group of people need not be part of a corporation in order to become a group agent. Family members may agree on family goals and beliefs, and form a group agent that acts on the basis of its goals and beliefs. Some rock bands may also count as group agents. Certainly one such rock band is Tom Petty and the Heartbreakers. Unlike many other bands, this one was not democratic: the other members gave their opinions, but Petty would have the last word as bandleader. So the decision-making procedure may have been dictatorial, but Petty himself was something like a benevolent dictator, taking into account the good of the whole group.

This was made easier by the fact that the band members shared many of the same ideas and values, like a taste for good music and the aim of maintaining musical integrity. These can be seen as beliefs and desires of Tom Petty and the Heartbreakers as a band, not just of Tom Petty as an individual. After their stint backing Bob Dylan in the Eighties, Dylan was so impressed by their unity that he remarked on how working with the Heartbreakers was like talking to just one person.

Rockin' Around (with You)

Philosophical theories of social action can help us to see whether Petty's actions should be analyzed as individual action or as participation in joint or group action. Michael Bratman's theory, in his 2014 book *Shared Agency,* states conditions for joint or shared action: the members have to have suitable intentions for the group to perform certain actions according to a plan, suitable beliefs about the action opportunities, interdependence of the members' intentions, common knowledge that the above conditions hold, and mutual responsiveness in actions.

The we-mode theory of Raimo Tuomela, presented in his 2013 book *Social Ontology,* poses even more demanding conditions, the satisfaction of which would make a strong case for questioning that Petty was acting alone for personal reasons and seeing him instead acting as a group member motivated by the group's interest. Tuomela distinguishes two ways of acting in social situations: the I-mode and the we-mode.

When people act in the I-mode, they typically are motivated by their own interests. This doesn't mean they are selfish, because their interests might be about other people's well-being, even exclusively. However, it means that they're acting their personal reasons, whatever those reasons may be and for whoever's benefit they are concerned with. That they are personal means only that they are the agent's own reasons that she considers valuable and for which she acts. When people act in the we-mode, by contrast, they act for group reasons. This means that they belong to a group that has, in one way or another, decided that these are reasons for which "we" should act, the subject "we" here referring to themselves.

For instance, when the Heartbreakers decide what to put on a set list for the next tour, they may first act as individuals (or in the I-mode), each suggesting songs they would personally prefer to play. In the course of discussion, they may take into account others' preferences to an increasing extent and are ready to make compromises and suggest songs that they all like personally and that they think others would like as well. In this phase, they are still acting as individuals but they are also motivated by the concerns of the whole group (this is called pro-group I-mode). Once they reach an agreement and make a decision to put certain songs on the set list for the tour, the group goal is in place, and they can start planning for the tour as group members.

They may still act individually, for instance, each packing their different instruments but they all share a goal and they act for the same reason, namely their goal to play concerts on the tour with the agreed upon set list. Such acting for a group reason is a central mark of acting in the we-mode, and thus as a proper group member in Tuomela's theory.

Another important thing about acting in the we-mode is that the group members are collectively committed to the goal. This means that because they have collectively accepted it as their goal, it binds them all and, moreover, they are not just individually committed to it, but each is committed to everyone else to do their part in pursuing the goal. No one can on their own legitimately change their mind about the set list plans. If someone wants to reconsider the order of songs or a surprise rarity, the band must meet and discuss, and possibly change the plan together.

A final condition for acting in the we-mode is so called collectivity condition, according to which the goal that they are aiming at can only be satisfied for all the members simultaneously. If the goal is to play the set list together at a particular concert then either this goal is satisfied for all of them or it is not satisfied for any of them. If for some reason one band member fails to join the others on stage for the show, then the original goal is not satisfied even for those who manage to spend the concert with the rest of the band members. After all, the original goal was to play the set list together as a band, and this cannot happen unless every band member gets on stage. The rest of the band can make a new decision and a new commitment to spend the concert on that same stage in spite of one band member missing—a problem they might've had to consider during the worst of Howie Epstein's heroin addiction—but this is a new goal and a different commitment from the original one that couldn't be satisfied.

We the Group

My point is to find room for an interpretation according to which Petty was not acting as a solitary individual but as a group member: It was not Tom Petty who fought the record companies, it was Tom Petty and the Heartbreakers, or perhaps even some larger group. Evidence for the idea that the whole group was involved in the actions, shared Petty's goals and was committed to them may be found in some of the interviews and biographical writings from the time of these events. My aim here is not to prove that this was actually the case. Philosophy aims to explore the space of possibilities, and my modest goal is to argue that the idea would be consistent with what we know about those cases, and perhaps not completely implausible.

In the interviews, Petty very often speaks in I-terms, saying what he personally was thinking and doing during the record company entanglements. However, on some occasions when he talks of these legal battles, he switches to we-talk. It's not always easy to say who exactly was the "we" Petty talks about during these events. The process involved not only Petty but the whole band. Even though Petty, as the bandleader and songwriter, was the central figure, the other band members must have been concerned and participated in various ways in the process. However, the band's role has probably been much stronger in the musical and creative aspects of Petty's life than in the courtroom situations.

In fact, there were severe problems within the band around the times of production of the *Damn the Torpedoes* album and the members weren't that much involved in the legal battles. Apparently, bass player Ron Blair spent a lot of time at the beach and keyboard player Benmont Tench spent quite a bit of time in the bar. Guitarist Mike Campbell went through a mental breakdown and drummer Stan Lynch had to take a lot of heat from producer Jimmy Iovine and engineer Shelly Yakus during those recording sessions. The conflicts and general frustration eventually and repeatedly led to Lynch being fired and replaced by session drummers, but he would later be re-hired.

That doesn't necessarily mean that the band wasn't united against the record company, at least in spirit. Just as family members may have occasional fights among themselves, an external threat tends to bring them together. Moreover, according to theories of collective action, it's possible for actions of individuals to count as actions of a group agent even in the absence of participation of other group members. A group can be dictatorial, and in limiting cases it may be the case that the dictator is the sole member acting for the group. Petty may have been in the position of a dictator deciding on the group's goals, but he has also insisted on group solidarity, a feature that Tuomela captures in his collectivity condition. For example, Petty occasionally defended Lynch from Iovine, who kept pushing for his firing, by saying that this is a band and bands are not in the business of firing people.

Even if the band may not have been actively involved in the legal battles, Petty was not acting alone. Of course there were hired lawyers who assisted him, but there were also other people working for and with the band who made important contributions well beyond their duties just because they cared so much. Iovine was very concerned with whether the record would ever come out due to the legal issues, so he and Petty conferenced by phone pretty much every night for a year in order to keep steering its course to proper completion.

Managers Tony Dimitriades and Elliot Roberts also supported Petty and the band in various ways. The latter even paid all the legal bills and came up with the plan that ultimately proved successful, wherein Petty filed for bankruptcy in order to void the contract with the record company. Assistant Mary Klauzer meanwhile kept the trains running on time and had a large role in organizing various practical matters in Petty's life. Alan "Bugs" Weidel, the band's road manager who was probably closest to Petty at the time, sometimes even accompanied him in the legal meetings. Weidel would also drive around California with the master tapes in the car so that Petty was able to truthfully say in court that he did not know where the tapes were located.

Such collaborative and interdependent participation in the execution of a shared plan is typical of joint action. Other necessary conditions of joint or shared action—regarding intentions, beliefs, mutual responsiveness, and interdependence of action—also seem to be in place. Even the stronger conditions of we-mode action mentioned above appear to be satisfied: the actions seem to have been done for group reasons with collective commitment in order to satisfy a collective goal.

Fooled Again (I Don't Like It)

In the second legal battle, Petty objected to the record company's plan to raise the price of their highly anticipated album *Hard Promises* by one dollar to $9.98, contrary to what the company had originally told the band. Here Petty seems to have identified with his fans and music lovers in general. In interviews, he explained that he was motivated to keep album prices low so that regular people could continue to afford to collect them. He felt the band didn't need the extra dollar and didn't want his fans to have to cough it up.

Petty threatened to put the originally planned price in the title of the album if the company were to follow their new plan, and even appeared in the cover of *Rolling Stone* tearing a dollar bill in half. Here again he did get support from people closest to him, but there was some grain of truth in this particular "one man's war" label, because Petty had expected support from other artists but was ultimately let down. Other musical acts facing the exact same price hike declined to lend their voices to Petty's revolt, even though he pitched the goal of it as being in their collective interest. Petty says it made him feel lonely. However, support eventually came from elsewhere: The reporters of *Rolling Stone* and *Musician* proposed a write-in campaign which led to fans writing directly to the record company to protest the price increase, and the company then decided to back down.

This kind of a campaign may not satisfy all the suggested conditions of joint action or we-mode action, because there probably wasn't common knowledge among all the participants about everyone's participation or collective commitment in the strictest sense. However, it clearly is a case of collective endeavor for a shared goal. Moreover, Petty seems to have identified with this group of music lovers and acted for group-based reasons—not for selfish or altruistic reasons, but for fairness and common good.

As he explained much later, even the corporation's interests were a consideration. Instead of trying to harm his own label, he was rather just objecting to its greed and short-sightedness. With hindsight, years later as music downloads began to over-take physical album sales, he attributed the crumbling of the old business model to that original failure to heed his warning about overpricing some two decades earlier. If albums still cost ten bucks, downloads would make less sense to broke fans. Petty didn't attribute his fight to noble motives, but to the long game of more effective sales strategy.

Reading Petty's interviews and biographies seems to pro-vide textual evidence suggesting that his actions have often been driven by group-based reasons, rather than by mere per-sonal reasons, and motivated by interests of a number of peo-ple including his band, the record buyers, or music lovers more generally. In addition, the actions themselves often involved other people like family members, band members, and friends who frequently figured as important supporters or even collab-orators sharing the same goal with Petty. Such cases make Petty's actions seem like contributions to joint actions, rather than individual actions as they have traditionally been pre-sented in the image of Petty created by the popular media.

Make It Better for You, and Me

Very few of us are pure "I-moders" who only act as self-inter-ested individuals. We all care about and have to deal with other people, we all belong to various groups, and most of as act as group members for large parts of our lives. In some contexts we act as family members, in others as employees, in yet others as citizens, and so on, and we are motivated by the well-being of those who we take to be part of our group. It's just that for some people the "we" includes themselves and possibly a few other people, while for other people the "we" is much more inclusive, even universal.

The difference between Tom Petty and the corporate guy is not in the type of intentionality or the type of action they are engaged in. They both act, sometimes individually and some-times jointly, for the good of themselves and the ones they care about or have to care about for the role they play at the time. Petty's court cases need not be seen as battles of an individual versus a corporation; they can be seen as battles between two group agents.

Where is the difference between Tom Petty and the corporate guy then? I learned to appreciate the difference gradually, like I learned to love Tom Petty's music after having been closed into a car for several hours with the music of Tom Petty and the Heartbreakers—a method I've used on my younger brother, my friends, and eventually my kids, with great success ever since.

The difference is in the size of the "we" they care about and act for. Everyone wants to pursue what is valuable for themselves and for the ones they care about. For some people the "we" is themselves, their family, or their company, and what they think is valuable is fame or money. For others—and Tom Petty was likely one of these—valuable things are the quality of the music they create and the joy and relief it can bring to people. For these people, the "we" includes anyone who loves rock'n'roll.

PART V

How to Rebel

14
Anything that's Spiked Is Fine

MEGAN VOLPERT

"Anything that's Rock'n'Roll" launched Tom Petty's career. It was the Heartbreakers' first hit single in the United Kingdom and the band did not become well known in the United States until almost a year after they enjoyed tremendous popular support and critical praise abroad.

This little two-and-a-half-minute, three-chord wonder ought to hold a special place in the heart of all Heartbreakers fans for lyrical reasons besides. As the final song on Side One of the original vinyl, this song is holding down the classic anthemic slot with a broad appeal to our desire for rebellions.

An exhaustive list of the things Petty sings that he is against on "Anything that's Rock'n'Roll": going to bed, going to work, going to school, bosses, parents, and rules. The only thing he favors? Rocking out with his friends to loud electric guitars on the radio until sunrise, which he characterizes as living free. Anything that rocks is fine. It's his highest good, but in this song's valuation, he lists it as merely fine. As long as the form—the sound of it—rocks. He invites some friends and his girlfriend to join him in the aural experience of rebellion. It's even possible that they could hip his girlfriend's mama to it, though she dislikes how they run around together.

Listening to rock music is often a group activity. So is playing it in a band. But riddle me this: You ever see two people trying to play one electric guitar? A few awkwardly punk or iconically hypersexualized stage stunts aside, me neither. It doesn't make sense, in the same way the excess of Cheap Trick's one and only Rick Nielsen playing his five-necked Hamer electric makes no sense. The ratio is fundamentally dumb when it comes to the technical rock action and only visually interesting for a hot minute. One to one is the correct thing here. To each her or his own guitar—at its root, it's a solo endeavor.

Where then is the rebellion located in "Anything that's Rock'n'Roll"? Is it in the individual guitarist making that music or in the group who is listening to it? Seems like we could just say it's both. We could call it a matter of chickens and eggs, sure, but let's consider it for fifteen more minutes instead because ultimately we should want to get at its implications for a rebellion's effectiveness. In our daily lives, we want to be the rebels who succeed.

Does Size Matter?

For a rebel, the opposite of success is not failure, but co-option. This is according to political theorists Michael Hardt and Antonio Negri in *Empire,* their well-known book that perhaps could be subtitled "How to Succeed in Revolution without Really Trying."

This book is frequently cited as a *Communist Manifesto* for the twenty-first century. It's concerned with how class systems consolidate against individuals to oppress them and how these individuals might best undermine such oppression. Negri served thirteen years in an Italian prison for his affiliation with a leftist guerrilla group that may have kidnapped and murdered some important government officials. You just don't find philosophers with those kinds of *bonafides* anymore.

In the music business, they refer to co-option as selling out. Musicians who fail just drop away, off their labels and out of sight, whereas musicians who sell out have chained their creativity to their marketability. Petty's work often depicted the temptation to sell out and its moral bankruptcy, most notably on *The Last DJ* album. Naturally, the album tanked because the industry tanked it—why would a business promote a message so highly critical of business interests? What could one man or one band do against that system? The deck is so stacked in favor of the financial investment that it's enough to make you want to escape back to mama.

The Last DJ came out in 2002, almost three decades into the Heartbreakers' *oeuvre*, when they had amassed plenty of power and had the privilege of complaining about their position. They were living the dream of "Anything that's Rock'n'Roll" by picking up the phone to call out the boss. But back in 1979, working on *Damn the Torpedoes* amidst the MCA contract dispute, they weren't sure whether they were stepping into big trouble for those same sentiments. Four out of that album's ten songs ultimately charted and "Century City" sure wasn't one of them.

"Century City" was Petty's first genuine stab at openly criticizing the music industry in a song. A glossy, up-tempo number whose lyrics go heavy on the repetition, it is sung in the voice of corporate music lawyers. Century City is the downtown Los Angeles business district where the band had to go to resolve their MCA contract, pushing paperwork and holding hearings among the skyscrapers. Petty sings each line from high in his nose, in the sneering tone that fans will come to recognize as his trademark way of pillorying authority figures (see also "Strangered in the Night," "Nightwatchman," "Something Big," "God's Gift to Man," and his cover of the Byrds' "So You Want to Be a Rock'n'Roll Star").

In undergoing co-option, a musician takes on the voice of the record company by pumping out their idea of monkey-making hits. When Petty takes on the voice of his record company's lawyers in "Century City," or any authority figure in any of these songs, he is making rebellious use of satire. He makes puppets of their voices through exaggerated imitation of their worst characteristics, showing he is criticizing their position, rather than acquiesce to making his voice into a puppet of their investments by ditching songs like "Century City" in favor of mass-producing more hits. The lawyer voice in his song purports to have everything covered, yet the desire to run back home sometimes still pokes through, even as the lawyer ominously warns the worried musician off of doing just that.

The mom and dad of "Anything that's Rock'n'Roll" offer a rather small villainy by comparison. Three years later, by the time he's writing "Century City," Petty is ready to acknowledge that those early teenage problems were so tame he actually misses them. He'd love to deploy the authority of some parental units against the giant fangs of the music business, but as the executive who constantly demeans him by calling him baby and honey makes plain, mama can't do anything to take down a system so big. The musician is led to expect that discouragement will be a recurring phase, so the musician should just accept cooption and not look for reasons as to how it happens. Modern musicians simply must live in the modern world, a euphemism for creative contracts in the corporate environment.

"Century City" slides back and forth between singular and plural pronouns just like "Anything that's Rock'n'Roll." In general, the angst is singularly belonging to an "I" while its action is owned by "we," whether that group is rebellious teenagers listening to the radio or a corporate legal team and the musicians who have sold out to it. Does this seem right? Do rebels need to travel in packs because their would-be oppressors do? When it comes to the success of a rebellion, does the number of rebels matter?

Obligatory Naziism Example

A rebellion should be tailored to the nature of its target. In referring to oppressive systems, should we use singular or plural pronouns? There is no basis for categorizing oppression as only the work of groups or only the work individuals. On the one hand you have the Nazi Party and on the other hand you have Adolf Eichmann (1906–1962), who oversaw the logistics of the Holocaust. Oppressors can be groups or individuals. This is one (not very debatable) conclusion reached by Hannah Arendt (1906–1975). She was a philosopher who left Nazi Germany in 1933, after being imprisoned by the Gestapo, and subsequently thought a lot about differing types of institutionalized, systemic oppression. Her body of work is often considered one of the most important contributions to twentieth-century political theory. Arendt lived to see her work amply torn apart, usually for evaluating the Holocaust too coldly.

In 1951, Arendt published *The Origins of Totalitarianism*, in which she identified Nazi ideology as the source of a new form of government tyranny. A totalitarian state rules through the proliferation of its propaganda, which the citizens come to actively embrace because of the gas chamber of terrors that awaits them if they do not. In a totalitarian political system, there is no freedom and plenty of force. What does totalitarianism look like in a corporate system? Perhaps we can characterize the music industry as totalitarian because it pushes a single goal—profitability of songs. It constantly imposes its will on all aspects of a band's production, and the musicians are expected to obey these directives, lest their contract be terminated.

But Tom Petty had this pesky notion that his individual creativity was the wellspring from which any profits ultimately derived, so therefore he could threaten to turn his artistic spigot off instead of playing 'fraidy-cat. Like Hardt and Negri, he had that different idea about who could do the strangling, since he was the true owner of the means of *his* production. Petty's uneasy alliance with the shady forces that helped his work find a wide audience shows that he considered the music business authoritarian, not totalitarian. Arendt defined authoritarian systems as those allowing some sense of freedom as long as the fundamental power at the top goes unchallenged. Music corporations conform to a model of authoritarianism because they purport to let the artist develop freely flowing waves of creativity, even though ultimately any artistry is all paddling around in the prospect of being able to sell out for more cash. One man's killer half-pipe is another man's tsunami.

This temptation to sell out is not offered by a lone dictator who makes the big wheels roll, but by a whole hierarchical cabal of enforcers—from the A&R man who says "son, I don't hear a single" to the lawyers in Century City. Arendt thought that collective resistance could put a dent in totalitarian regimes run by one CEO Joe. But is this group process a similarly rebellious antidote to authoritarianism, in light of the fact that authoritarians themselves run in packs?

In some limited sense, all groups are authoritarian. Even among the Heartbreakers, the creative contributions of individual members were given with the general understanding that Petty, as bandleader, always got the final say. It's uncomfortable. Whenever conflicts flared up between the band and its corporate keepers, as leader, Petty held the front line as a matter of course. But then he was also the gatekeeper of their creativity.

Arendt's most famous turn of phrase is "the banality of evil," which she coined in 1961 during her coverage of Adolf Eichmann's trial in Jerusalem. She meant basically that this particular Nazi was no great mastermind and not especially cruel. Instead, she said he was a rather ordinary bureaucrat who thought of his crimes as just doing his job. She characterized him as vapid, dull, and tame. A lot of folks took justifiable umbrage with this characterization, which I only mention to try to get at some reflection on whether banal evil has an opposite. Is there such a thing as the banality of an individual's rebellion?

Sex and Death in Baton Rouge

Here we must make a brief detour so that I can charm you with a shocking thing I did in graduate school at Louisiana State many moons ago. I wore a spiked dog collar every day for about two years. Just picture me: shaking hands with faculty, moderating panel discussions, teaching classes of undergrads, and generally aiming to be full-blown scholarly and serious while wearing this profound visual disturbance. The leather strap was an inch wide and had one-inch stainless steel spikes going around the whole way, with the buckle resting on the back on my neck.

Not sure what possessed me to do it, but it was a great social experiment. Sometimes it delivered me into the hands of surprises both good and bad; a lot of days it amused me at least a little, but just as often I could go all day without really thinking about it. Is this a potential starting point for identifying the banality of rebellion? My unscientific study basically concluded that ninety percent of people will not mess with you when you have a spiked dog collar on. The other ten percent are people you do not yourself want to mess with, trust me. This experiment actually took place well before I ever noticed Petty's excellent *Southern Accents* b-side, "Spike," an underrated gem to which we will now turn emphatically detailed attention.

The Strife of Spike on Daily Strike

Spike is likely the most successfully rebellious character Petty ever created—although since "Spike" is based on a real person, perhaps it's fairer to say that Petty's imaginative interpretation of Spike's life indicates that he viewed Spike as an individualist role model. The plot is simple: a punk wearing a spiked dog collar walks into a bar where he is then confronted by a dumb redneck. In interviews, Petty himself referred to these characters as punk and redneck, so if either of those loaded words stirs a bee in your bonnet, you'd have to take it up with the man himself; I'm just reporting here.

The lyrics for "Spike" are comprised of the various threatening and pontificatory inquiries made by the redneck, who has been shaken up by the mere existence of the punk within the space of the dive bar. Though it's no longer called the Cypress Lounge, you can still find the pool table and the almost comically darkened scene inside Munegin's On 13th, predictably located on 13th Street in Gainesville. No jukebox though.

The original 1986 studio recording of "Spike" is only about three and a half minutes, but in live performance the runtime consistently doubles and even sometimes comes close to touching eight minutes. The two most widely circulated live recordings were also made in 1986 shortly after *Southern Accents* came out, in Portland in July (available on 2006's *The Live Anthology*) and at Farm Aid in September (available on 2015's *Transmission Impossible*). It's not a jam-based song; the extra time is exclusively due to Petty giving a lengthy introduction before the first verse and another equally long interruption toward the end.

The nameless redneck talks to Spike and also about him with other regulars at the bar. Spike does not seem to be a regular and he never utters a word in reply other than the exceptionally banal and somewhat sweet "doo doo, dee dee, dee dee." That's the oral equivalent of thumb-twiddling, is it not? Petty assumes the voice of the redneck for the entire song, delivering the talky lines with a cartoonishly amped up Floridian accent as another satirical act of musical puppetry. The longer the redneck's queries are met with silence while Spike just bobs along on the current of the redneck's animosity and confusion, the more freaked out and broken down the redneck becomes. He has numerous points of reference for this encounter with Spike, derogatorily listing him as another: badass, troublemaker, misfit, Jimmy Dean, and likely motorbike driver. Those are all species of rebels that he has met with in this bar before.

The redneck is not necessarily characterized as a biker, but listeners do easily get the feeling that the character is a pack animal. Most of his lines are not said to Spike, but are instead loud, one-sided conversations with his friends meant to needle at Spike while he is within earshot. With many plural pronouns, the redneck makes clear that the bar is full of his own people, that he has a posse assembled to discreetly threaten

Spike by sheer force of numbers. He refers to his friends as boys, calling Spike a man in order to undercut him by distinction, to indicate that wearing a dog collar does not in fact make Spike a man. The redneck perceives that Spike is elitist, assumes that the collar makes him feel superior to the regulars. This is a projection of the redneck's own feeling of inferiority with regard to Spike—said every psychotherapist ever.

He also speculates that Spike is mad about the future, ominously offering some kind of help to show Spike that the future is not what it used to be. This is where things start to go off the rails for the redneck, who has perhaps begun to cogitate on why the future is not what he himself had expected. He then turns his words directly to Spike for the refrain, inching closer to confrontation: "Hey Spike, what do you like?" This is a commonly heard question in any bar.

Spike Wins without Bite or Bark

So, would you let this dude buy you a drink? Is the redneck the bartender who owns the joint, taking Spike's order? Is he about to start a fight? Or is he asking in the broadest possible way for Spike to volunteer the name of any thing that he is not mad about? What in the world can gratify Spike? Spike still doesn't answer. In the live performances, Petty shouts the redneck's own response to this question: Nothing! The redneck thinks the punk will never be satisfied, that he will be critical of everything.

Spike must be a rebellious army of one. He's a guerrilla on their turf. The redneck jokes around that his wife is afraid of people like Spike, but sliding around under that is the acknowledgment that the redneck himself is thrown off by Spike's silent, solo form of steadfast resistance. The studio recording concludes with the redneck pleading for Spike to tell him about life. Again, it's meant to be a ribbing on the literal level, but underneath, the redneck clearly sees that Spike has figured out something he hasn't. How will Spike respond to this philosophical inquiry? The studio recording leaves it hanging there with nothing more than the vague feeling that Spike is far from joyless.

In live performance, Petty improvised the redneck's second wind. In an attempt at empathy, the redneck begins to imagine himself wearing Spike's collar. He thinks one might see the world anew with the collar on, might turn into a brand new man or at least a more toughened guy. Or he might be demeaned into a dog. Petty's bow-wow howling during this portion of the redneck's monologue was generally understood by his audience as a call and response activity. His wailing is answered by the wailing of the crowd. What is everybody bow-wowing about? They join the redneck in his expression of existential angst.

The redneck is easy. We all know that guy. But Spike's pretty opaque to us; he doesn't seem to display any angst, even in a dive bar situation with strong potential to turn out scary. At concerts, Petty always delivered a happy ending for Spike. He slides off his bar stool with ease, marches straight into the sunlight outside, and hitchhikes away down Interstate 75. His first, last, and only words: "Doo doo, dee dee, dee dee."

All we ever get to truly know about him is this meaningless little ditty and the spiked dog collar—and the impact he made on a group of alleged tough guys he once encountered. Is Spike fighting for something? Is he rebelling against anything? The simple assertion of his existence is enough to set a gang of rednecks on edge. Up until Spike walked in to silently challenge them, these guys likely thought of themselves as quite the rebels. But they've still got a pack mentality.

Their jabs at Spike resemble a form of hazing. Imagine a parallel universe where Spike does open up to them in whatever fashion and then ends up being accepted among these grizzled regulars as one of their own. It's totally plausible and perhaps even a kind of happy ending for all concerned, but he's Petty's character. Spike persists in exuding a sense of individualism that causes the group to angle for his further ostracism as a sort of defense against their assumption that he has already rejected them first. Okay, rednecks, Dr. Freud will see you now.

You get the sense that this kind of thing happens to Spike a lot. He just goes about his day-to-day business, often running into jackasses on high horses who, for whatever reason, perceive his horse to be higher than theirs. But he just kind of lets it roll off of him, strolling purposefully out of these antagonistic scenes without any hint that they've broken through to hurt him. The redneck's group process leaves Spike undefeated.

They have tried to oppress him and yet he remains buoyant. Petty thinks of Spike as a heroic figure, as the winner that day and probably on most days.

Cool Against Co-option

So Spike is the ultimate cool, right? Coolness means many things to many people, but let me direct you to the banal, canonical example of Bartleby. Like Spike, he was hip enough to go by one name only. Bartleby was a scrivener, which is just a fancy way of saying he clerked for some finance guys. He was the main character in a good little short story, "Bartleby, the Scrivener: A Story of Wall Street," written by Herman Melville (1819–1891). Melville is best known for a super long and boring book about a pissed off captain who hunts for the whale that took his leg. In *Moby Dick*, Captain Ahab is your classic hot-tempered bro who would prefer to hold a grudge so tightly it (spoiler alert?) kills him, rather than sit at the dock lobbing wooden leg jokes while tossing back some pints with his crew.

Bartleby doesn't have a sense of humor either, but he remains calm for fully one hundred percent of the time. The Wall Street lawyer guys ask him to do all kinds of tasks and at first he does really good work. But then he does no work whatsoever, and when they ask him to do even the simplest things, he just keeps repeating that he would prefer not to do those things. No reason given; now that's *cajones*. So Bartleby is just there, in their space, freaking out these brokers who had no doubt fancied themselves a very clever pack of wolves up until that point. At first they talk tough to him, but as outrage settles on them and the fog of confusion persists, they make some honest efforts to understand him. The rest of Bartleby's story diverges from Spike's, but you see the type of individualist vibe I'm after.

Is it on the same wavelength as James Dean? The rednecks throw the name of this dead movie star at Spike mainly as a way of calling him a poser, a way of assuming a kid in a dog collar cannot reach the awesome levels of defiance attained in *Rebel Without a Cause*. Dean's movie and Melville's story both end happily to the extent that any parental and financial oppressors in them do receive a shock to their system. (See also: *Cool Hand Luke*, which in my not terribly humble opinion is a much better piece of both cinema and argument than *Rebel Without A Cause*, but I digress.) Dean, Bartleby, and Spike hover on the periphery of the system. They won't do as they're told, but they're not going to get all up in your face about it either. These plots each hinge their drama on the same simple fact: coolness is an often surprisingly successful strategy for putting authoritarians on tilt.

How to Be Cool

First of all, it's super uncool to ask me that—but I will tell you because you've purchased this book. Just stay chill and occasionally insert yourself among powerful crews who assume their system can remain unchecked. You don't have to go looking for trouble if you're cool, because it'll find you pretty easily. You'll naturally stick out a bit, spiked dog collar or not. As long as an individual is not imposing her or his viewpoint upon others in a totalitarian manner, then everything the individual does constitutes rebelliousness, whereas everything a group does constitutes authoritarianism. That's how norms are made. So individuals can rebel against authoritarianism, but groups—as systems whose formations always melt down into authoritarianism—inherently cannot. Spike is cool, and groups never truly are.

It's pretty hard to stay cool. Jimmy Dean died trying and so did Bartleby. Who knows what happened to the real-life Spike? He probably found other means of making his point and eventually laid the dog collar to rest, same as me. Is that selling out? It's the responsibility of any elder statesmen among rebels to suffer the accusations of co-option. Is this not the battle that Tom Petty always fought? An aging rebel walks a fine line on the hot seduction of selling out through the strategic deployment of coolness, which is precisely that same permissiveness found in the sentiment of "Anything that's Rock'n'Roll."

But the kids themselves are not quite capable of feeling anything is fine. They have such totalitarian impulses to police each other, it's like infighting among band members. Individual resistance is best. It stocks the world full of rebels. Let's not try to get together for a rebellion because systems inevitably suck, whether they're a well-oiled MCA Records machine or merely some stupid gaggle of locals in a dive bar. Just go get yourself a guitar—none of those double-neck monstrosities—and learn how to play three-chord "doo doo, dee dee, dee dee" ditties. Might seem low key, but that'll keep you plenty cool. It worked for Tom Petty for forty years.

15
Clueless Rebels

Eric v.d. Luft

"Rebels," the first song on Tom Petty's 1985 album, *Southern Accents*, expresses the regional pride of a native-born Southerner. He obviously felt this pride deeply. In the 1980s he used a huge Confederate battle flag in his shows as an emblem of his regional pride. As soon as he realized that it was also a racist symbol, he stopped using it and apologized. But what really made him do that?

The Ethical Rock Star

Ethical rock stars are rare. Like most people, most rock stars are happy just to take whatever they can get, do whatever they want, and have as much as fun as they can along the way, without much thought to anyone else outside their own family and close friends. Those with a social conscience are rare.

The first inkling we had that Petty was one of this rare breed was in 1981 when he launched a crusade against greedy promoters, distributors, and record companies. The July 1981 cover story of *Rolling Stone* told of his principled fight against their gouging of music lovers and other customers. Other popular musicians would gladly ignore the price increase and pocket the difference.

Thereafter Petty had the well-deserved reputation of being an unusually ethical, fair-minded, and socially conscious artist. Even during those brief periods in the classic rock era when the overt display of such traits was considered good for a star's career, he seemed more sincere than most about doing the right thing, along with George Harrison, Bruce Springsteen, and very few others.

Humans have no greater calling than to work toward making this world a better place when they leave it than it was when they entered it. Petty took this calling seriously and met its challenge, through solid introspection, sympathetic encounters, and ethical action, all of which came out in his words, his music, and his life.

Who Were Those Blue-Bellied Devils?

In "Rebels," Petty sang of his character's ongoing outrage at the "blue-bellied devils," the invading Union soldiers in the American Civil War, 120 years after the fact. But Petty hardly invented this phrase himself. It was in common usage throughout the South both during the Civil War and in the decades immediately afterward, not only among Southern whites, but also among brainwashed Southern blacks who had acquiesced to slavery.

In their 1883 account, *The Blue and the Gray*, Theodore Gerrish and John S. Hutchinson report an incident that happened near Fort Monroe, Virginia: A black slave yelled at the Union soldiers who had just fired in his direction. He said, "Quit your foolishness, you blue bellied devils." Petty's use of this epithet in "Rebels" is not only an obvious reference to the Civil War, but also, and more significantly, an expression of continuing regional pride.

A Question of Justice

Justice is one of Plato's Four Cardinal Virtues, along with courage, temperance, and wisdom. Combined with the Three Christian Graces—faith, hope, and charity—they make the Seven Cardinal Virtues. These are the antidote to the Seven Deadly Sins: greed, wrath, lechery, sloth, envy, gluttony, and pride.

Plato says in the *Republic* that justice is giving us all what we each deserve, doing no harm, and minding our own business. Aristotle says in the *Nicomachean Ethics* that justice is the greatest virtue, that the best people are those who provide justice to others as well as to themselves, and that therefore justice is whatever serves the common good and creates friendship.

A key source of information about Tom Petty's sense of justice is his July 2015 interview with Andy Greene of *Rolling Stone*. Besides Petty's commitment to justice, this interview also provides insight into his fight against greed. It shows his courage in admitting his mistakes and in seeking to do the right thing in every circumstance.

Petty's further awakening of his already well-developed sense of justice is what moved him to repudiate his use of the Confederate flag. He told Greene that he had doubts about the flag almost immediately in 1985. It was sending and validating the wrong message, and attracting people to his shows for the wrong reasons. Thus he explicitly rejected it in 1987. By then, he had clearly shown that he was always open to new ideas, not afraid to change, and not ashamed to admit when he was wrong. From 1981 until his death in 2017, he revealed himself over and over again as a lover of justice, willing to learn about it, to implement it, to fight for it, and to put self-interest behind it.

In the interview with Greene, Petty called his use of the Confederate flag "downright stupid." He explained that "Rebels" created a character, rather than expressed his own point of view. This character was raised with certain Southern traditions and still blames the North for his family's discomfort, and the flag was only meant to illustrate this point. Petty reported to Greene that back in 1987, he was telling audiences this flag display was on behalf of the persona in the song, not a reflection of Petty's own values. He frowned upon audiences bringing Confederate imagery to his shows.

Are We Worth Defending?

Our kneejerk reaction when attacked is to defend ourselves, our homes, our families, our way of life. We do this without thinking, and usually self-defense is easy to justify if we're questioned about it later. If we kill a burglar in our home and can prove to a court that we did so in self-defense, then we're innocent. If we're camping and we kill a grizzly bear in our tent, then we're innocent, even though this bear belongs to an endangered species.

Likewise, Petty's constant conflict with the record industry, especially his positive assertion of ethical arguments against it, could be seen as innocent self-defense of his integrity. His outspokenness could have derailed his career at any time, but he seemed not to care whether it did or not. David Wild's 2002 *Rolling Stone* article, "10 Things that Piss Off Tom Petty," demonstrates that Petty was more interested in being fair than in being rich. Five of the ten things that pissed him off involve greed. The other five involve such problems as censorship, corporate conformity, misogyny, obscenity, pedophilia, propaganda, violence, lack of empathy, and loss of human values. All ten involve injustice.

However, sometimes we make mistakes. Sometimes we kill what ought not to be killed. Sometimes we defend what isn't worth defending. Sometimes we even defend what ought to be attacked and destroyed. How can we determine what is and what isn't worth defending?

The answer to this question also has to do with justice. As humans, we seek to establish and preserve justice. Most times justice is served by defending ourselves when attacked, but not always. If we deserve to be attacked, then defending ourselves is wrong. But who or what decides whether we deserve to be attacked?

Before embarking on self-defense, we should consider whether ourselves are worth defending, or whether justice, or some other greater good, would be better served by our capitulation, defeat, or even death. Obviously we shouldn't let the burglar rob us or the bear eat us; but, in less obvious situations, if we have time, we should try to find out whether justice lies on our side or the other. Considering only our clear and present danger is not always good enough.

It didn't serve justice to rip Africans out of their native land, chain them in boats, fetch them into a strange land, and enslave them in the fields of Dixie. Therefore, to defend this practice was equally unjust. Yet millions of Southerners defended it with their lives in the Civil War. Why?

There was at least one prominent reason for antebellum Southerners to believe that slavery was a kind of justice. Overt racism was part and parcel of the various Protestant denominations of Southern Christianity, which were very powerful, both culturally and politically. Any number of Southern preachers in that era proclaimed biblical support for natural white mastery and natural black servitude in their sermons and tracts. A clear case in point is Reverend Josiah Priest's *Bible*

Defence of Slavery, or, the Origin, History, and Fortunes of the Negro Race, which went into several editions in the late 1840s and early 1850s. The title says it all. Southern whites believed this stuff. It was dangerous to doubt the Bible.

Self-Sacrifice for the Greater Good

Both history and fiction are full of examples of people who, for the sake of some higher goal, refuse to defend themselves. Such instances are all case-specific, so it would be difficult to formulate a general principle or maxim that would apply to all of them. Even though their reasons for self-sacrifice vary, they all have in common a high level of commitment to some ethical ideal.

Socrates refused to defend himself against capital charges of impiety, even though it was quite clear that the citizens would have preferred not to execute him. They would rather have had him confess, promise to mend his ways, and be wrist-slapped or exonerated. But Socrates freely chose to stick by his principles and make a martyr out of himself. A bit later, Crito offered him an easy and foolproof plan of escape, but Socrates refused. He remained consistent that living with honor, ethics, and righteousness is more important than merely living.

Jesus refused to defend himself, either against the Roman soldiers who arrested him in Gethsemane or against Pilate. Self-sacrifice was an integral part of his moral message. He practiced what he preached, turning the other cheek.

Or take the case of Njal Thorgeirsson, the hero of the medieval epic, *Njal's Saga*. He's sick and tired of the bloodshed in several longstanding feuds involving his family and friends. In loyalty to them, he doesn't take their side against their enemies, but tries to make peace. Frustrated by the failures of his efforts over many decades, he finally commands his three warlike sons not to defend themselves or their families when their home is attacked and surrounded. As a result of his decision, Njal and his household are burned alive. Eventually, however, his tactic works, since the lone survivor of the burning, Kari Solmundarson, and the leader of the burners, Flosi Thordarson, forgive each other, become friends, and thus end the series of feuds, sealing the deal with Kari's marriage to Flosi's niece Hildigunn.

J.K. Rowling's teenage wizard hero, Harry Potter, sacrifices himself to begin the chain of events that dooms Voldemort. In *Harry Potter and the Deathly Hallows*, Harry finally realizes that he is a Horcrux and therefore must die if Voldemort is to die. He has unraveled the mystery of the inscription "I open at the close" on the Snitch that Dumbledore gave him. Since he chooses to die in order to save others, he fearlessly welcomes death. He calmly stands and allows Voldemort to perform the Avada Kedavra killing curse on him. But Harry doesn't die completely; only the part of Voldemort's soul that was linked to Harry dies. Thus Harry is able to rise up and kill Voldemort in their last duel, since Harry is now the master, not only of himself, but also of Voldemort's wand.

Petty's song, "I Won't Back Down," praises remarkably ethical people like Socrates, Jesus, Njal, and Harry, who embody tremendous personal courage as they defy even the very gates of hell for the sake of peace, justice, integrity, or some other high ideal. The song expresses the hope that he might be one of them.

Such altruistic self-sacrificers have many things in common, but perhaps the main thing is their unshakable defense of whatever they perceive is worthy of their ultimate loyalty.

Loyalty to What?

Justice is inextricably tied up with loyalty. In his 1908 book, *The Philosophy of Loyalty*, Josiah Royce asks three important questions about human life: What is our purpose? What is our duty? What is our ideal? The answers to all three involve an understanding of loyalty. He believes that genuine loyalty is to an ideal, a cause, a universal, or an absolute—not to a person, a group, or anything finite. Justice is not only intimately related to loyalty, but also an indispensable aspect of ethics. Royce connects loyalty with the eternal values which humans express in their beliefs, ethical decisions, and everyday practical actions. Thus loyalty expresses itself as justice.

In his 1993 book, *Loyalty: An Essay on the Morality of Relationships*, George P. Fletcher also shows the close connection between loyalty and justice. Any theory of justice must include a theory of loyalty. Both loyalty and justice are necessary for coherent society, secure nations, and good government. Both show concern for others as the basis of our common human bond. Nevertheless, if loyalty is limited to a small group, a distinct entity, or a particular ideal, then it can be at odds with justice. That is, limited loyalty sets us against other groups, entities, and ideals besides our own. Justice must be universal, with no limits and no exceptions. Allowing conflicting loyalties to influence our concept of justice distorts both loyalty and justice. For example, although xenophobia and racism demand loyalty, they can never be consistent with justice.

Royce and Fletcher agree that commitment to justice is a kind of loyalty and that loyalty to a worthy cause is a kind of justice. But the value of loyalty isn't determined by the intensity of the emotion of loyalty, no matter how sincere or heartfelt that emotion might be. Rather, the value of loyalty is determined by the object of loyalty. To what are we loyal? To what ought we to be disloyal? Lukewarm loyalty to worthy causes such as liberation, fairness, or equality is better than fervent loyalty to unworthy causes such as slaveholding, ethnic cleansing, or organized crime, or to unworthy people who nevertheless commanded powerful loyalty, such as Adolf Hitler or Charles Manson.

Simon Keller writes in his 2010 book, *The Limits of Loyalty,* that loyalty without justice is an example of bad faith. This means that it is immoral to hold something as right just because it is ours. Rather, we should hold something as ours because it is right, and if it isn't right, then we shouldn't allow it to remain ours. Loyalty to ourselves, our families, our homes, our land, our friends, or our country should always entail trying to make them ethically better, not merely striving to protect them, enrich them materially, or preserve their status quo.

I Won't Back Down

While self-preservation should indeed usually be our main goal, we're sometimes justified in sacrificing our own lives in the name of loyalty when the situation demands it. Sometimes the situation even dictates that it would be unethical or cowardly to choose to preserve our own lives rather than serve the greater good. For examples, a courageous soldier in combat falls on a live grenade to save the rest of the platoon, or an obedient soldier heads back into a war zone on the commander's orders to search for stranded civilians.

Neither courage nor obedience is a virtue in itself. They are only virtues if what is being served is worthy of being served. Sometimes courage in the face of overwhelming odds, or even certain death, is the only honorable course. Sometimes disobedience is the only ethical option.

We honor the courageous and disobedient sacrifice of conscientious subordinates who put their loyalty to principles ahead of their duty to obey their superiors. Grady Scott Davis discussed in his 1992 book, *Warcraft and the Fragility of Virtue*, the case of a soldier who was court-martialed and shot for disobeying orders to execute noncombatant civilians. He asks whether we call this soldier heroic because we suspect that we couldn't do what he did. Recognizing courage in others is often tantamount to recognizing cowardice in ourselves, and perhaps the best that could come of such recognition is that we appreciate even more the heroism and nobility of courage, especially self-sacrificing courage, and set it as a moral goal to which we may aspire.

While disobedience, the opposite of obedience, is sometimes the proper course of ethical action, cowardice—as the opposite of courage—is never right. Whatever situation we find ourselves in, we must face it bravely. Don't back down!

All the Wrong Reasons

We see from "Into the Great Wide Open" that Petty had some sympathy for clueless rebels. Clueless rebels is what the rank and file Confederate soldiers mostly were. Poor and middle-class Southern whites didn't benefit from slavery; only the upper class did. But regional pride, kneejerk self-defense reactions, and perhaps also a quest for excitement and adventure, prompted them to fight for the Confederacy.

The outcome of the "War between the States" or the "War of Northern Aggression" still rankles many Southerners, adding defiance, obstinance, and self-satisfied bravado to their regional pride. This unexamined pride of heritage does little credit to the region. Petty, on the other hand, was sufficiently reflective to see eventually that the Civil War, from the Southern point of view, wasn't only about defending their homeland from invaders and their traditional way of life from Yankee legislative and judicial influences, but also about propping up an essentially evil and anti-human institution: slavery.

Then what should Southern citizens have done? Should they have refused to enlist? Disobeyed their superiors? Fragged their officers? Plotted to assassinate Jefferson Davis? Bucked their churches? Allowed the blue-bellied devils to destroy their livelihood, burn their homes, and murder, rape, loot, and pillage throughout Dixie at will? People faced with the immediate threat of home invaders aren't likely to worry about ideologies before pulling the trigger in self-defense—nor should they. Scarlett O'Hara was surely right to blow the head off the Yankee soldier who was advancing on her up the staircase in *Gone with the Wind*.

Is it farfetched to think that individual slaveholders could have defied the Confederacy, freed their slaves, and thereby removed the *casus belli*, the reason for the North to invade? This last question might seem ludicrous, but it is really quite complex. In considering it, let's not forget that the South fired the first shots of the war and that the North was fighting, not to abolish slavery, but to preserve the Union.

Unexamined regional pride declares that whatever is ours is right, but introspective regional pride doesn't decide that something is right because it is ours, but adopts it as ours only after deciding that it is right. A Southern farmer who joined the Confederate army to defend his home from the invading Yankees was innocent; but if he joined in order to defend slavery, then he was guilty, or, if not guilty, then at least ignorant.

Misplaced Loyalty and Its Correction

Petty came to realize that although many of the "blue-bellied devils" were individually diabolical, they were in fact agents of the ethically superior position: the abolition of slavery. If he had been around in the 1850s, perhaps he would have been a conductor on the Underground Railroad, even though a proud native Southerner. His rejection of the Confederate flag not only attests to his personal growth, but also raises quite a few important questions about the nature of loyalty.

Should we be primarily loyal to home, family, native land, parochial values, tradition, and ethnic heritage, or to broad ethical principles, general human values, and whatever "the common good" might turn out to be? How can ideals of loyalty best be served? How can loyalty best be attuned to justice? When is being loyal not the best course? Since loyalty entails being willing to defend whatever I am loyal to, how can I reconcile loyalty to some higher ideal with my natural inclination to defend my family, friends, and homeland, even when they are wrong?

There are strong arguments on most sides of these issues, but in the end, the greater—or more nearly universal—good must be served, as Petty recognized.

16
I Should Have Known It

Ashley Watkins

Throughout his career, we could count on Tom Petty for rock music with a human heart and an American soul, communicating universal themes with beauty, simplicity, and specificity. Among the stories he told us were the personal and the fictional, but one story stood out in his work since *The Last DJ*, culminating in the hard-hitting *Hypnotic Eye*.

Petty chronicled in his lyrics a disturbing change in our culture that's all too familiar to us now, and traced in that change the role of our beliefs, the truth, and our responsibilities to ourselves and to each other.

Petty never shied away from standing his ground against those who would use money and influence to erode the integrity of rock'n'roll. He resisted the relentless commodification of music and the transformation of a community of musicians and fans into a faceless, heartless market. This resistance appeared in his work alongside tales of love, growth, and letdowns. But as we listen to *Mojo* and *Hypnotic Eye*, his work during the 2010s, it's clear that money has become king far beyond the scope of the music industry. And part of the reason for this lies in what people know and believe, or what philosophers would call their *epistemic* situation.

In these later albums we find lyrical kernels of conflicts that philosophers spend their lives grappling with: the powerful versus the overpowered, rights versus responsibilities, comforting feelings versus cold hard facts. Songs like "Power Drunk," "Burnt Out Town," "Playing Dumb," and "Shadow People" tell the story of how greed and fear tempt us away from the truth, and we lose ourselves along with the high standards we once held ourselves to as a result. In other songs, especially the anthemic "I Should Have Known It" and even in "U Get Me High," Petty sets us straight with the refreshing practical wisdom we've come to expect. If we don't want to be sold down the river and left for dead, we have to look at what's right in front of us.

Between Two Worlds

If you eavesdrop on a few debates, either in person or online, it won't be long before you encounter the cliché that everyone is entitled to an opinion. When people say they're entitled to an opinion in response to fact-checking or evidence contrary to what they've said, it's considered a fallacy—a flawed pattern of reasoning. You can't justify the truth of what you've said by appealing to your right to believe in it. Hell, I might believe that dogs have wings, but my alleged entitlement to that opinion shouldn't convince anyone else to run out looking for a winged dog. But what about that supposed right to believe in something, despite being presented with evidence to the contrary?

The cliché itself, separate from any argument, is held up as a sort of sacred principle. If everyone doesn't have the right to believe whatever they want, so this reasoning goes, we'll end up in a demented dystopia run by tyrannical thought police where all freedoms are lost. Behind this is the idea that there's something uniquely private about what's in our minds that protects us from scrutiny, particularly ethical scrutiny. We might be told that our beliefs are wrong in the sense of being false in reality, but surely we can't be told that it's morally wrong just to think whatever we please within our own minds. If we can be told that we can't believe something, some kind of fundamental power over ourselves is lost—can't we even be king of our own little town?

But the hold of the cliché is tenuous. The same arguments that include an assertion of entitlement to opinions also include calls for the other person to read a book or get some life experience before they express their opinion. Despite purportedly believing everyone is entitled to an opinion, they've participated in a debate to try and bring about a change of heart. Isn't that a violation of the sacred right to believe whatever? Isn't it a way of saying that they *should* believe something else?

This popular conversation exists between two worlds, asserting a principle to avoid criticism in one instant and violating that same principle egregiously in the next. But if we turn to Tom Petty's songs for a little enlightenment, he'll remind us of a simple truth: that being king of your own little world is an escape, a dream to have from time to time. Isolating your mind from what's around you is no way to live your life.

Shadow Land

In a reversal of the dystopia imagined above, *Hypnotic Eye* shows how a radically permissive practice of thinking and believing whatever we want has resulted in a real-life shadow land. When thinking about the fraught relationship between the powerful and those they've overpowered, we typically pinpoint *feelings*, like greed, fear, or hatred, as the source of the problem. But Petty reminds us how central the *epistemic* dimension—what people believe and know, or don't know—is to the quickening spread of this American divide. Plenty of hate is thrown around, but knowledge is at the heart of it. The scary man is the one who'll destroy everything he don't *understand*.

It's easy to think that the epistemic dimension in the struggle to get out from under the feet of the rich and powerful comes down to straightforward deception and lies. The rich have the means both to spread misinformation and to suppress the truth. They manipulate beliefs, foster misunderstanding, create distracting conflicts, and thereby retain and amplify their power and wealth to the detriment of everyone else. But in Petty's music we can find a story that's more complicated, more human, and more insidious.

In the case of the powerful, "Power Drunk" and "Burnt Out Town" offer some strong, clear indictments. The powerful begin to believe their own lies as part of the cost of their upkeep, compromising their own epistemic integrity along with everyone else's. No one thinks they're the villain in the story, and to fully accept that they're deceiving others in order to maintain an illegitimate hold over them would be tantamount to admitting that they're the bad guys. They come to sincerely believe that nothing's out of their range, that they're entitled to swallow up the world around them, even the painted hills that no rich man can claim.

Power Drunk

'Power drunk' is not just an insulting euphemism, it's a genuine epistemic impairment with a hangover that hurts as bad as a gallon of moonshine. They've forfeited their own mental clarity in the pursuit of more riches and influence. They've burnt out towns to keep up the flow of crooked money, and had to create an entirely new realm of reality to sustain their position—a reality in which the truth has become indecent and must be kept hidden even from themselves. They better sober up not only for the people they've left in the wind, but for their own good as well. If it's the *truth* within that makes a good man rise, then this self-deception sinks the powerful lower and lower into drunkenness and immorality. They're responsible for the dishonest way they've come to believe in their own superiority and are therefore accountable for the pain they've left behind in their wake.

The idea that it's morally wrong to suppress doubts rather than honestly investigate them is at the center of William K. Clifford's famous 1877 essay "The Ethics of Belief." In it, he devises a thought experiment, or a fictional story that illustrates his point. In the story, the owner of a ship wants to sell tickets for a trip across the ocean. He knows that his ship may not be seaworthy, but since that would be difficult and expensive to resolve, he suppresses his doubts about his ship, much like the powerful push aside their doubts about their right to lord over others. Rather than really investigating the condition of his ship, he talks himself out of his doubts until he has formed the sincere belief that it's all good. Then he sends the ship out, it sinks, and he goes on his merry way with insurance money in hand.

Clifford first makes the point that the shipowner is responsible for all those who died in the wreck because his way of forming the belief that it was seaworthy was unethical. He then asks us to imagine that, by sheer luck, the ship makes it to its destination. In this case, the shipowner was still just as wrong as he was in the other scenario. He was *not entitled to his opinion* that his ship was seaworthy. It was all right there in front of him, and he should have known it was dangerous. His failing was epistemic, but it was also a moral failing.

Clifford's position is a form of "evidentialism." It's considered particularly strict, as he argues that we're obligated to have sufficient evidence for every one of our beliefs. Is there a philosophical counterpart to the entitlement we described, in which we have the right to believe anything regardless of evidence? Not really. Clifford's essay is usually discussed alongside William James's 1896 response, "The Will to Believe." James concludes that in some cases we're not only entitled to hold beliefs without sufficient evidence, but we may even be obligated to hold those beliefs. But he narrows this down to only some cases, particularly regarding religious beliefs, in which the evidence is missing or insufficient in either direction.

The closest we can get is a radical form of what's called "fideism," in which we can believe something on faith even if we have strong evidence against it. But even the biggest names in fideism, such as Tertullian (c. 160–c. 220 C.E.), Blaise Pascal (1623–1662), and Søren Kierkegaard (1813–1855), focused particularly on matters of religious faith. It's not a stretch to suppose that they'd object to the use of their position to justify a rich man's "faith" that he can claim the painted hills, or the man with a badge who believes nothing is out of his range.

When Petty says the power drunk better sober up, it's a moral imperative of the sort Clifford was aiming at. It's an ethical obligation to hold themselves to some kind of evidentiary standard in the formation of their beliefs, a standard that excludes suppressing doubts and self-deception. If the thoughts in another man's head can't possibly be wrong in the ethical sense, why would we need God to protect us from them? Sobering up—getting a handle on your belief formation by seeing what's right there in front of you—is part of being a good person.

Fooled Again

The motivation for the rich and powerful to adopt lax standards of belief formation is pretty clear: it allows them to retain their position while also believing that they deserve it and are acting rightly. After all, it's good to be king and have your own way, especially when you've found means of eliminating any pesky guilt. They've dug themselves in deep enough that they can sleep at night. In the end, playing dumb works for them.

But how could everyone else—those who are trampled in the drunken bar crawl of the powerful—be tempted to play along? What is the motivation for everyone else to buy into the cliché that they're entitled to an opinion, no matter the evidence?

For one thing, acknowledging that someone has done something wrong is often followed up by some kind of punishment. You might be horrified by the thought that you can be punished not for *doing* anything but for just believing something, hence the slippery slope to dystopia. This kind of fear-mongering that the state will reach too far is paradoxically advanced by those in the very position to do such overreaching. But the connection between what's unethical and what's punishable just isn't that direct. As a society, we recognize that all sorts of things are unethical without making them illegal or punishable. Just think about all the ways we do each other badly—we tell lies, leave people in the dust, drag hearts around. The state doesn't punish us for any of that.

Even the distinction between doing and believing is questionable. Granted, having a belief doesn't seem like the kind of thing you can just do on demand. I can't make myself believe in angels, even when faced with a ruler-wielding nun. Individual beliefs don't seem to work that way. But it's reasonable to think that at least some of how we form beliefs is up to us—that belief formation is a kind of *doing*, as Clifford argued.

I can choose to stick my head in the sand and turn my eyes away from the evidence, as the powerful have done in the grip of their drunkenness. It's difficult and intimidating to challenge the order of things. It's humiliating to admit that every promise handed down from the rich and powerful was just a runaround. The world will break your heart to pieces, and you may not want to see. But doubling down on the fantasy isn't the easy way out that it first appears. That denial of the truth is what turned us into shadow people, refugees from reality.

We can choose instead to face up to all the information that's available to us. After all, we can be blamed for being wrong when the evidence has been thrown in our faces over and over again. No matter how hard to believe, *we should have known it*; 'should' here indicative of the most robust, moral sense.

Even if forming beliefs is a sort of doing, or action, perhaps it's not the kind of action that counts as moral or immoral. It's tempting to reply to a charge like Clifford's by insisting that it wasn't the belief or even the formation of the belief that was unethical, but the act of sending a dangerous ship out to sea. Just the belief on its own didn't kill anyone. Likewise, perhaps, just the belief that one person is superior to another doesn't hurt anyone until it's acted upon. It isn't what we believe or don't believe that got us into this mess, it's what we've done.

But this distinction is artificial. The most basic account of voluntary actions requires both a belief about the way the world is and a desire to bring something about. If I want to listen to "Magnolia" and I believe it's on *You're Gonna Get It*, my action will be to put that record on. We always act in accordance with our beliefs; there's no separating the two. To deny that beliefs have the power to cause harm is to deny their essential role in action. It's even plausible that we have just as much power over our belief formation as we do over our actions once those beliefs are in place.

It's the Last Time You're Gonna Hurt Me

For the overpowered, then, there's both accountability and hope to be found. We don't have to sit around and wait for the power-drunk to sober up, because much of the responsibility lies with us. When all the evidence was there in front of us, no matter how hard it was to believe, we *should have known* what was going down. We're just as responsible for our belief-formation practices as the powerful, even if we may not share quite as much responsibility for the current shadow land we all live in. It's our duty not only to see what's in front of us, but also to seek out and expose the indecent truth. We have to resist the pull into that alternate reality, otherwise we either become crooks ourselves or we go out and destroy what we don't understand.

Ultimately, it's up to us to throw up that rotten food our minds were fed and *stop playing dumb*. The lesson to be found in these songs is to give up living in a dream world and join reality. To stop bending the rules governing our beliefs. To really reach for the truth that can set us free and make us rise. As always, we can take the example straight from Petty himself, one of our last human voices. Let go of easy, vacuous clichés and get right down to the meat of life in the real world.

This accountability, the idea that we don't have the right to just believe whatever we want despite the evidence, is precisely why we're merely overpowered and not powerless. Petty isn't afraid of the great deception because those bad dreams turn to smoke when he really looks. We don't have to be afraid of it either.

Taking hold of our responsibility to seek out evidence, giving matters the close inspection that they deserve, and exposing the truth is the first step toward telling the power-drunk that it's over now, that it's the last time they're going to hurt us. Short of God protecting us from the thoughts in another man's head, holding our own belief formation to high evidentiary standards is what will let the sun shine straight overhead.

We don't have to be shadow people in a shadow land anymore.

The Meditation of St. Thomas (Petty)

RANDALL E. AUXIER AND MEGAN VOLPERT

Fans, make mine an instrument of your peace of mind.
Where there is hatred, let me sow love songs.
Where there is insult, also pardon the injury.
Where there is doubt, let me not shout it.
Where there is despair, let's be hopeful rebels.
Where there is darkness, let me light one up.
Where there is heartbreak, joy gives back an echo.

Oh, brother bandmates, grant that I may not so much
seek the board console as the amplifier knobs,
seek to understand as to understate,
seek to be loved as to love music.
For it is in singing that we find the harmonies,
it is in rocking that we are rocked,
and it is in jamming that we have sworn a fraternal life.
Rock on.

Bibliography

Auxier, Randall E. 2013. *Time, Will, and Purpose: Living Ideas from the Philosophy of Josiah Royce*. Open Court.

Balaguer, Mark. 2014. *Free Will*. MIT Press.

Bataille, Georges. 1985. *Visions of Excess: Selected Writings, 1927–1939*. University of Minnesota Press.

———. 1991. *The Accursed Share: An Essay on General Economy. Volume 1: Consumption*. University of Minnesota Press.

Beauvoir, Simone de. 2011 [1949]. *The Second Sex*. Vintage.

Bratman, Michael E. 2014. *Shared Agency: A Planning Theory of Acting Together*. Oxford University Press.

Cassirer, Ernst. 1946. *Language and Myth*. Harper.

———. 1961 [1946]. *The Myth of the State*. Yale University Press.

———. 2009 [1932]. *The Philosophy of the Enlightenment*. Princeton University Press.

Clifford, William K. 1999 [1876]. *The Ethics of Belief and Other Essays*. Prometheus.

Davis, Grady Scott. 1992. *Warcraft and the Fragility of Virtue: An Essay in Aristotelian Ethics*. University of Idaho Press.

Descartes, René. 1993. *Meditations on First Philosophy*. Hackett.

Empiricus, Sextus. 1990. *Outline of Pyrrhonism*. Prometheus.

Fletcher, George P. 1993. *Loyalty: An Essay on the Morality of Relationships*. Oxford University Press.

Friedman, Michael. 2000. *A Parting of the Ways: Carnap, Cassirer, and Heidegger*. Open Court.

Frye, Marilyn. 1983. The *Politics of Reality: Essays in Feminist Theory*. Random House.

Gerrish, Theodore, and John S. Hutchinson. 1883. *The Blue and the Gray: A Graphic History of the Army of the Potomac and That of Northern Virginia Including the Brilliant Engagements of These Forces from 1861 to 1865*. Hoyt, Fogg, and Donham.

Greene, Andy. 2015. Tom Petty on Past Confederate Flag Use: "It Was Downright Stupid." Interview with Tom Petty. *Rolling Stone* (July 14th).

Hardt, Michael, and Antonio Negri. 2001. *Empire*. Harvard University Press.

Harman, Graham. 2007. *Heidegger Explained: From Phenomenon to Thing*. Open Court.

Heidegger, Martin. 1962 [1927]. *Being and Time*. Harper and Row.

Husserl, Edmund. 2012 [1931]. *Ideas: General Introduction to Pure Phenomenology*. Routledge.

Jameson, Fredric. 1984. Postmodernism: Or the Structural Logic of Late Capitalism. *New Left Review* 146 (July–August).

———. 1991. *Postmodernism: Or the Structural Logic of Late Capitalism*. Duke University Press.

James, Aaron. 2012. *Assholes: A Theory*. Random House.

Kahn, Charles H., ed. 1981. *The Art and Thought of Heraclitus: An Edition of The Fragments with Translation and Commentary*. Cambridge University Press.

Keller, Simon. 2010. *The Limits of Loyalty*. Cambridge University Press.

Kierkegaard, Søren. 1986. *Fear and Trembling*. Penguin.

Kornfield, Jack. 2009. *The Wise Heart: A Guide to the Universal Teachings of Buddhist Psychology*. Bantam.

———. 2011. *Bringing Home the Dharma: Awakening Right Where You Are*. Shambhala.

Lamarche, Pierre, Max Rosenkrantz, and David Sherman, eds. 2011. *Reading Negri: Marxism in the Age of Empire*. Open Court.

Marx, Karl H. 1974. *Capital: A Critical Analysis of Capitalist Production*. Progress.

McClary, Susan. 1991. *Feminine Endings: Music. Gender, and Sexuality*. University of Minnesota Press.

Melville, Herman. 2001 [1851]. *Moby-Dick: Or, The Whale*. Penguin.

———. 2016. *Billy Budd, Bartleby, and Other Stories*. Penguin.

Moeller, Hans-Georg. 2004. *Daoism Explained: From the Dream of the Butterfly to the Fishnet Allegory*. Open Court.

Moore, G.E., 1939. *Proof of an External World*. Milford.

Nietzsche, Friedrich. 1961 [1872]. *The Birth of Tragedy: Out of the Spirit of Music*. Penguin.

———. 1961 [1883]. *Thus Spoke Zarathustra: A Book for Everyone and No One*. Penguin.

———. 1967 [1872, 1888] *The Birth of Tragedy and The Case of Wagner*. Random House.

———. 2017 [1901]. *The Will to Power*. Penguin.

Origen. 1953. *Contra Celsum*. Cambridge University Press.

Pascal, Blaise. 2004 [1670]. *Pensées*. Hackett.

Plato. 1997. *Plato: Complete Works*. Hackett.

———. 2003. *The Last Days of Socrates*. Penguin.

Priest, Josiah. 2010 [1848]. *Bible Defense of Slavery and the Origin, History, and Fortunes of the Negro Race*. Kessinger.

Rahula, Walpola. 1974 [1959]. *What the Buddha Taught: Revised and Expanded Edition with Texts from Suttas and Dhammapada*. Grove Press.

Ratcliffe, Matthew. 2012. Phenomenology as a Form of Empathy. *Inquiry* 55:5.

Royce, Josiah. 1908. *The Philosophy of Loyalty*. Macmillan.

Russell, Bertrand. 2000 [1967]. *The Autobiography of Bertrand Russell*. Routledge.

Sartre, Jean-Paul. 1989. *No Exit and Three Other Plays*. Vintage.

Tertullian. 2014. *The Apology*. Beloved.

Tuomela, Raimo. 2013. *Social Ontology: Collective Intentionality and Group Agents*. Oxford University Press.

Van Inwagen, Peter. 2017. *Thinking about Free Will*. Cambridge University Press.

Heartbreakers and Refugees

S. KELLER ANDERS is a philosopher and instructor in Portland, Oregon, who always strives to keep things weird. Her focus is on Applied Ethics, particularly why people do the things they do—on their own and with other people. She's currently working on a secondary degree in Behavioral Economics examining the ideologies of charitable giving and monetary donation. She lives with a rambunctious dog and several towering stacks of books, often with a Heartbreakers album on the record player.

RANDALL AUXIER once backed down, on the playground in second grade, and has regretted it ever since. A mean old teacher named Miss Hopper had slapped him, for no good reason, right across the face. He wasn't humiliated because he hadn't done anything wrong, on *that* occasion. So he learned to generalize. From that day forward he began to reflect of the problem of assholes and heroes. The outcome of all this reflection was a fairly self-indulgent set of habits, so, after failing as a professional musician, he studied philosophy, bought books, acquired cats and a patient spouse, and set about to see if anyone would pay him to live like an Epicurean. Illinois has a century and a half of corrupt state government to build upon, so Randy went to SIU Carbondale and demanded special treatment and excellent pay. It worked. So he ran for Congress. That didn't work but no one can discover why. It may have failed due to the books he published with Open Court, which is about the number of your fingers and toes, if you are hegemo-dactylic. Randy has the same number of digits as Tom Petty had. It's his proudest accomplishment.

BRIAN BERKEY is Assistant Professor in the Department of Legal Studies and Business Ethics in the Wharton School at the University of Pennsylvania, with a secondary appointment in the Department of Philosophy at Penn. He received his PhD in Philosophy from the University of California, Berkeley, in 2012, and did his undergraduate work in Philosophy and Politics at New York University. Before moving to Penn, he was a Postdoctoral Fellow at the Center for Ethics in Society at Stanford University. His academic work is in moral and political philosophy, and he has written about issues such as the demandingness of morality, individual obligations of justice, climate change mitigation obligations, effective altruism, and entitlements of justice for non-human animals.

MATTHEW CRIPPEN is following leads from pragmatists, who progressed by wedding old and new ideas and developing interdisciplinary trajectories. His research integrates a number of schools and eras, including embodied cognitive science, phenomenology, Greek thought, and more, while drawing resources from psychological, biological and occasionally physical sciences. Much of it also revolves around value theory, especially aesthetics but also ethics and politics, again with pragmatic approaches at its core. Matthew has published in top journals on American philosophy and aesthetics, and is currently in the midst of a book project with Jay Schulkin, titled *Ecologies of Self: Embodiment, Neurobiology and Valuations of Life.* Outside the academy, he has worked as a musician, mandolin and guitar instructor, and gymnastics coach. He is currently in the Einstein Group at Humboldt University's Berlin School of Mind and Brain, with a focus on aesthetic perception of popular arts, and more generally relations between pragmatism and cognitive science.

MATTHEW DIXON is a Toronto-based court reporter, with a background in cultural studies. Actively interested in the fine arts, he has mounted and acted in a number of plays and worked as a musician. An admirer of Tom Petty's music, he is enthusiastic about this volume. He sees his contribution as a small tribute to Petty's music and also to Petty himself.

MARY L. EDWARDS is a Teacher in Philosophy in the School of English, Communication and Philosophy at Cardiff University. She received her PhD from University College Cork, Ireland, in 2017. Her main research and teaching interests are in existentialism, feminist philosophy, phenomenology, and philosophy of the imagination. She is currently working on a monograph, provisionally titled *Sartre and Knowing Others.*

DON FALLIS is Professor of Information and Adjunct Professor of Philosophy at the University of Arizona. He has written many philosophy articles on lying and deception, including "What Is Lying?" in the *Journal of Philosophy* and "The Most Terrific Liar You Ever Saw in Your Life" in *The Catcher in the Rye and Philosophy: A Book for Bastards, Morons, and Madmen*. But to be perfectly honest, like many other fans, Fallis often feels that Petty is writing about his life. While he grew up with "a freeway runnin' through the yard" in Southern California, his parents came from the Ozarks. So, he is very familiar with those "southern accents." And he "got lucky" that "Here Comes My Girl" pretty much describes his relationship with his spouse.

RAUL HAKLI is a long-time fan of Tom Petty and the Heartbreakers. He stubbornly considers himself the number one TPHB fan in Finland on the grounds that he was the first in line queueing for the concert tickets the one and only time Tom Petty and the Heartbreakers ever played in Finland, as both opening act and back-up band for Bob Dylan in 1987. In addition to listening to Tom Petty records, Hakli works as a university researcher in practical philosophy at the University of Helsinki. He obtained his PhD thesis in theoretical philosophy from University of Helsinki in 2010. His research interests include social ontology and collective intentionality, social and collective epistemology, and philosophy of technology.

CHRISTOPHER M. INNES got his PhD from Goldsmiths College. This is the coolest college in the University of London. This is where Princess Beatrice of York, Mary Quant, Malcolm McLaren, Goldierocks and many others got their inspiration. He now teaches philosophy at Boise State University in Idaho. The move to the US was a creative one. Creativity is often assisted by listening to music. Dr. Innes remembers well Tom Petty's *Free Fallin'*, and *I Won't Back Down* while an undergraduate. Both sum up some of the feelings students have when grasping the fundamentals of philosophy. (This is when he was an undergraduate at Hull University gaining his BA, later to gain his MA at Kent at Canterbury University) The fundamentals are still perplexing, but this does not stop him revising his text book that he uses in his undergraduate philosophy classes, which will be published later this year. His specialism is in social and political philosophy where the questions about the mysteries of government and who should be in charge go unanswered.

ERIC V.D. LUFT earned his BA magna cum laude in philosophy and religion at Bowdoin College in 1974, his PhD in philosophy at Bryn Mawr College in 1985, and his MLS at Syracuse University in 1993. From 1987 to 2006 he was Curator of Historical Collections at SUNY Upstate Medical University. He has taught at Villanova University,

Syracuse University, Upstate, and the College of Saint Rose. He is the author, editor, or translator of over 640 publications in philosophy, religion, librarianship, history, history of medicine, and nineteenth-century studies, including *Hegel, Hinrichs, and Schleiermacher on Feeling and Reason in Religion: The Texts of Their 1821-22 Debate* (1987), *God, Evil, and Ethics: A Primer in the Philosophy of Religion* (2004), *A Socialist Manifesto* (2007), *Die at the Right Time: A Subjective Cultural History of the American Sixties* (2009), *Ruminations: Selected Philosophical, Historical, and Ideological Papers* (Volume 1, 2010; Volume 2, 2013), and *The Value of Suicide* (2012). He owns Gegensatz Press and is listed in *Who's Who in America*.

JOHN SEWELL is Assistant Professor of Convergence Journalism for the Department of Mass Communications at The University of West Georgia. He received his PhD in public critical theory from Georgia State University in 2012. His work in critical cultural studies, queer theory, and post-structuralism has appeared in several academic journals and scholarly collections. Sewell got his start in music writing as a scribe for umpteen fly-by-night, xeroxed punk rock zines of dubious quality in the 1980s. Since these inauspicious beginnings, his music journalism, columns, feature writing and cultural criticism have appeared regularly in a host of music magazines and alternative weeklies including *Metro Pulse* (Knoxville, Tennessee), *Baltimore City Paper*, and *Mean Street* (Los Angeles). Presently he is a music writer for *Stomp and Stammer* in Atlanta, Georgia, where he lives with his wife, Stacy Fentress.

MEGAN VOLPERT is the author of many books on communication and popular culture, including two Lambda Literary Award finalists. After seven years as a nationally competitive debater, she competed in poetry slams for several more. Her MFA in Creative Writing is from Louisiana State University and she writes regularly for *PopMatters*. She has been teaching high school English in Atlanta for over a decade and was 2014 Teacher of the Year. She edited the American Library Association–honored anthology *This Assignment Is So Gay: LGBTIQ Poets on the Art of Teaching*. Volpert is a theory junky who cannot resist rock'n'roll. She used to drive a scooter and has "What would Tom Petty do?" literally tattooed over her heart.

ASHLEY WATKINS is a doctoral candidate in philosophy at the University of St Andrews. Originally from Las Vegas, he graduated from California State University, Northridge before exchanging the desert heat for the wind and rain of Scotland's east coast. His research interests include the philosophy of fiction, the aesthetics of popular culture, and everyday aesthetics. He is particularly attracted to topics in which metaphysics and aesthetics collide. A lifelong fan, he got his first Tom Petty cassettes for his eighth birthday— *Wildflowers* and the *Greatest Hits*. He first saw Tom Petty and the Heartbreakers live at the age of fourteen and enjoys reminding everyone that he's seen them perform with both Howie Epstein and Ron Blair. He's been an avid listener since and is always up for one more listen of Mojo.

DANIEL ZELINSKI fell in love with Petty's music while growing up in THE valley not far from Mulholland Drive and Ventura Boulevard with the bad boys, good girls, and all the vampires, and he credits Petty with helping him let all that go and adjust to life in the South. He's spent the last eighteen years in Virginia, utilizing pop culture to attempt to convey philosophy to introductory students as Professor of Philosophy and Religion at Richard Bland College of the College of William and Mary.

Index